Field Experience

Strategies for Exploring Diversity in Schools

Richard R. Powell
Texas Tech University

Stanley Zehm
University of Nevada, Las Vegas

Jesus Garcia
University of Illinois, Champaign-Urbana

Merrill,
an imprint of Prentice Hall
Englewood Cliffs, New Jersey   Columbus, Ohio

Library of Congress Cataloging-in-Publication Data

Powell, Richard R.
    Field experience : strategies for exploring diversity in schools /
  Richard R. Powell, Stanley Zehm, Jesus Garcia.
      p. cm.
    Includes bibliographical references and index.
    ISBN 0-02-396311-5
    1. Multicultural education.   2. Teaching.   3. Action research in
education.   I. Zehm, Stanley J.   II. Garcia, Jesus
   III. Title.
   LC1099.P69   1996
  370.1996—dc20
                                          95-14111
                                           CIP

Cover photo: ©Phil Matt
Editor: Debra A. Stollenwerk
Developmental Editor: Linda Ashe Montgomery
Production Editor: Louise N. Sette
Photo Editor: Anne Vega
Text Designer: Anne D. Flanagan
Cover Designer: Julia Zonneveld Van Hook
Production Manager: Pamela D. Bennett

This book was set in Usherwood Book by Carlisle Communications, Ltd. and was printed
and bound by R. R. Donnelley & Sons Company. The cover was printed by Phoenix Color
Corp.

 © 1996 by Prentice-Hall, Inc.
A Simon & Schuster Company
Englewood Cliffs, New Jersey 07632

Photo credits: Richard R. Powell

Printed in the United States of America

10 9 8 7 6 5 4 3

ISBN: 0-02-396311-5

Prentice-Hall International (UK) Limited, *London*
Prentice-Hall of Australia Pty. Limited, *Sydney*
Prentice-Hall of Canada, Inc., *Toronto*
Prentice-Hall Hispanoamericana, S. A., *Mexico*
Prentice-Hall of India Private Limited, *New Delhi*
Prentice-Hall of Japan, Inc., *Toyko*
Simon & Schuster Asia Pte. Ltd., *Singapore*
Editora Prentice-Hall do Brasil, Ltda., *Rio de Janeiro*

✼ Preface

In our diverse and varied experiences as teacher educators, we have worked with dozens of teachers at both preservice and in-service levels. We have worked with these teachers in locations where school classrooms contain students who are richly diverse in ethnicity, religion, economic class, family background, and nationality. Our interactions with teachers in these settings, coupled with recent reports on multicultural teacher education, suggest that beginning teachers in general lack preparation for meeting the challenges of teaching in contemporary classrooms that are culturally diverse.

Although many beginning teachers are required to take university courses in multicultural education to fulfill their teacher education requirements, these teachers' beliefs, values, and attitudes about teaching, as well as their awareness of cultural differences in classrooms, are mostly unchanged by teacher education courses. Consequently, beginning teachers are often experientially naive and uninformed about classroom cultural issues when they begin actual classroom teaching.[1] Our primary purpose with this book is to help preservice, novice, and veteran teachers to develop a firsthand awareness of multicultural classroom issues through interacting with students in real classroom settings, rather than to acquire a vicarious awareness through university courses that teach objectively about multicultural principles. By helping educators increase their cultural awareness and by helping them develop a deeper understanding of muticultural classrooms, we hope this book fosters the development of positive, helpful, and culturally sensitive learning experiences for all students.

A major premise we adopted for this book is that multicultural education coursework housed in colleges and universities is but one part of a greater process of becoming a multicultural person. We hold the view that becoming such a person is by no means limited to experience in university multicultural education courses, nor is a multicultural person shaped, for example, from reading a list of books about cultural experiences.[2] The process of becoming a multicultural person and transferring a multicultural perspective to the classroom involves many factors that continuously interact in each of our lives. We have sought to acount for these factors in this book and to help readers explore how these factors collectively influence classroom instruction.

A second related premise, which is supported by biographical studies of teachers, is that teacher education is a lifelong process, beginning far in advance of any formal teacher preparation and extending the entire professional life of a teacher. Related to this premise is our assumption that experiences both inside and outside school classrooms and inside and outside teacher education programs contribute equally to the wisdom and experience that foster effective teaching. Therefore, teachers' personal theories for teaching, constructed partly from many life experiences outside teacher preparation programs, are powerful guides for classroom decision making.

By beginning with personal theories, as we do in this book, multicultural education is moved away from an objectivist to a phenomenological process; that is, we move away from the perspective that multicultural theory is comprised of a body of knowledge apart from teachers' lived experiences. By endorsing a phenomenological approach to multicultural education, we further align with two frameworks: (a) personal practical knowledge as a way of teacher knowing[3] and (b) construct psychology as a way of describing how teachers acquire personal theories about teaching.[4] These two complementary frameworks support our belief that teachers are active agents in the construction of their professional knowledge about teaching and that meaningful learning occurs when teachers are actively engaged in inquiry, action, and continuous reflection. Personal knowledge about cultural diversity, when constructed in this way, is not static and objective, but rather is dynamic and ever changing.

From the frameworks of constructivism and personal practical knowledge, we have designed this book to help educators become active inquirers of their own teaching. Throughout this book, we ask teachers to explore their teaching context; to observe it closely; to interview students, other teachers, and administrators; and to study the relationship between schools and communities. Perhaps most important, we ask teachers to explore the origins of their own beliefs about teaching in multicultural classrooms to determine the efficacy of their beliefs for working with culturally diverse students. Because this book aligns with a phenomenological perspective, we do not offer a list of prescribed methods or an algorithm for teaching in multicultural classrooms; rather, we suggest activities and action research projects, combined with background information and sources for further reading, that will encourage preservice and in-service teachers to look deeper into their teaching context, to explore the complexities of teaching in multicultural settings, and to examine their personal philosophies for teaching.

We do not intend this book to replace existing multicultural theory books that provide a basis for multicultural courses offered in teacher preparation programs. Many excellent works have provided some of the framework for this book. Our hope is that this book can supplement other related works by situating multicultural discourse in school classrooms. The dialogue on multicultural education should not end when final grades are posted at the end of the semester course on multicultural education, but rather should continue as beginning teachers enter and experienced teachers reenter their classrooms. This book is intended to extend multicultural discourse to school classrooms and to help teachers construct personal practical philosophy for teaching diverse students.

The activities, research projects, and background information in this book are organized into three parts. Part I contains five chapters that collectively provide an understanding of how personal beliefs and biographical predispositions to interacting with other persons influence teaching in important ways. A model for doing site-based research, which is central to this book, is presented. This first part also provides an overview of the developmental nature of multicultural education and related terms.

In Part II, which contains six chapters, readers explore school and classroom learning environments while focusing on diversity issues. School district policies about diversity issues are considered. The last chapters of this part explore curricular and instructional issues related to student diversity. Strategies for teaching culturally diverse students, for choosing and creating culturally sensitive curriculum, and for assessing diverse learners are discussed.

In Part III, readers reflect carefully on the activities and research projects completed in earlier chapters. This part helps readers synthesize their personal practical philosophies for teaching diverse students.

ACKNOWLEDMENTS

The authors are grateful to many persons who, in various ways, contributed to the development of this book. For the site visits to the three exemplary schools described in Chapter Six, thanks are extended to Roy Ford, principal of Hollibrook Elementary School in Houston, Texas, Camille Barr, principal of Brown Barge Middle School in Pensacola, Florida, and Linda Maryott and Rudy Chavez, administrators at Mark Keppel High School in Alhambra, California. These persons were instrumental in facilitating our visits to these schools. Thanks also go to the four teachers whose personal biographies and instructional strategies are highlighted in Chapter Seven, including Linda Fussell at Brown Barge Middle School, Gissella Castro at Mark Keppel High School, Joanie Phillips at Las Vegas High School, and Karen Donathen at Hollibrook Elementary School. Each of these teachers gave up valuable time for us, and they opened their classroom doors so we could study their classroom instruction. We are also indebted to the preservice teachers who provided us with their biographies that we included in Chapter Three, including Amy Owens, Jennifer Gosse, and Karrie Terrill. Appreciation is extended to Linda Skroback-Heisler for granting permission to use her action research project in Chapter Two. Tom Dickinson was helpful in the initial phases of locating Brown Barge Middle School, and to him we owe sincere gratitude. Various portions of the book were pilot tested in teacher education classes at the University of Nevada, Las Vegas. We are grateful to the postbaccalaureate preservice teachers who participated in this pilot testing of the book. Ellen Ebert recommended special background readings for this book; quotations from her recommendations are included throughout the book, particularly in the final chapter. A very special thanks is extended to Porter Troutman, University of Nevada, Las Vegas, who assisted us on all site visits to the schools described in Chapter Six, and to Dale Anderson, Dean of the College of Education, University of Nevada, Las Vegas, who supported these trips. During the final phases of preparing the manuscript for this book, five chapters were lost because of technological problems. The diligence and hard work of Peggy Attaway and Margaret Graham, College of Education, Texas Tech University, to reenter these lost chapters in a timely and patient manner allowed us to meet final deadlines for the book. Gratitude is also offered to Kim Perry, who compiled the index. Finally, we offer thanks to the reviewers of the book, including Debra Baird de DeVega, Ph.D., Austin College; Lowell J. Bethel, The University of Texas at Austin; Leigh Chiarelott, Bowling Green State University; Noble R. Corey, Indiana State University; Beatrice S. Fennimore, Ph.D., Indiana University of Pennsylvania; Max Ferguson, Southern Utah University; Karen L. Ford, Ball State University; Maureen Gillette, Ph.D., College of St. Rose; Hilda Hernandez, Ph.D., California State University, Chico; Tom Savage, California State University, Fullerton; and Elizabeth P. Quintero, Ph.D., University of Minnesota, Duluth, who provided ongoing and pertinent feedback during the formative stages of manuscript development.

NOTES

1. One of us (Garcia) has discussed this more extensively elsewhere. See Garcia, J., & Pugh, S. (1992). Multicultural education in teacher preparation programs. *Phi Delta Kappan, 74,* 214-219.

2. Ibid. Mary Dilworth also presents this argument eloquently in the preface of her edited book. See Dilworth, M. (1992). *Diversity in teacher education: New expectations.* San Francisco: Jossey-Bass.

3. Clandinin, J. (1985). Personal practical knowledge: A study of teachers' classroom images. *Curriculum Inquiry, 15,* 361-385.

4. For example, see Fosnot, C. (1989). *Enquiring teachers, enquiring learners: A constructivist approach for teaching.* New York: Teachers College Press.

Introduction to Readers

This book is about being a teacher in a society that has become increasingly pluralistic. You might be thinking that because you are now teaching or are planning to teach in a remote area perhaps away from the kind of ethnic diversity found in most urban settings, this book doesn't apply to you. We believe, and we think you will soon come to realize, that in today's society every classroom in every location contains various kinds of diversity; ethnic diversity is but one kind. Examples of other kinds of diversity are socioeconomic class, religion, nationality, exceptionality, and geographical location (urban, suburban, rural). Understanding how diversity influences your ability to teach all students effectively and how diversity influences your ability to interact with them throughout each day in ways that are personally respectful and academically productive is a necessary first step to being an effective teacher in every classroom.

Whether you are just beginning your teacher education program, completing student teaching, beginning your first year as a teacher, or adding another year to an accomplished career as an educator, this book will engage you in deeper thinking about the practical realities of teaching students who represent many different backgrounds. To engage you in this way, we, like Hunt (1987), believe that you must begin with yourself. By this we mean that you must first develop a better understanding of your beliefs, convictions, attitudes, personal theories about teaching and learning, and students. You must also realize how your teaching perspectives influence your ability and willingness to implement culturally relevant curriculum and instruction.

Throughout this book are many activities and classroom-based action research projects intended to help you develop a deeper understanding of your beliefs about teaching in culturally diverse settings. Developing this understanding moves you toward gaining a multicultural perspective. Moving toward this perspective, however, does not ensure that you will reach that goal by the time you finish this book. We would be foolish to have that expectation for you and to think this book alone could accomplish that.

To deepen and extend cultural sensitivity in your classroom curriculum and instruction, you must continuously think about teaching in diverse classrooms. This thinking certainly can begin with this book and its many activities. At some point, however, you must decide to move well beyond what we ask you to consider in the following pages. Examples of things you must do regularly in order to move toward a culturally sensitive classroom include (a) reading other books and research reports about diversity in schools, (b) talking with peers and colleagues about diversity issues, and (c) thinking about the strengths and weakness of your own teaching.

Additional strategies should include recognizing stereotypes you have for certain students, however unintentional these stereotypes might be, and recognizing culturally insensitive curriculum and instruction.

We realize that culturally sensitive teaching further depends on the overall goals of your school and school district, as we discuss in Chapter 8. It is you, however, the classroom teacher, who interfaces daily on personal, academic, and social levels with students; you are the one who, by your classroom teaching strategies, either engages students in or disengages them from meaningful learning of the content you teach. If you ask most experienced teachers, you will hear them say that knowing the content to be taught is one thing but that knowing how to engage all students in learning the content in personally relevant ways is altogether another dimension of teaching. It is this dimension we focus on in this book.

Just how do you know when you are or when you are not engaging your students in personally and culturally relevant teaching? Might you be distancing some of your students unintentionally from your classroom curriculum and not know you are doing this? We have designed this book to help you clarify, build on, extend, and, if necessary, reconstruct your personal practical philosophy for teaching diverse learners. We believe we can help you find personally meaningful responses to the questions raised in this introduction.

Although personal practical philosophy as described by Connelly and Clandinin (1986) is one way to think about your teaching, it is not always something you can easily and clearly state. For example, you might say, "Her teaching aligns with my personal philosophy." But when asked to state your philosophy for teaching, you might not know what to say; this uncertainty is because personal practical philosophy is embedded deeply in classroom practice and deeply in your biographical experiences. In this sense, personal practical philosophy is the fabric of your teaching life; it is interwoven with your actions, thoughts, behaviors, beliefs, and values for teaching. Personal practical philosophy is not something you ordinarily think about; rather, it is something you act out on the basis of what you know about teaching and what you have experienced inside and outside school. When viewed in this way, personal practical philosophy is embodied within your life's story. Connelly and Clandinin (1986) write, "Personal practical philosophy contains the notions of beliefs and values but goes beneath their surface manifestation to their experiential narrative origin" (p. 6).

To understand your personal practical philosophy for teaching diverse learners, you must share your teaching perspectives with peers and colleagues, and you must compare their perspectives with those you hold. Think of your personal practical philosophy, therefore, as being socially constructed; you acquire it over time as you exchange your perspectives with peers and colleagues, as you gain practical experience teaching students in school classrooms, and as you continue exploring related literature on diversity. By acquiring new information over time about teaching in culturally diverse classrooms, your personal practical philosophy will very likely change; we hope this change, if it occurs, helps you better understand the relationship between students' personal backgrounds and your classroom instruction.

We say more about personal practical philosophies in Chapter 12, the final chapter of the book. In this introduction, we want you to begin examining your personal practical philosophy; you continue this process in various ways throughout the book. Then, in Chapter 12, you reexamine your initial personal philosophy in order to chart changes in your perspectives for teaching diverse students, to provide some synthesis for what you learned throughout the book, and to provide direction for your future teaching.

To begin examining your personal practical philosophy, consider some of your beliefs about teaching in general and about teaching students with diverse backgrounds in particular. Write out these beliefs and then compare them with the beliefs of your colleagues and peers. Remember that an essential part of discovering your own personal practical philosophy for teaching diverse learners and how this philosophy may affect your interactions with students is to compare your beliefs and perspectives with those expressed by peers. Make this comparison with an open mind and with a willingness to learn about the strengths and limitations of your own beliefs.

In most of the activities and research projects in the following chapters, we ask you to think independently and reflectively on various aspects of school life. We also ask you to engage in many conversations with your peers. In these conversations, which are intended to help you share your personal insights about teaching, you begin to clarify your personal practical philosophy for teaching diverse learners. This clarification, in turn, may help you expand your repertoire of teaching strategies for helping all students engage in meaningful and relevant learning.

REFERENCES

Connelly, F. M., & Clandinin, D. J. (1986). On narrative method, personal philosophy, and narrative unities in the story of teaching. *Journal of Research in Science Teaching, 23* (4), 293-310.

Hunt, D. (1987). *Beginning with ourselves.* Cambridge, MA: Brookline Books.

✤ *Brief Contents*

✦ Contents

Chapter 3   *Examining Your Autobiography and Beliefs About Cultural Integration   43*

Chapter 4   *Assessing Your Readiness for Teaching in Culturally Diverse Classrooms   63*

PART I

Preparing for Field Experience

Chapter 1
Moving Toward a Multicultural Perspective

Chapter 2
Exploring Culturally Diverse Classrooms:
Becoming Teacher as Researcher

Chapter 3
Examining Your Autobiography and Beliefs
About Cultural Integration

Chapter 4
Assessing Your Readiness for Teaching in
Culturally Diverse Classrooms

Chapter 5
Using Multicultural Concepts in Diverse Settings

Chapter 1

Moving Toward a Multicultural Perspective

Sometimes it gets pretty damn difficult trying to understand the human race, don't it?
(Castillo, 1988, p. 30)

And that reminds me of a story. *(Walker, 1992, p. 3)*

DISCOVERING CULTURAL DIVERSITY IN THE CLASSROOM

I sat in the back of the classroom, watching Jennifer Crowley (not her real name), a beginning teacher, teach her sixth-period class. I (Powell) was observing Jennifer as part of a longitudinal study on factors that influence how teachers develop classroom curriculum. Jennifer, a White middle-class teacher, was in the 3rd year of my longitudinal study, and I thought I knew her potential as a teacher. In my previous observations of Jennifer during this same school year, I thought she was doing very well in her beginning year.

Jennifer's beginning year was in an urban high school that had a large percentage of minority students.[1] Jennifer had mentioned to me in one of our earlier conversations that she was uncertain how to teach her sixth-period class of ninth graders, which was the last period of the day; she wanted me to observe her during that class so that I could give her some suggestions on management and student discipline. I arrived at Jennifer's classroom early enough to watch her sixth-period students come into class. I said hello to Jennifer, who was standing at the door to greet students as they entered her room, and then I went to the back of the classroom as I usually did when I observed her. In a few moments, students entered and shuffled around the classroom, talking with each other, and a few male students chased each other around the room. When the tardy bell rang, most students were in their seats, but a few were still moving around the room and talking loudly. Jennifer reminded them to be seated and to begin writing the objectives and the daily assignment from the chalkboard into their logbooks. A few students began writing, but most remained off task.

I thought to myself that the noisiness of the class might be a result of this period being the last one of the day. I remember from my own teaching that certain periods challenged my ability more than others as a teacher of a subject area and as a classroom manager. The last period usually was one of them. As I watched Jennifer teach and as I observed this class of rowdy students, I searched through my own prior experiences as a teacher and teacher educator to understand and interpret what was happening in Jennifer's class. I began to feel uneasy, however, when I couldn't seem to draw from any of my former experiences.

The students in sixth period represented various groups. Of the 22 students I was observing in Jennifer's classroom, 8 were Hispanic, 5 were Black, 4 were Asian, and 5 were White. Three students had limited English proficiency. I couldn't recall from my prior public school teaching experiences any classrooms with such diversity. That could have been why I was unable to draw from my former teaching experiences to explain the dynamics of Jennifer's sixth period; I had taught classes of mostly White middle-class suburban and rural students.

Jennifer told me that three females in the class were members of street gangs and that she had not been successful teaching these students the course content or communicating with them on a personal level. I observed all of sixth period and noticed that Jennifer did have trouble keeping the students on task. Most of them talked loudly; a few threw paper as she turned her back to write on the chalkboard. They were generally unruly for the whole period.

After class Jennifer and I sat together for over an hour, exploring possibilities to improve the situation in her classroom. Jennifer was very concerned about the class, and she immediately wanted to know what she should do to get this class on task. I admitted openly to Jennifer that I wasn't sure how to go about teaching this class. I was both disturbed and disquieted by my lack of helpful suggestions and by my inability to understand the dynamics of this class.

As we talked about the problems in the class (throwing paper, loud talking, off-task behavior), we considered whether Jennifer's teaching strategies, including her expectations for classroom behavior and her classroom curriculum, might be culturally inappropriate for some members of the class. As we talked about this possibility, Jennifer reflected on how she had more difficulty communicating with the Hispanic females in the class than with White or Asian females. She also thought the Hispanic females were giving her the most management problems.

In trying to understand the deeper factors contributing to the challenges Jennifer had with her last-period class, we asked whether the main problem underlying her inability to maintain an effective learning environment for this class might be her lack of understanding for teaching in a culturally diverse classroom. Ending our conversation with this question, we agreed to think about this during the next few days and then to meet again to consider cultural diversity factors in her teaching.

As I drove back to the university, I thought more carefully about the relationship Jennifer had with her sixth-period class. My thoughts kept returning to the cultural and ethnic differences between Jennifer and her students. Why does Jennifer have more difficulty interacting personally and academically with the Hispanic female students? How does this difficulty influence her ability to teach them content? Could she be having difficulty with students in her other classes but not be aware of it? Complicating these issues was yet another factor: Jennifer might be having problems because she may not relate well to Hispanic American girls, but it was possible that each of these girls, as human beings, had a separate need, issue, or problem that had to be addressed apart from ethnicity.

Thinking carefully about Jennifer's experience with cultural diversity and her seemingly limited multicultural perspective caused me to think about my own experiences as a teacher and teacher educator. I had to admit honestly that, like Jennifer, I am limited, with my White middle-class perspective, in my repertoire of strategies for working in classrooms that are culturally rich and ethnically diverse. I wondered whether this was why I was unable to provide helpful suggestions to Jennifer at the end of her last-period class. Although my experiences as a teacher and writer have provided me with opportunities to travel extensively overseas, including working for several years in the Middle East, my experiences with Jennifer nonetheless helped me discover that my multicultural perspective for classroom teaching is yet limited, particularly with the diversity found in U.S. schools.

Jennifer's experience, along with those of other preservice teachers I have worked with, caused me to think about Jennifer's teacher education program, of which I was part. Perhaps this program failed to offer her meaningful opportunities to explore issues surrounding student diversity or to offer her a practical understanding of how multicultural classrooms pose special circumstances for all teachers. As part of her teacher education program, Jennifer was required to take a 1-hour course in multicultural education. This course was comprised of a few hours of lecture and discussion at the university; in this context, the course was removed from the real-life setting of school classrooms.

I suddenly became aware of the concerns now being expressed over preparing teachers for culturally diverse classrooms: that White middle-class preservice teachers with primarily monocultural schooling experiences are being prepared by teacher educators with similar backgrounds to teach in classrooms that are ethnically and socioculturally diverse.[2] Jennifer and I were classic examples of this phenomenon. This type of teacher education (e.g., monocultural middle-class teacher educators and monocultural middle-class preservice teachers) is essentially unable to help preservice teachers like Jennifer develop curriculum and instruction that meet the needs of all student cultural groups and that foster academic success for students whose cultural backgrounds differ from those of their teachers.

Because Jennifer and I were both viewing her class with limited cultural perspectives, we were at first unable to connect some of her classroom concerns to the cultural disparity between her and the students. After we began thinking in terms of cultural diversity, we were then able to pinpoint ways for enhancing her classroom learning environment and for strengthening her rapport with students.

Realizing that society is experiencing rapid demographic shifts nationally and globally that are changing the social fiber of local communities, I'm aware that the chasm between the cultural, biographical, and social class heritages of teachers and their students will continue to widen, just as it widened the gap between Jennifer and many of her sixth-period students. Bridging this gap can be done only if teachers and teacher educators are willing to explore together, as Jennifer and I did, the profound relationship between cultural diversity and classroom teaching. This book is intended to foster that exploration.

ACTIVITY 1.1   Assessing Your Cultural Sensitivity

Jennifer had few prior experiences with groups other than her own. In the classroom, this limited her sensitivity for how to best communicate with some students in her classroom, especially Hispanic females. Think about significant former experiences that you've had both inside and outside schools or about experiences you're now having that involve interactions with cultural groups other than your own. List these experiences in Figure 1–1.

Regarding the experiences you listed, respond to these questions:

1. Which of these former experiences have enabled you to acquire sensitivity for the lifestyles of various cultural groups?
2. Like Jennifer, if you have limited cultural sensitivity for some of the students you teach, how can you develop this sensitivity? How can you acquire a readiness for teaching in culturally diverse classrooms?

A. Experiences with cultural group(s) other than your own:

School experiences:

_____

_____

_____

Nonschool experiences:

_____

_____

_____

B. Experiences with your own cultural group(s):

School experiences:

_____

_____

_____

Nonschool experiences:

_____

_____

_____

Figure 1–1   Prior experiences with student social group(s)

TOWARD A MULTICULTURAL PERSPECTIVE

This book is intended to help you explore diversity within the practical reality of school classrooms. It is designed to help you explore how your autobiographical experiences have given you a socially constructed framework for communicating information to your students. The exploratory activities throughout the book involve a research process intended to help you develop a new perspective, a multicultural perspective, for fostering student success in school.

Acquiring a multicultural perspective is a challenging journey that takes you through the byways of your beliefs and biases for cultural diversity. Many preservice and in-service teachers we have worked with have taken this journey. They discovered that some of their classroom practices interfered with their ability to communicate content and positive social messages to students from other cultural groups. Taking exploratory journeys that cause you to stop and self-reflect on teaching in culturally diverse classrooms is a prerequisite for effective classroom teaching today.

Activities such as self-reflection move you toward acquiring a multicultural perspective. Another way to acquire this perspective is to explore schools and their communities over time. These exploratory activities include, for example, focused observations of classroom teaching, interviews and conversations with experienced educators, collaborative site-based teacher research projects, and reflective thinking about cultural diversity in schools.

Although activities like these help you move toward a multicultural perspective for teaching, they won't ensure that you will reach this goal. To actually construct a multicultural perspective, you must be willing to reflect carefully on your own beliefs and values, to acknowledge honestly any beliefs that limit your perspective, and to take action on restructuring those beliefs that limit effective classroom interaction with all of your students. Freire (1972) gives the name *praxis* to this kind of reflection and action. According to Freire, emerging from social forces that limit your view of the world is "done only by means of praxis: reflection and action upon the world in order to change it" (p. 28).

Having a multicultural perspective means understanding, just as Jennifer needed to understand, how to effectively teach students whose cultural backgrounds differ from your own. Becoming a multicultural teacher means

1. looking at students, schools, and communities from multiple viewpoints
2. knowing how to take advantage of ethnic and cultural diversity in your classroom
3. searching for and building on the strengths of students from all social groups
4. viewing multicultural education as positive and beneficial
5. knowing how your beliefs about cultural diversity influence your ability to effectively communicate content to students
6. reflecting on and continuously examining your beliefs about teaching that interfere with your relationships with students

To develop learning environments that meet the needs of all students, you need to understand how classroom instruction and student learning are influenced by social, economic, historical, and cultural factors.[3] If you are unclear of your own cultural background and how it socializes you into ways of interacting with students in the classroom, and if you have had only limited cross-cultural experiences prior to teaching,[4] as Jennifer had in the story above, you might unknowingly use ethnocentric teaching practices that limit learning for some students.[5]

ACTIVITY 1.2   Assessing Your Multicultural Perspective

The six features listed above collectively contribute to a multicultural perspective. This activity asks you to determine how you align with these features. In Figure 1–2, place a check in the space that best represents your level of alignment with each feature.

Persons who have begun moving toward a multicultural perspective will answer yes to these statements. After completing the checklist, determine which of the features, if any,

Alignment			Feature
Yes	No	Some	
_____	_____	_____	1. I am able to look at schools, students, and communities from multiple viewpoints.
_____	_____	_____	2. I know how to use in positive ways the cultural diversity that exists in my classroom.
_____	_____	_____	3. I am able to identify and build on the cultural strengths of all students.
_____	_____	_____	4. I view multicultural education and cultural diversity as positive parts of teaching.
_____	_____	_____	5. I know how my beliefs about cultural diversity influence my ability to communicate content effectively to students.
_____	_____	_____	6. I now reflect on and continuously examine my teaching beliefs and practices for interacting personally and academically with students.

Figure 1–2   Features contributing to a multicultural perspective

need further development. Compare your checklist with those of your peers and discuss differences and similarities in your responses.

WHY EXPLORE CULTURAL DIVERSITY IN SCHOOL CLASSROOMS?

Because society and its social groups influence school classrooms in profound ways,[6] we are surprised to find the topics of multicultural education and cultural diversity to be only marginal in many teacher education programs.[7] In Jennifer's teacher education program, only a brief academic experience in multicultural education was required. Girabaldi (1992) notes, however, that learning about all forms of student diversity should be central to teacher education. He further argues that diversity issues should also comprise more than a single course on multicultural principles or human relations.[8]

From our personal experiences in schools and from various reports on multicultural education, we describe below specific reasons for making cultural diversity central to your development as a teacher.

1. *Facilitate successful learning for all students.* A primary goal for multicultural education is to foster the academic success of all students, especially students who historically have been marginalized in the schools by the mainstream culture.[9] Ogbu (1992, p. 6) notes that all educators should explicitly address the question, To what extent will multicultural education improve the academic performance of those minorities who have not traditionally done well in school? On the surface, this question may seem simple and straightforward, but on deeper levels it is complex. Answering this question requires you to examine the relationships you develop with all student groups in your classroom. The question also requires you to consider how race, social class, gender, and religion influence your classroom learning environment. Helping students in all cultural groups succeed in school requires you to develop a deeper understanding of each of these groups. Bullivant (1993) writes: "Teachers cannot rely on the cultural knowledge appropriate to their own social groups if they want to work effectively in the multicultural classroom, in which children from many ethnic groups may be present" (p. 42).

2. *Consider the human dimensions of teaching.* Multicultural education focuses on the human dimensions of teaching.[10] Teachers who have a multicultural perspective understand that cultural diversity is part of the human dimension of life, not just a political instrument.[11] When you affirm diversity in your students, you acknowledge the gifts that each student has, the gifts inherent within race, culture, and gender. By focusing on the human dimensions of teaching, you communicate positive messages to students on academic and personal levels.

3. *Assess the impact of global and local shifting populations on teaching.* Some people in various parts of the world view the United States, with its emphasis on democratic ideals and equal opportunity for all, as an attractive place to live. Consequently, immigrants and refugees from various parts of the world seek residency in the United States.[12] The arrival of new immigrants (e.g., from Asia and Latin America), coupled with ongoing urban migration of Black Americans, Native Americans, and native-born Hispanic Americans, is rapidly reshaping the face of communities and schools in irreversible ways.[13] Schools in the 1990s have therefore become more linguistically, culturally, and racially diverse than at any other time in history. Whether you teach in urban[14] or rural schools,[15] your teaching will be influenced by this increased diversity. Being aware of your beliefs about teaching other cultural groups and having a good understanding of the nature of cultural diversity will help you teach culturally diverse student populations.[16]

4. *Address the growing disparity between cultural backgrounds of teachers and students.* That the cultural backgrounds of teachers, including their socioeconomic status, contrast markedly with those of their students is clear.[17] Students of color are the majority in 23 of the 25 largest school districts in the United States.[18] By the year 2000, students of color are projected to reach as high as 40% of the student population in U.S. public schools.[19] The teaching profession, however, has become increasingly White and middle class.[20] The implications of this disparity become obvious when we account for the powerful influence that biography (culture, family, prior schooling experiences, social class) has on the daily life in classrooms.[21]

Research suggests that the instructional strategies you use in your classroom are influenced strongly by your former teachers. Moreover, your decisions about what and how to teach are influenced as much by biographical experiences outside school as experiences inside school.[22] Most of the teaching profession, according to Fuller (1992a), "will teach as though their students are middle-class, White children exhibiting the behaviors and values of that population" (p. 91). Fuller further suggests that teachers need to understand and appreciate diversity among students. She notes that if teachers fail to "understand and appreciate children whose cultural and socioeconomic backgrounds are different from their own [then] future K–12 students will feel that schools are inattentive to their needs and that teachers [will] neither understand nor value them" (p. 91).

5. *Move multicultural education from marginal status to central status in teacher development.* Multicultural education historically has been relegated to marginal status in teacher education at both preservice and in-service levels.[23] This status is highlighted by Garcia and Pugh (1992). They ask, "Why is it that, after more than a decade of rhetoric and official declarations, multicultural education remains a segregated enterprise in schools of education, with little or no impact on the curricula of preservice teachers?" (p. 214). Haberman (1991) writes that teacher awareness about cultural diversity is unlikely unless teacher education programs (e.g., the one Jennifer completed at the beginning of this chapter) have increased philosophical commitment toward multicultural education.[24]

This book is intended to move you beyond only brief academic exercises that predominate multicultural education in most teacher preparation programs. The activities and research projects throughout the book are designed to help you learn about cultural diversity in school through posing and solving real site-based problems in school classrooms. Solving these problems helps you think about cultural diversity and fosters the construction of personal knowledge that is embedded in real-life teaching experiences. Hunt (1987) reports that this kind of personal knowledge has a significant influence on your classroom instruction.[25]

This book moves multicultural education to the center of your development as a teacher. The book by itself, however, is a limited tool. When this book is combined with the real life of school classrooms, with group/peer discussions about cultural diversity, with site-based problem posing, and with ongoing reflective activities, it can provide meaningful learning experiences that change the way you view school classrooms.[26]

6. *Examine your biases, stereotypes, and misconceptions about cultural groups.* One of the first conditions you must meet to become an effective multicultural educator is to look honestly at the beliefs you now have for other cultural groups of students.[27] Looking honestly at these beliefs helps you identify and clarify personal values that either knowingly or unknowingly constrain your willingness to teach all students.[28] The activities in this book help you examine the strengths and limitations of your beliefs about teaching in multicultural classrooms. Many of these activities, which are conducted in schools and communities,[29] help you see cultural diversity "as a reality and not an academic exercise—a reality [you] experience through interactions with a diverse . . . student body" (Hixson, 1991, p. 18). When you choose to affirm diversity and to acknowledge modes of living other than your own, the lifelong commitments you have to your beliefs, including your misconceptions, are illuminated and more easily explored (Gergen, 1991).[30] Developing a multicultural perspective and becoming a multicultural person then begins to become a reality.

Engaging in classroom-based and community-based activities that require you to reflect on your existing teaching beliefs, including your misconceptions, can help you clarify who you are as a teacher.[31] Engaging in a series of these activities over a period of time fosters an understanding for how you reinforce the stereotypes you may have for other cultural groups. Then you can counteract these stereotypes with culturally sensitive instruction.[32]

7. *Make your classroom curriculum culturally sensitive.* Given the diversity of students in many schools, how can you implement a curriculum in your classroom that is culturally sensitive? As you seek an answer to this question, you'll engage in two activities. First, you will actually develop, implement, and refine curriculum materials for classrooms of diverse students. This task helps you develop a working understanding of a culturally sensitive curriculum. Second, you will engage in awareness building. You'll become aware of the many cultural and political factors that influence your classroom instruction.[33] You'll learn about the value-laden nature of selected curriculum materials, the politics surrounding the knowledge that school administrations want their students to acquire, the social dimensions inherent in the selected curriculum, and the subtle messages hidden within curriculum frameworks (the hidden curriculum).

ASSUMPTIONS FOR EXPLORING DIVERSITY

Guiding the organization of this book is a set of assumptions that frames the overarching theme of exploration. First, we assume that multicultural education is not a one-time effort. It is not something you do once, generate a product (e.g., a report for a university course or for a professional development course), and then move on to another topic. Multicultural education is an ongoing process.[34] It is also a way of thinking about how to create culturally sensitive classroom curriculum materials and activities.

Second, although research is limited on what actually helps teachers become multicultural educators,[35] we nonetheless assume that site-based activities focusing on cultural diversity help you examine your personal beliefs about teaching in contemporary classrooms. These activities help you in three distinct ways: (a) to assess your readiness for teaching culturally diverse students, (b) to consider multicultural principles and theoretical constructs, and (c) to connect these principles and constructs to your classroom teaching.

Third, we assume that as you use the activities in this book and as you discuss the results of your work with peers, you'll begin to construct new beliefs about diversity. You'll also be able to try out new instructional strategies that are culturally appropriate.

Fourth, we assume, as do Karen Noordhoff and Judith Kleinfeld, the designers of the Teachers for Alaska (TFA) program,[36] that learning about the relationship between cultural diversity and teaching is most effective when it is placed within the daily life in school classrooms.[37] This kind of multicultural education is activity based, reflective, collaborative, and problem posing.[38]

Finally, we assume that the approach taken in this book helps you become an informed professional capable of conducting site-based research in your own classroom. This approach mirrors the one used by the TFA program. TFA emphasizes three dimensions of learning about student diversity:[39]

1. Attending to contexts of teaching and learning, rather than overgeneralizations about groups of students.
2. Making connections between diverse students' background experiences and frames of references with academic subject matter.
3. Learning how to learn from one's students, communities, and practical experience.

These dimensions are central to the activities and research projects that we've included in the following chapters.

The assumptions noted above, especially those related to TFA, suggest that exploring cultural diversity in school classrooms is best conducted with a series of site-based activities that occur over time in schools and their communities. These activities, according to Ogbu (1992), help you compare and contrast minority and mainstream cultures in schools. He notes that "the crucial issue in cultural diversity and learning is the relationship between the minority cultures and the American mainstream culture" (p. 50). This book helps you explore this relationship and helps you reexamine the mainstream culture within school classrooms.

ACTIVITY 1.3   Further Considerations of Diversity and Classroom Life

In this chapter, you have encountered several key concepts related to classroom diversity. These concepts include cultural diversity, multicultural perspective, multicultural person, multicultural education, biases and stereotypes, ethnic groups, and culturally sensitive classroom curriculum. To help you reflect on these key concepts and to assess your level of awareness for the implications these concepts have for classroom instruction, complete the following activities.[40]

1. Write a paragraph about what these words mean to you.
2. In group discussions, determine how your paragraphs are similar to and different from those of your peers.
3. Write a statement describing how much these key concepts influence the way you think about teaching in contemporary classrooms.

SUMMARY

Never before has the challenge been greater for you, as a classroom teacher, to develop a deeper understanding for the academic and social needs of students whose backgrounds vary from each other's and from yours. And never before has the challenge been greater to connect what you do and what you teach in your classroom to the larger global community.

Developing an appreciation for cultural diversity means acquiring a multicultural perspective. Teachers who have this perspective affirm many types of diversity[41]— including learning diversity, pedagogical diversity, language diversity, social class diversity, and racial diversity—in their students. When students perceive your classroom to be a caring community where these diversities are valued, they will be more likely to feel like they are part of your classroom learning environment. The stage is then set to foster successful learning for all students.

NOTES

1. The school ethnicity where Jennifer began teaching was 35% Hispanic, 35% White, 24% Black, 5% Asian, and 1% American Indian.
2. Fuller, M. (1992a). Monocultural teachers and multicultural students: A demographic clash. *Teaching Education, 4*(2), 87–93.
3. Ogbu, J. (1992). Understanding cultural diversity and learning. *Educational Researcher, 21*(8), 5–14.
4. *Cross-cultural experience* is used here to represent, for example, living in other cultures for extended periods of time or spending formative years living around other ethnic groups.
5. Zeichner, K. (1993, April). *Educating teachers for cultural diversity.* Paper presented at the Annual Meeting of the American Educational Research Association, Atlanta.
6. For example, see Heath, S. B. (1983). *Ways with words: Language, life, and work in communities in classrooms.* New York: Cambridge University Press. See also Ogbu, J. (1992). Understanding cultural diversity and learning. *Educational Researcher, 21*(8), 5–14.
7. Grant, C., & Secada, W. (1990). Preparing teachers for cultural diversity. In W. R. Houston (Ed.), *Handbook of research on teacher education* (pp. 403–422). New York: Macmillan; Zeichner, K. (1993, April). *Educating teachers for cultural diversity.* Paper presented at the Annual Meeting of the American Educational Research Association, Atlanta.
8. Girabaldi, A. (1992). Preparing teachers for culturally diverse classrooms. In M. E. Dilworth (Ed.), *Diversity in teacher education: New expectations* (pp. 23–39). San Francisco: Jossey-Bass.
9. Sleeter, C., & Grant, C. (1986). Success for all students. *Phi Delta Kappan, 86*(12), 297–299.
10. The human dimensions of teaching we include here are more fully described by Zehm, S., & Kottler, J. (1993). *On being a teacher: The human dimension.* Newbury Park, CA: Corwin Press.
11. Trachtenberg (1990) notes that teachers who effectively teach all students are willing to admit, "Nothing human can be alien to me." This statement supports our position that multicultural education represents the human dimension of teaching.
12. As an example of this phenomenon, see Trueba, H., Jacobs, L., & Kirton, E. (1990). *Cultural conflict and adaptation: The case of Hmong children in American society.* New York: Falmer Press.

13. See, for example, the following ethnography: Horton, J. (1992). The politics of diversity in Monterey Park, California. In L. Lamphere (Ed.), *Structuring diversity: Ethnographic perspectives on the new immigration* (pp. 215–245). Chicago: University of Chicago Press.

14. Goode, J., Schneider, J-A., & Blanc, S. (1992). Transcending boundaries and closing ranks: How schools shape interrelations. In L. Lamphere (Ed.), *Structuring diversity: Ethnographic perspectives on the new immigration* (pp. 173–213). Chicago: University of Chicago Press.

15. Stull, D., Broadway, M., & Erickson, K. (1992). The price of a good steak: Beef packing and its consequences for Garden City, Kansas. In L. Lamphere (Ed.), *Structuring diversity: Ethnographic perspectives on the new immigration* (pp. 35–63). Chicago: University of Chicago Press.

16. Banks, J. (1991). Teaching multicultural literacy to teachers. *Teaching Education, 4*(1), 135–144; Gay, G. (1989). Ethnic minorities and educational equality. In J. Banks & C. Banks (Eds.), *Multicultural education: Issues and perspectives* (pp. 171–194). Boston: Allyn & Bacon; Ogbu, J. (1992). Understanding cultural diversity and learning. *Educational Researcher, 21*(8), 5–14; and Zeichner, K. (1993, April). *Educating teachers for cultural diversity.* Paper presented at the Annual Meeting of the American Educational Research Association, Atlanta.

17. Fuller, M-L. (1992a). Monocultural teachers and multicultural students: A demographic clash. *Teaching Education, 4*(2), 87–93. See also Grant, C., & Secada, W. (1990). Preparing teachers for cultural diversity. In W. R. Houston (Ed.), *Handbook of research on teacher education* (pp. 403–422). New York: Macmillan. See Dilworth, M. (1990). *Reading between the lines: Teachers and their racial/ethnic cultures.* Washington, DC: Clearinghouse on Teacher Education and American Association of Colleges for Teacher Education.

18. National Center for Educational Statistics. (1987). *Digest of education statistics 1987.* Washington, DC: Government Printing Office. See also Fuller, M. (1992a). Monocultural teachers and multicultural students: A demographic clash. *Teaching Education, 4*(2), 87–93; Fuller, M. (1992b). Teacher education programs and increasing minority school populations. In C. Grant (Ed.), *Research and multicultural education: From the margins to the mainstream* (pp. 184–200). Washington, DC: Falmer Press.

19. Hodgkinson, H. L. (1985). *All one system: Demographics in education–Kindergarten through graduate school.* Washington, DC: Institute for Educational Statistics.

20. Fuller, M-L. (1992a). Monocultural teachers and multicultural students: A demographic clash. *Teaching Education, 4*(2), 87–93.

21. Refer to the story of Jennifer Crowley at the beginning of this chapter.

22. Powell, R. R. (1992). The influence of prior experiences on pedagogical constructs of traditional and nontraditional preservice teachers. *Teaching and Teacher Education, 8*(3), 225–238. See also Goodson, I. (1980). Life histories and the study of schooling. *Interchange, 11*(4), 62–76.

23. Numerous claims have been made about the marginalization of multicultural education throughout teacher education. See, for example, the recent discussions offered by Zeichner, K. (1993, April). *Educating teachers for cultural diversity.* Paper presented at the Annual Meeting of the American Educational Research Association, Atlanta; Grant, C., & Secada, W. (1990). Preparing teachers for cultural diversity. In W. R. Houston (Ed.), *Handbook of research on teacher education* (pp. 403–422). New York: Macmillan; Zeichner, K. (1989). Preparing teachers for democratic schools. *Action in Teacher Education, 11*(1), 5–10; Banks, J. (1993b). Multicultural education: Development, dimensions, and challenges. *Phi Delta Kappan, 75*(1), 22–28; Gay, G. (1993). Ethnic minorities and educational equality. In J. Banks & C. Banks (Eds.), *Multicultural education: Issues and perspectives* (2nd ed., pp. 171–194). Boston: Allyn & Bacon; Noordhoff, K., & Kleinfeld, J. (1993). Preparing teachers for multicultural classrooms. *Teaching and Teacher Education, 9*(1), 27–39.

24. Haberman, M. (1991). Can cultural awareness be taught in teacher education programs? *Teaching Education, 4*(1), 25–31. Haberman defines *cultural awareness* as sensitivity to issues of cultural diversity, sexism, racism, handicapism, classism, religious differences, and multilingualism.

25. Hunt, D. (1987). *Beginning with ourselves.* Cambridge, MA: Brookline Books.

26. Zeichner, K. (1993, April). *Educating teachers for cultural diversity.* Paper presented at the Annual Meeting of the American Educational Research Association, Atlanta.

27. Sonia Nieto writes that becoming a multicultural person requires one first to confront one's own racism and biases. See Nieto, S. (1992). *Affirming diversity: The sociopolitical context of multicultural education.* New York: Longman, p. 275.

28. Banks, J. (1991). Teaching multicultural literacy to teachers. *Teaching Education, 4*(1), 135–144.

29. See Noordhoff, K., & Kleinfeld, J. (1993). Preparing teachers for multicultural classrooms. *Teaching and Teacher Education, 9*(1), 27–39. The importance of moving field experiences and teacher development activities beyond school classrooms is discussed in Zeichner, K. (1990). Changing directions in the practicum: Looking ahead to the 1990s. *Journal of Education for Teaching, 16*(2), 105–132.

30. Gergen, K. (1991). *The saturated self: Dilemmas of identity in contemporary life.* New York: Basic Books.

31. Bullough, R., & Stokes, D. (1993, April). *Analyzing personal teaching metaphors in preservice teacher education as a means for exploring self and encouraging development.* Paper presented at the Annual Meeting of the American Educational Research Association, Atlanta.

32. New, C., & Sleeter, C. (1993, April). *Preservice teachers' perspectives of diverse children: Implications for teacher education.* Paper presented at the Annual Meeting of the American Educational Research Association, Atlanta.

33. These factors were drawn from multiple sources, including Apple, M. (1993). *Official knowledge: Democratic education in a conservative age.* New York: Routledge; Garcia, J. (1993). The changing image of ethnic groups in textbooks. *Phi Delta Kappan, 75*(1), 29–35; Gay, G. (1988). Designing relevant curricula for diverse learners. *Education and Urban Society, 20*(4), 327–340; Gay, G. (1990). Achieving educational equality through curriculum desegregation. *Phi Delta Kappan, 72,* 56–62; Nieto, S. (1992). *Affirming diversity: The sociopolitical context of multicultural education.* New York: Longman; Suzuki, B. (1984). Curriculum transformation for multicultural education. *Education and Urban Society, 16*(3), 294–322.

34. The view that multicultural education is a process is also held by James Banks: Banks, J. (1993a). Multicultural education: Characteristics and goals. In J. Banks & C. Banks (Eds.), *Multicultural education: Issues and perspectives* (pp. 3–28). Boston: Allyn & Bacon.

35. Grant, C., & Secada, W. (1990). Preparing teachers for cultural diversity. In W. R. Houston (Ed.), *Handbook of research on teacher education* (pp. 403–422). New York: Macmillan; Zeichner, K. (1993, April). *Educating teachers for cultural diversity.* Paper presented at the Annual Meeting of the American Educational Research Association, Atlanta.

36. Kleinfeld, J., & Noordhoff, K. (1988). Getting it together in teacher education: A "problem-centered" curriculum. *Peabody Journal of Education, 65,* 66–78.

37. Noordhoff, K., & Kleinfeld, J. (1993). Preparing teachers for multicultural classrooms. *Teaching and Teacher Education, 9*(1), 27–39.

38. Education that is activity based, reflective, collaborative, and problem posing is described in Kemmis, S., & McTaggart, R. (1988). *The action research planner* (3rd ed.). Victoria, Australia: Deakin University Press.

39. Noordhoff, K., & Kleinfeld, J. (1993). Preparing teachers for multicultural classrooms. *Teaching and Teacher Education, 9*(1), p. 37.

40. These questions were taken, in part, from Grant, C., & Sleeter, C. (1993). Race, class, gender, and disability in the classroom. In J. Banks & C. Banks (Eds.), *Multicultural education: Issues and perspectives* (2nd ed., pp. 48–68). Boston: Allyn & Bacon.

41. See the discussion on reconceptualizing teacher education toward diversity offered in Zimpher, N., & Ashburn, E. (1992). Countering parochialism in teacher candidates. In M. E. Dilworth (Ed.), *Diversity in teacher education: New expectations* (pp. 40–62). San Francisco: Jossey-Bass.

REFERENCES

Apple, M. (1993). *Official knowledge: Democratic education in a conservative age.* New York: Routledge.

Banks, J. (1991). Teaching multicultural literacy to teachers. *Teaching Education, 4*(1), 135–144.

Banks, J. (1993a). Multicultural education: Characteristics and goals. In J. Banks & C. Banks (Eds.), *Multicultural education: Issues and perspectives* (pp. 3–28). Boston: Allyn & Bacon.

Banks, J. (1993b). Multicultural education: Development, dimensions, and challenges. *Phi Delta Kappan, 75*(1), 22–28.

Bullivant, B. M. (1993). Culture: Its nature and meaning for educators. In J. Banks & C. Banks (Eds.), *Multicultural education: Issues and perspectives* (2nd ed.). Boston: Allyn & Bacon.

Bullough, R., & Stokes, D. (1993, April). *Analyzing personal teaching metaphors in preservice teacher education as a means for exploring self and encouraging development.* Paper presented at the Annual Meeting of the American Educational Research Association, Atlanta.

Castillo, A. (1988). *My father was a Toltec.* Novato, CA: West End Press.

Dilworth, M. (1990). *Reading between the lines: Teachers and their racial/ethnic cultures.* Washington, DC: Clearinghouse on Teacher Education and American Association of Colleges for Teacher Education.

Freire, P. (1972). *Pedagogy of the oppressed.* Auckland, New Zealand: Penguin Books.

Fuller, M. (1992a). Monocultural teachers and multicultural students: A demographic clash. *Teaching Education, 4*(2), 87–93.

Fuller, M. (1992b). Teacher education programs and increasing minority school populations. In C. Grant (Ed.), *Research and multicultural education: From the margins to the mainstream* (pp. 184–200). Washington, DC: Falmer Press.

Garcia, J. (1993). The changing image of ethnic groups in textbooks. *Phi Delta Kappan, 75*(1), 29–35.

Garcia, J., & Pugh, S. (1992). Multicultural education in teacher preparation programs. *Phi Delta Kappan, 74*(3), 214–219.

Gay, G. (1988). Designing relevant curricula for diverse learners. *Education and Urban Society, 20*(4), 327–340.

Gay, G. (1989). Ethnic minorities and educational equality. In J. Banks & C. Banks (Eds.), *Multicultural education: Issues and perspectives* (pp. 171–194). Boston: Allyn & Bacon.

Gay, G. (1990). Achieving educational equality through curriculum desegregation. *Phi Delta Kappan, 72,* 56–62.

Gay, G. (1993). Ethnic minorities and educational equality. In J. Banks & C. Banks (Eds.), *Multicultural education: Issues and perspectives* (2nd ed., pp. 171–194). Boston: Allyn & Bacon.

Gergen, K. (1991). *The saturated self: Dilemmas of identity in contemporary life.* New York: Basic Books.

Goode, J., Schneider, J-A., & Blanc, S. (1992). Transcending boundaries and closing ranks: How schools shape interrelations. In L. Lamphere (Ed.), *Structuring diversity: Ethnographic perspectives on the new immigration* (pp. 173–213). Chicago: University of Chicago Press.

Goodson, I. (1980). Life histories and the study of schooling. *Interchange, 11*(4), 62–76.

Grant, C., & Secada, W. (1990). Preparing teachers for cultural diversity. In W. R. Houston (Ed.), *Handbook of research on teacher education* (pp. 403–422). New York: Macmillan.

Grant, C., & Sleeter, C. (1993). Race, class, gender, and disability in the classroom. In J. Banks & C. Banks (Eds.), *Multicultural education: Issues and perspectives* (2nd ed., pp. 48–68). Boston: Allyn & Bacon.

Haberman, M. (1991). Can cultural awareness be taught in teacher education programs? *Teaching Education, 4*(1), 25–31.

Heath, S. B. (1983). *Ways with words: Language, life, and work in communities in classrooms.* New York: Cambridge University Press.

Hixon, J. (1991, April). *Multicultural issues in teacher education: Meeting the challenge of student diversity.* Paper presented at the Annual Meeting of the American Educational Research Association, Chicago.

Hodgkinson, H. L. (1985). *All one system: Demographics in education–Kindergarten through graduate school.* Washington, DC: Institute for Educational Statistics.

Horton, J. (1992). The politics of diversity in Monterey Park, California. In L. Lamphere (Ed.), *Structuring diversity: Ethnographic perspectives on the new immigration* (pp. 215–245). Chicago: University of Chicago Press.

Hunt, D. (1987) *Beginning with ourselves.* Cambridge, MA: Brookline Books.

Kemmis, S., & McTaggart, R. (1988). *The action research planner* (3rd ed.). Victoria, Australia: Deakin University Press.

Kleinfeld, J., & Noordhoff, K. (1988). Getting it together in teacher education: A "problem-centered" curriculum. *Peabody Journal of Education, 65,* 66–78.

National Center for Educational Statistics. (1987). *Digest of education statistics 1987.* Washington, DC: Government Printing Office.

New, C., & Sleeter, C. (1993, April). *Preservice teachers' perspectives of diverse children: Implications for teacher education.* Paper presented at the Annual Meeting of the American Educational Research Association, Atlanta.

Nieto, S. (1992). *Affirming diversity: The sociopolitical context of multicultural education.* New York: Longman.

Noordhoff, K., & Kleinfeld, J. (1993). Preparing teachers for multicultural classrooms. *Teaching and Teacher Education, 9*(1), 27–39.

Ogbu, J. (1992). Understanding cultural diversity and learning. *Educational Researcher, 21*(8), 5–14.

Powell, R. R. (1992). The influence of prior experiences on pedagogical constructs of traditional and nontraditional preservice teachers. *Teaching and Teacher Education, 8*(3), 225–238.

Sleeter, C., & Grant, C. (1986). Success for all students. *Phi Delta Kappan, 86*(12), 297–299.

Stull, D., Broadway, M., & Erickson, K. (1992). The price of a good steak: Beef packing and its consequences for Garden City, Kansas. In L. Lamphere (Ed.), *Structuring diversity: Ethnographic perspectives on the new immigration* (pp. 35–63). Chicago: University of Chicago Press.

Suzuki, B. (1984). Curriculum transformation for multicultural education. *Education and Urban Society, 16*(3), 294–322.

Trachtenberg, S. (1990). Multiculturalism can be taught only by multicultural people. *Phi Delta Kappan, 71*(9), 610–611.

Trueba, H., Jacobs, L., & Kirton, E. (1990). *Cultural conflict and adaptation: The case of Hmong children in American society.* New York: Falmer Press.

Walker, A. (1992). *Possessing the secret of joy.* New York: Pocket Books.

Zehm, S., & Kottler, J. (1993). *On being a teacher: The human dimension.* Newbury Park, CA: Corwin Press.

Zeichner, K. (1989). Preparing teachers for democratic schools. *Action in Teacher Education, 11*(1), 5–10.

Zeichner, K. (1990). Changing directions in the practicum: Looking ahead to the 1990s. *Journal of Education for Teaching, 16*(2), 105–132.

Zeichner, K. (1993, April). *Educating teachers for cultural diversity.* Paper presented at the Annual Meeting of the American Educational Research Association, Atlanta.

Zimpher, N., & Ashburn, E. (1992). Countering parochialism in teacher candidates. In M. E. Dilworth (Ed.), *Diversity in teacher education: New expectations* (pp. 40–62). San Francisco: Jossey-Bass.

Chapter 2

Exploring Culturally Diverse Classrooms: Becoming Teacher as Researcher

Self-teaching is one of the most profound reasons that humans live.   (Storm, 1994, p. xiv)

But something can be done to empower some teachers . . . to reflect upon their own life situations, to speak out in their own voices about the lacks that must be repaired, the possibilities to be acted upon in the name of what they deem decent, humane, and just.   (Greene, 1978, p. 171)

INTRODUCTION

Almost every day that you interact with students, you teach yourself something new about classroom life. This is especially true during your beginning years as a teacher, when your personal practical philosophy for teaching develops most rapidly. As you interact with students in the classroom, self-teaching helps you generate many hypotheses, sometimes in only a few seconds, about things like disciplining a student, asking questions in a discussion, or assessing student learning. Forming these hypotheses is a very important process because they help you construct a personal knowledge[1] base for classroom teaching. Over time, these hypotheses develop into a set of personal theories that frame and enrich your personal philosophy for teaching and that guide your instruction.[2]

Teachers are not always able to state explicitly the nature of their personal theories. And because classroom life is so fast paced, spontaneous, and demanding, teachers rarely have time alone to think intentionally and in a reflective way about their teaching. When you take time to look purposefully into your classroom instruction, to look at it deeply and critically, you see the underlying dimensions of your teaching and begin entering the small spaces of your teaching you might otherwise overlook. When you engage in this process regularly and with meaningful intention, you likely will acquire an empowering awareness of your teaching. From this awareness, you'll speak out in your own voice, as Greene (1978) notes above, about possibilities for making your classroom learning environment humane and equitable for all students. You'll also illuminate the values and attitudes you hold toward your students' cultural backgrounds, explore these values and attitudes, and consider the consequences of enacting personal values in your teaching.[3]

This chapter provides you with a systematic means for asking intentional questions about your school, your classroom, and your teaching relative to diversity issues. Drawing from recent discussions of site-based teacher research[4] and from an action research model,[5] we define **systematic classroom research** as an orderly way for gathering and recording information about your teaching.

The following discussion first introduces you to teacher-directed research. The benefits to you of this research are described. The final portion of the chapter is devoted to the process of actually doing teacher-directed research. A systematic research model is explained, and strategies for conducting research are suggested.

WHO ARE TEACHERS AS RESEARCHERS?

The form of research you spontaneously and informally do in the classroom each day provides you with a practical knowledge base[6] for developing a deeper understanding about teaching. Suggested in this chapter, however, is a type of research that is more explicit and systematic. **Systematic teacher research** focuses purposefully on one aspect of teaching, with the intention of developing a better understanding and greater awareness of that aspect.[7] Teachers who fill the role of purposeful researcher ask carefully crafted questions about classroom instruction. Finding answers to these questions can help you

- identify alternative strategies for classroom instruction
- clarify your existing beliefs about schooling
- explore your personal values and attitudes toward students
- reflect carefully on your classroom life
- search for more effective ways for reaching students

Teacher as classroom researcher is not the only role you assume when you look purposefully into your classroom life. When you study your own teaching and when you study the teaching of a peer or colleague, you become teacher as student and teacher as learner.[8] Teacher researchers pose problems about their teaching and consequently ask practical questions that inform and enhance their instruction, hence teacher as informed pedagogue. And when you develop the habit of posing problems about teaching, you become teacher as informed problem solver.[9] These metaphors collectively indicate what you become when you strive to thoughtfully improve your practice. When you share with your peers the insights and deeper understandings you develop from doing research, you help them develop informed and autonomous voices for their teaching too.

WHAT PURPOSEFUL RESEARCH DOES FOR YOU

Systematic classroom research that is purposeful moves you toward new ways of thinking. Some of these ways are described below.[10]

Toward Autonomy, Empowerment, and Emancipation

Fosnot (1989) notes that teacher research should be problem based and involve specific activities, including exploring, problem posing, and problem solving. This process, Fosnot holds, leads to teacher empowerment. She notes, "Prospective teachers who have been taught to question and construct creative, possible solutions will be empowered as individuals and will be able to facilitate such empowerment of children" (p. 13).

Self-empowerment helps you become more autonomous in your classroom decision making. Moreover, by (a) reflecting critically on the results of classroom-based research and weighing the results against existing norms, practices, and beliefs, (b) taking account of your increased understanding of teaching that results from doing classroom-based research, and (c) changing your teaching actions as a result of your research, you become more aware of the constraints that your own beliefs impose on your teaching. Teacher research also helps you become more aware of the constraints imposed on your teaching by social and bureaucratic factors.[11] Lather uses the concept of emancipation to describe this process.[12] Emancipation relates to the greater ownership you assume for your teaching and to the increased awareness you acquire for your classroom actions. An outcome of these actions is for you to view your teaching critically and to see teaching as an ever-changing, dynamic process always becoming something new.[13]

Toward a Vivid Picture of Classroom Teaching

When you do systematic teacher research, you have to somehow make strange the familiar terrain of the classroom. You must interpret the depth of the classroom landscapes that you tend to see with regularity. You spent literally thousands of hours in school classrooms as a student earlier in your life. During this time, you became socialized into the norms and practices of schools. Consequently, you already have many personal theories about good and bad teaching. With this familiarity, how can you begin looking deeper into the teaching process? How can you ask interesting questions about the very classroom instruction that has become commonplace? Purposeful research is one strategy for asking important questions about teaching and for moving beyond the barrier of extreme familiarity.

Making the familiar terrain of the classroom strange by doing purposive research helps you develop a more vivid picture of life in your classroom. It enables you to see beyond the normal events of daily classroom life. Kemmis and McTaggart (1988) note that doing purposive research helps you build "a more vivid picture of life and work in the situation, [of] constraints on action and more importantly, of what might now be possible" (p. 14).

Toward Reflective Thought and Action

Classroom research that involves focused reflective thinking helps you go beyond your everyday teaching experiences. It helps you think more carefully about your classroom instruction by asking you to reflect on your own beliefs about teaching. This kind of reflective thinking can turn practical, everyday problems into interesting research questions with important theoretical significance. Reflective thinking is discussed more in Chapter 12.

Toward Patterns of Change and Transformation

As you learn about teaching to culturally diverse students through research projects, you become aware of how, when, and why you should change your teaching strategies. As you make changes in your teaching, you observe the consequences of these changes, evaluate these consequences critically, and then make further modifications as needed.[14] Using this process continuously helps you develop patterns of ongoing improvement in your teaching. You then enter an almost continuous stream of transformation, of moving to a state that is more informed, more studied, more thoughtfully approached. Regarding the relationship between purposive research and transformation in teachers' classroom lives, Allen and her colleagues (Allen, Combs, Hendricks, Nash, & Wilson, 1988) note that when teachers do purposive research, their classroom instruction is "transformed in important ways: [teachers] become theorists, articulating the intentions, testing their assumptions, and finding connections with practice" (p. 386).

Toward an Increased Celebration of Diversity

The work of Garibaldi (1992) and Zeichner (1993) suggests that doing research in your classroom helps you understand factors that limit student success and that marginalize students in school. Teacher education programs have been criticized for not helping preservice teachers become more aware of the influence of cultural factors on their classroom instruction.[15] The activities and projects throughout this book are intended to address these criticisms by engaging you over time in exploring and examining specific issues surrounding diversity in schools.

Toward an Understanding of Teacher as Researcher

As you engage in the research projects in the following chapters, you develop a fuller understanding of the value of becoming a classroom researcher. You learn that systematic research is

- classroom based
- practice oriented
- problem focused
- needs focused

You also learn that teacher-directed classroom research fosters

- practical theory
- theoretical practice
- greater levels of teaching expertise
- deeper understandings about classroom dynamics
- critical analysis of practice
- habits of critical thinking
- collaborative teaching
- classroom autonomy (through careful observation, thoughtful reflection, and corresponding action)

BENEFITS FROM DOING RESEARCH

You get two key benefits from doing teacher research.[16] First, doing research helps you develop intercultural competence as a classroom teacher. Bennett (1990) describes intercultural competence as "the ability to interpret communications (language, signs, gestures), some unconscious cues (such as body language), and customs in cultural styles different from one's own" (p. 293). Zeichner (1993) suggests that because of our personal histories and unique family backgrounds, we are all intercultural beings. Being intercultural, however, doesn't ensure the ability to be sensitive to cultural styles different from your own, especially if you have limited involvement with other cultures.

Intercultural competence is requisite to effective communication in classrooms with diverse student populations. Developing a sensitivity toward, an appreciation of, and respect for other cultural groups in the classroom helps you develop intercultural competence by connecting with students in meaningful ways.[17] The research projects in this book, therefore, are intended to help you acquire intercultural competence in the classroom by increasing your sensitivity toward individual classroom needs of all students.

Second, doing research that focuses specifically on diversity issues helps you examine any discriminatory beliefs you might unknowingly have for teaching culturally diverse students. Such attributes can have subtle, yet powerful, influences on your classroom learning environment.[18] Some cultural biases you have might be so subtle that you don't even know how the biases influence student learning in counterproductive ways. Exploring how your stereotypes influence classroom instruction provides benefits for you and your students. These benefits include

- fostering academic equity in your classroom
- developing cultural respect for other persons in the classroom
- placing value on students' cultures
- establishing high academic expectations for all students
- acknowledging individual needs of students
- viewing all students as capable learners
- developing a culturally sensitive classroom curriculum

THE PROCESS OF PURPOSIVE TEACHER RESEARCH

Discussed below is one process for doing teacher research. First, following the work of Evans and Winograd (1992), two types of teacher research are described.[19] Second, a cognitive model that explains how you acquire new knowledge about teaching as you do research is discussed. Third, a five-phase model for conducting research projects on cultural diversity is suggested. Finally, strategies for gathering information as you carry out the projects are recommended.

An important note needs to be made about the model of action research we describe below. The model, though useful and current, is not the only model you may use. A major premise of action research and other forms of classroom-based, teacher-directed inquiry is that new models evolve with each project and with each new group of participants. When conducting action research, you should also use strategies that fit you best, that fit your personality and style. And always remember to remain flexible throughout the process: What works great with one group or one project might not work for another.

Types of Teacher Research

Interventionist Research. In interventionist research,[20] you develop a specific plan to initiate, explore, and examine change in some aspect of your teaching. You then determine how this change influences the nature of your instruction. For example, you might develop a plan to determine which cooperative learning strategy works best with your students. You would actually try out several strategies over time, documenting the effects of each. Not all readers of this book, however, have their own classrooms and thus do not have the freedom to effect change in classroom teaching. Consequently, these persons are unable to implement freely the interventionist model of doing classroom research. For this reason, we include noninterventionist research projects in various chapters.

Noninterventionist Research. Noninterventionist research examines teaching and learning within preexisting instruction. This form of research does not involve changes in the instructional environment; rather, it explores existing classroom phenomena. Noninterventionist research helps you develop a deeper understanding of classroom action and provides you with time to reflect carefully on your existing beliefs about teaching, perhaps reconstructing your beliefs throughout this process.[21] As an example of noninterventionist research, you can observe how different teaching styles (e.g., student centered, subject centered) influence students' classroom participation. You wouldn't actually alter classroom instruction for this research. You would make observations of teachers who demonstrate different teaching styles and then compare and contrast the results of your observations.

A Cognitive Model for Teacher Research

The research projects in this book are developed around a five-phase model,[22] as shown in Figure 2–1.[23] The model is intended to reflect research that is developmental,

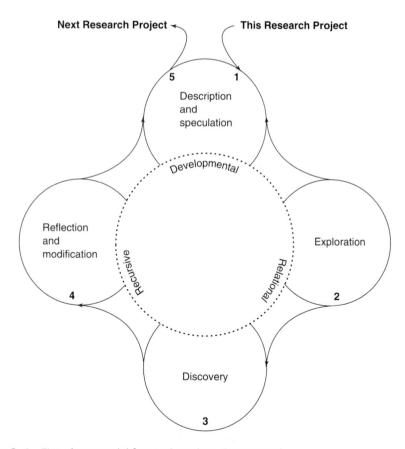

Figure 2–1 Five-phase model for site-based teacher research

recursive, and relational.[24] The model is developmental because the research you undertake continuously redefines itself during the study; that is, as you undertake a research project, you pose questions that lead to focused observations. Your observations and the other information you gather as you carry out the research cause you to revise your original questions or develop entirely new questions so that they are more relevant to your immediate school or classroom context. The model is recursive in that any phase of the research can be repeated numerous times during the study. The relational quality of the model suggests that each phase relates to all other phases. No phase, then, is independent of other phases, but all phases are collectively dependent on each other.

Five-Phase Model for Doing Research

Description and Speculation.   The first phase of the research process is description and speculation. In this phase, you choose a research topic by asking questions (posing problems) about some dimension of your teaching. You also speculate on what topics are most beneficial to explore. This phase begins with your personal awareness of teaching, which includes your beliefs, assumptions, personal practical knowledge, and personal theories for teaching. To begin this phase, ask yourself open-ended questions about a specific topic, what Spradley (1979) calls "grand tour questions." Examples of these questions: For the topic I've selected, what is happening here? What are the dimensions of the topic I might study? What specific dimension seems to be the most pressing and most salient? What might happen if I change something in my teaching?

Asking yourself these questions gives you the freedom to explore topics based on your informational needs and perceived teaching problems.[25] Kelsay (1991) reports that teacher researchers usually make decisions about what to explore on the basis of what they perceive to be the most useful in their classrooms. As an example of this decision-making process, Skroback-Heisler conducted a classroom-based research project based on perceived needs of the local school context.[26] This project, described briefly in the Appendix to this chapter, was conducted to determine the informational needs that limited-English-speaking Hispanic parents have for determining the academic progress of their children.

To help you explore culturally diverse learning environments, we have posed problems for selected chapters.[27] These problems have been turned into research projects. We've assumed that these projects have universal appeal to preservice and in-service teachers and are generalizable to most school contexts. The obvious limitation of this assumption is that teaching situations vary greatly for teachers. School contexts differ in their local cultures and in the diversity of their students. For example, school contexts and student diversity differ considerably between schools in rural Alaska[28] and Nogales, Arizona.[29] Therefore, you may need to modify the questions we ask and the topics we suggest to better suit your immediate needs.

Exploration.   Following the description and speculation phase is the exploration phase, during which you actually conduct research. As you describe a research topic and speculate on its potential to improve your practice, ask yourself additional questions, such as, How will I find out more about the topic I've identified? What strategies will I use to explore the topic? What other research has been done on my topic? After you've considered these questions and located additional readings related to your topic, you'll be more informed to carry out the research.

In the exploration phase, you develop a plan for gathering information and a schedule for carrying out the study. Included in this plan are strategies for gathering and analyzing information and for monitoring the study closely over time. You also must consider the ethical implications of involving key stakeholders in your study. This is especially true for students whose position of deference to you must be safeguarded with anonymity in any reports you develop about your study and in any conversations you have with peers and administrators.

Discovery. Although the discovery phase is third in our model, it actually occurs throughout the research project. In the discovery phase, you begin thinking more about what you've discovered during the study. This step aligns with what Schön (1987) calls "reflection in action." A hoped-for outcome of this kind of thinking is a careful consideration of your practice, thus setting the stage for the reconstruction of your teaching practice.

Reflection and Modification. You begin reflecting on your study during the exploration phase. In the reflection and modification phase, however, you think more directly about your research project and develop a formal or informal report of your analysis (see the Appendix to this chapter). As you construct your report, you reflect on (a) your personal beliefs and assumptions about teaching that you recorded prior to the study, (b) your teaching practice or your views of what practice should be, and (c) your classroom and school environments. As you reflect on these three areas, you will have opportunities to modify your teacher beliefs and your practice.

Description and Speculation. For the final phase of the research, you return to the description and speculation component of the research. You begin thinking about additional studies related to the one you just completed. In this phase, you ask, Given what I've learned from this project, what do I now need (or want) to know more about? What additional questions can I ask about my original problem? These questions bring closure to your present study while serving as a stepping stone to your next project.

Strategies for Doing the Research

In the description and exploration phases of doing research, you will choose strategies for gathering information, for monitoring the study, and for charting changes in your beliefs. The list of strategies below follows the suggestions of New and Sleeter (1993), who report that a first step toward doing classroom research on diversity issues should be the acquisition of ethnography skills by teachers—that is, "collecting and interpreting data as an ethnographer would" (p. 5).[30] Similarly, Delpit (1988) claims that "we must become ethnographers in the true sense" (p. 297) if we are to fully understand the implications of cultural diversity on classroom instruction.

Observations.   *Observations of specific aspects of the classroom, school, or community context.* You make observations as a participant observer or as a nonparticipant observer. As a participant observer, you observe classroom activities while fulfilling the duties associated with the role of teacher, student teacher, school counselor, or administrator. As a nonparticipant observer, you are not an interactive part of the process you are observing. For example, you make observations from a particular location in the classroom as you watch a lesson being presented.

Anecdotal Records and Field Notes.   *Descriptive detailed accounts over time of specific events, actions, or expressions of students, teachers, other professional school staff, parents, and community members.* Each entry you make in your field notebook is dated and contains enough background information so that you can revisit, vicariously and with rich meaning, each record at a later date. Anecdotal records and field notes are also important places to record insights you might have while making observations.

Theoretical Memos.   *Reflective analytical statements about the research topic.* Unlike anecdotal records and field notes, theoretical memos are written away from the actual observation site. They are best written when you are alone, after you've talked about your research with others or read other information about your study. The memos you write should be more general in scope and reflect deeper insights you have about your study.

Document Analysis.   *Close examination of materials such as school policy statements, classroom rules, student work, bulletin boards, handouts, tests, curriculum materials, and classroom and school decorations.* School documents are valuable sources of information for helping you understand many dimensions of schooling. Classroom instructional materials are especially helpful in understanding the nature of the curriculum.

Personal (Reflection) Journal.   *Personal account, in narrative form, of your insights, thoughts, perceptions, and attitudes about what you are observing and learning from your study.* Like theoretical memos, personal journals are intended to help you reflect on your study and record your personal thoughts that only you (or other privileged persons) will read. This kind of reflection is helpful, as Gonzalez (1993) found, for you to critically examine your attitudes and educational philosophies. Personal journals also help you become more aware of your influence on the educational success of your students (p. 38).

Interviews and Conversations.   *Structured and unstructured dialogue with other persons for gathering the perceptions, insights, and personal views of participants in your study.* Structured interviews are conducted with a set of predetermined questions to be asked each research participant. Unstructured interviews are open ended and allow research participants flexibility in responding to and participating in the interview.

Interviews may be planned or unplanned. Unplanned interviews are spontaneous. They can be very rich with information. Note taking during unplanned interviews is unlikely. You should be prepared to capture key quotes from these interviews immediately after leaving the site. Planned interviews usually require you to plan the basic structure of the interview before you actually conduct it. Therefore, you very likely will begin planned interviews with questions prepared in advance; these questions are intended to find out specific information. Do not think, however, that planned interviews consist only of structured dialogue. Rather, as interviewees begin answering questions, you should further explore their responses. There will always be an element of spontaneity in planned interviews. Not only should you take notes during these interviews, but you should also be prepared to audiotape them if permission is granted. Listening to the tapes at a later time can help you reflect more carefully on what was said, thus providing further insights.

Interviews conducted with persons from other cultural groups or another gender can be a challenging adventure even for the experienced researcher. Subtle cultural and gender differences can interfere with open communication. Cultural and/or gender sensitivity training might be beneficial prior to conducting interviews.

Conversational interviews, as described by Oakley (1981), can be useful for conducting your interviews. These interviews are spontaneous and interactive, with you as researcher giving as much information about yourself as you get from your research participant.

Audio- and Videotape Recording.   *Taped records of conversations, interviews, or events.* Audio- and videotape recordings can be indispensable to your research. Audiotapes allow you to revisit your interviews with more attention. Videotapes enable you to watch events carefully and repeatedly if necessary. Before doing any type of taping, however, you should obtain permission from research participants and school officials.

Tests of Student Performance.   *Records of student achievement on classroom or school exams.* Records of student performance are central to some research projects, especially tests that determine the efficacy of modifying instructional strategies.

DEVELOPING A RESEARCH SUPPORT SYSTEM

A research support system is very useful for carrying out your research project. In a study of action research, Evans and Winograd (1992) found that teachers overwhelmingly thought the presence of a support system was an important factor in enriching the quality of the research experience. One type of support system is a group of peers who are exploring the same or similar research topics as you. The model of action research proposed by Kemmis and McTaggart (1988) is based solely on group collegiality and collaboration. Moreover, Gonzalez (1993) reported that one group of teachers who worked in groups doing research projects, rather than work alone, had opportunities to listen to others' beliefs and personal philosophies for teaching diverse students and thus increased their awareness of the strengths and limitations of their own beliefs about multicultural classrooms. In research support groups, you develop insights in talking with peers about your study, receive moral and technical support for doing the research, and share your experience with peers doing similar research.

Your support system should extend beyond your immediate peer group. University professors, expert teachers, scholarly literature, and community resources can all be part of your support network when doing site-based teacher research. Broadening your support network helps you gain additional insights into your study as you hear informed and experienced views on your topic.

ACTIVITY 2.1   Description and Speculation

Begin thinking about a specific research topic related to classroom diversity issues you might undertake. Working alone, write out several topics that interest you.

1. _____
2. _____
3. _____
4. _____

Select one of these topics, perhaps one you know the most about or one that has the most interest for you, and pose a problem for your teaching. For example, one topic you might consider is classroom social interactions between students with different ethnicities. To pose a problem for this topic, ask yourself specific questions for description and speculation.

1. For the social interactions among students in my class (or for the class I'm observing) who have other cultural backgrounds, what is happening here?
2. What are the dimensions of social interactions relative to cultural diversity that I might study?
3. What studies have been done on social interactions among students in culturally diverse classes?
4. What specific dimension of social interaction seems to be the most pressing and most salient?
5. What might happen to the social interactions between culturally diverse students in my classroom if I change from large group work to small group work?

ACTIVITY 2.2   Research Support Group

Share the problem you posed in Activity 2.1 with a group of peers. Ask for their insight into your problem and seek advice for how you might conduct your study. Discuss these items with your peers:

- value of the topic for informing classroom teaching
- related topics that might also be worthy of exploration

- sources of information (e.g., research reports, books) that can give you further understanding about the topic
- methods for gathering information
- persons who will participate in your study
- ways of reporting the results of your study

Record insights about your research problem that you gain from your peers.

SUMMARY

In this chapter, we introduced you to systematic teacher research, which forms the basis for many of the activities you will do in the remaining chapters. Our intention was to help you develop a better understanding of teacher research as a means for deepening your personal knowledge about teaching in culturally diverse classrooms.

By becoming a classroom-based researcher, you will be continuously assessing your own beliefs about how and what to teach. Bissex and Bullock (1987) summarize what purposeful research can do for you as a teacher:

Research in this way can be transforming because it changes the way we see others and ourselves (p. 15). . . . [D]oing classroom research changes teachers and the teaching profession from the inside out, from the bottom up, through changes in teachers themselves. And therein lies its power. (p. 27)

NOTES

1. Constructing a personal knowledge base for teaching and becoming a "scientist" of one's own teaching are derived from the work of George Kelly on construct psychology. See Kelly, G. (1970). A brief introduction to personal construct theory. In D. Bannister (Ed.), *Perspectives in personal construct theory* (pp. 1–29). New York: Academic Press. The notion of personal practical knowledge of teaching used in this chapter and throughout this book is grounded in the work of Clandinin and Connelly. See, for example, Clandinin, J. (1985). Personal practical knowledge: A study of teachers' classroom images. *Curriculum Inquiry, 15*(4), 351–385; Connelly, M., & Clandinin, J. (1990). On narrative method, personal philosophy, and narrative unities in the story of teaching. *Journal of Research in Science Teaching, 23*(4), 293–310.
2. For a discussion of personal theories, see Hunt, D. (1987). *Beginning with ourselves.* Cambridge, MA: Brookline Books.
3. Banks, J. (1991). Teaching multicultural literacy to teachers. *Teaching Education, 4*(1), 135–144.
4. For example, see Lytle, S., & Cochran-Smith, M. (1992). Teacher research as a way of knowing. *Harvard Educational Review, 62*(4), 447–474. See also Zeichner, K. (1994, April). *Action research and issues of equity and social justice in preservice teacher education.* Paper presented at the Annual Meeting of the American Educational Research Association, New Orleans.
5. Kemmis, S., & McTaggart, R. (1988). *The action research planner* (rev. 3rd ed.). Victoria, Australia: Deakin University Press.

6. See Lee Shulman's discussion of the forms of knowledge that teachers construct: Shulman, L. (1987). Those who understand: Knowledge growth in teaching. *Educational Researcher, 15*(2), 4–14.

7. For example, see Catherine Fosnot's discussion of teachers as field researchers: Fosnot, C. (1989). *Enquiring teachers enquiring learners: A constructivist approach for teaching.* New York: Teachers College Press, pp. 21–28. See also Lytle, S., & Cochran-Smith, M. (1992). Teacher research as a way of knowing. *Harvard Educational Review, 62*(4), 447–474.

8. Fosnot, C. (1989). *Enquiring teachers enquiring learners: A constructivist approach for teaching.* New York: Teachers College Press, p. 15.

9. Kelsay, K. (1991). When experience is the best teacher: The teacher as researcher. *Action in Teacher Education, 13*(1), 14–21.

10. The various ways we discuss are derived mainly from the following sources: Kemmis, S., & McTaggart, R. (1988). *The action research planner* (rev. 3rd ed.). Victoria, Australia: Deakin University Press; Lather, P. (1986). Research as praxis. *Harvard Educational Review, 56*(3), 257–277; Lather, P. (1991). *Getting smart: Feminist research and pedagogy with/in the postmodern.* New York: Routledge, Chapter 1; Lytle, S., & Cochran-Smith, M. (1992). Teacher research as a way of knowing. *Harvard Educational Review, 62*(4), 447–474.

11. See, for example, Goodman, J. (1987). Factors in becoming a proactive elementary school teacher: A preliminary study of selected novices. *Journal of Education for Teaching, 13*(3), 207–227.

12. Lather, P. (1991). *Getting smart: Feminist research and pedagogy with/in the postmodern.* New York: Routledge.

13. The notion of transformation in teaching that we are using was taken from Freire, P. (1972). *Pedagogy of the oppressed.* Auckland, New Zealand: Penguin Books.

14. Kemmis, S., & McTaggart, R. (1988). *The action research planner* (rev. 3rd ed.). Victoria, Australia: Deakin University Press, p. 44.

15. For example, see Irvine, J. J. (1992). Making teacher education culturally responsive. In M. E. Dilworth (Ed.), *Diversity in teacher education: New expectations* (pp. 79–92). San Francisco: Jossey-Bass. See also Grant, C., & Secada, W. (1990). Preparing teachers for diversity. In W. R. Houston (Ed.), *Handbook of research on teacher education* (pp. 403–422). New York: Macmillan.

16. These benefits are described more fully in Bennett, C. (1988, April). *The effects of a multicultural education course on preservice teachers' attitudes, knowledge, and behavior.* Paper presented at the Annual Meeting of the American Educational Research Association, New Orleans.

17. See Heath, S. B. (1983). *Ways with words: Language, life, and work in communities and classrooms.* New York: Cambridge University Press.

18. For example, see the classic study by Ray Rist: Rist, R. (1971). Student social class and teacher expectations: The self-fulfilling prophecy in ghetto education. *Harvard Educational Review, 40,* 411–451. An excellent discussion of the influence of racism, bias, and stereotype on classroom instruction is found in Chapter 3 of Nieto, S. (1992). *Affirming diversity: The sociopolitical context of multicultural education.* New York: Longman.

19. Evans and Winograd (1992) identify two types of research that you can do: interventionist and noninterventionist.

20. The premises of the interventionist approach align closely with those of the action research model described by Kemmis and McTaggart, 1988.

21. We used the noninterventionist research approach to develop Chapters 6 and 9 of this book. Using many of the strategies for gathering information we suggest in this chapter,

we examined the contexts of three schools. By engaging ourselves in this process, we were able to examine our own beliefs and assumptions about multicultural schools and have conversations with each other about our observations at these schools. This process caused us to refine our thinking about teaching in classrooms with ethnic diversity and gave us a fuller and richer view of multicultural classrooms than was possible from reading others' accounts.

22. The model in Figure 2–1 is based partly on the work of Neisser (1976). Neisser describes a three-part perceptual cycle for acquiring new knowledge. The cycle begins with anticipatory schemata (what you already know and what you believe to be true based on your prior experiences) that guide what you see and what you come to know in any situation. When applied to teacher research and cultural diversity, Neisser's perceptual cycle provides a framework for describing how and what you learn from doing the research. Anticipatory schemata guide classroom-based research in that these schemata guide what questions you will ask about cultural diversity and what information from the classroom you will actually gather. Finally, as you acquire information from the exploration process and as you compare new information with what you already know, you may modify your existing schemata and construct new understandings of the classroom.

23. See Strudler and Powell (1993). The model prescribed in Figure 2–1 developed by Strudler and Powell is a variation of the action research process suggested by Kemmis and McTaggart (1988).

24. See Allen et al., 1988, p. 380.

25. Informational needs and perceived problems are mentioned by McKernan (1988) and by Kemmis and McTaggart (1988) as reasons that teachers select research problems.

26. This research project was conducted to fulfill requirements of a graduate-level class in qualitative research.

27. Kemmis and McTaggart (1988) hold that teacher research should be comprised mostly of problem posing, rather than problem solving. Problem posing provides teachers with opportunities to think beyond daily problem solving and to look carefully at their teaching and at the classroom learning environment. See Kemmis and McTaggart, 1988, p. 21.

28. Noordhoff, K., & Kleinfeld, J. (1990). Shaping the rhetoric of reflection for multicultural settings. In R. Clift, W. R. Houston, & M. C. Pugash (Eds.), *Encouraging reflective practice in education: An analysis of issues and programs* (pp. 163–185). New York: Teachers College Press.

29. Lucas, T., Henze, R., & Donato, R. (1990). Promoting the success of Latino language-minority students: An exploratory study of six high schools. *Harvard Educational Review, 60*(3), 315–340.

30. See also Kemmis and McTaggart (1988) and Lather (1991).

APPENDIX	*Site-Based Teacher Research Project* *Latino Parents' Perspectives of Student Assessment* Linda Skroback-Heisler

Teaching experience for Linda Skroback-Heisler:

12 years junior high school reading
 4 years elementary school ESL
 4 years elementary school reading
 2 years high school adult education

Current teaching position:

Elementary ESL teacher

Languages spoken:

English, Spanish

Phase One: Description and Speculation

The questions for my study came about as a result of reflection about my classroom practice. Components of my multi-age (ages 6 to 10) primary English-as-a-second-language (ESL) classroom include developmentally appropriate integrated curriculum, immersion in English with inclusion of students' native languages, risk-free classroom climate, and authentic assessment. Students in my classroom work in groups for varying amounts of time on the basis of their own needs. If students who are 10 years old need to work with students who are 6 years old, then they do.

Within my classroom context, the school district's report card didn't seem to adequately describe ESL children's progress, so I developed an alternative form of reporting progress. During the last 4 years, I added comments to the district report card that initially began as several short paragraphs but that eventually grew into two pages of descriptive comments for each child in the classroom. The comments to parents were written in English, but I orally translated them into Spanish for Spanish-speaking parents during quarterly parent conferences.

Because I wasn't sure how my alternative form of reporting progress was working for parents, I decided to examine my alternative reporting strategies more formally. I selected seven families of my first graders because their children would remain in my classroom for another year, and we, as a collaborative group, could continue refining the reporting strategy over time. The questions I asked for this study were, What do Latino parents of my students understand about school district grade reports? Do parents understand my comments written in English and translated orally into Spanish? In what ways, if any, do I need to simplify or modify this practice? What do Latino parents want to know about their children's progress? What can we invent together (Latino parents and I) that will better help them understand their children's progress in school?

For some of these questions, I had background knowledge from an earlier project I had conducted. In addition to learning about the school system in one state in Mexico, I had learned much about the home life of one Latino family. By spending time in the home of one family, I had opportunities to meet families of several other students in my classroom. Now that I had some personal knowledge about the life of one family, I was better prepared to conduct this study. Moreover, the questions I posed were very important to me because I had moved from being dependent on a translator outside the immediate classroom to being able to interact on my own with the families in their native language.

Phase Two: Exploration

After posing specific questions noted above, I then needed to actually choose the families who participated in my study. I had several criteria for choosing families. First, they needed to be parents of the first graders I had in class all year. Also, as the younger students, the first graders would continue for another year in my multi-age classroom. The possibility of working with Latino parents for a second year was crucial to this research project. A majority of the parents spoke only Spanish, and I wanted to ascertain their concerns and suggestions about student assessment. Second, I needed their permission and time to answer the questions I posed. Six families met these criteria. I was pleased when a seventh parent of one of my second graders heard that I was talking with parents about schooling and asked to be involved in the study.

I developed a theoretical understanding for my study by reading literature about Latino demographics and Latino education. I also read literature on alternative assessment and ESL instruction (both theory and practice). Through one of my classes at the university, I also developed an interest in critical theory and in the work of Paulo Freire, and I found this particular body of literature to be relevant to my study. From my theoretical understanding and from the questions I posed, I then generated questions for my interviews with the parents and determined a timeline for completing the study.

During the exploration phase, I found that interviewing parents worked better if I used a conversational format, rather than a structured interview format. These informal conversational interviews led to a far wider range of questions and answers with the parents than I had initially anticipated. For a teacher researcher looking for specific answers to questions, our tangential conversations were often overwhelming for me, though in a positive way. Our interviews and conversations went far beyond answering my questions and not only have made a difference in my classroom practice but also have given me further directions to explore.

In my fieldwork for this study, I conducted the interviews with parents in their homes. This tactic was very helpful in allowing me to observe the family relationship at home relative to what we talked about in our interviews. Although I audiotaped all of the interviews, I nonetheless wrote field notes immediately after leaving the homes in order to remember as much as possible from our conversations. I also recorded anecdotal records in my field notes as often as I could during the interviews.

Many interesting anecdotes occurred after the tape recorder was turned off; I knew that these anecdotes would be important for my study, so I included them in my notes.

I reflected carefully on my study on a weekly basis throughout the project to review my progress, to consider what I was finding, to examine my own thoughts, and to maintain a fresh connection with my study. I taped all of the interviews and then transcribed them in Spanish. I looked for themes in the transcripts and in my field notes that linked parents' comments together and that provided me with further insight into my alternative strategy for reporting student progress.

Phase Three: Discovery

Most of the discoveries I made from this project were in learning about the home lives of my students. Specifically, I learned about parents' concerns and questions and found that their families were the most valuable issues in their lives. All of my students live in small apartments in two separate areas of the city. Near all of the apartment buildings I visited were grass, trees, and areas where children could play safely. Their apartments had varying numbers of televisions, VCRs, and stereos. Parents' concerns about their children were as diverse as knowing how math was taught, seeking advice for helping with homework, discussing absences caused by chicken pox, and regretting that they did not have sufficient time to spend with their children after working all day.

The parents viewed their children's education to be successful if it would help them ultimately get a job and support a family. Having their child attend college was not a goal for most of them, but being *buen educado* (well educated) was important. Within the seven families, one parent had been to high school in another country, several had completed junior high school, and most had completed up to the sixth grade. With a sixth-grade education, the parents thought they were *buen educado* and stated they were not limited by their own education. From these conversations, I learned to appreciate their values and to learn about people who had received an education different from mine or my colleagues'.

One interesting discovery from my study was what the parents said about learning the English language. The parents I interviewed stated that they did not find the English language necessary to learn because they could usually find a friend with English skills or simply look for a Spanish-speaking clerk in a store. One parent mentioned that not speaking English was a problem for her, but several others said they did not need English or would not consider going to English classes even if they were offered in a convenient location. About learning English, one mother noted:

> *Que crée que solo su inglés ya es suficiente. Y no, porque esta en un país libre, es un país donde pueden aprender. No solo en español, si no el portugués, el francés, el italiano, aquí hay la; oportunidad.* (They [Americans] believe that only English is sufficient. And it is not, because it is a free country, a country where they can learn not only in Spanish but in Portuguese, French, Italian. Here [in the United States] there is opportunity.)

An important benefit of this study, and something that to me was a major discovery, was the collaborative spirit I developed with the parents. The answers to my questions in our conversations were obviously important to my study, but the answers took on a minor importance, compared to the personal connections the parents and I made throughout this process. I also learned that even if parents did not communicate much orally during the actual interview, a strong connection between us was still made. I realized this when I received letters and phone calls further verifying that the interview time was well spent. As a result of this study, I received more notes and phone calls from the 7 families I worked with than from all the other 25 families in my classroom.

In response to the parents' answers, I changed several things in the area of assessment so that the parents would better understand their children's progress. The first and perhaps most obvious change involved reporting progress in Spanish. The parents wanted the comments written in Spanish on the forms. Because I translated the comments orally for several grading quarters, I was ready to take a risk and write them in Spanish and then write an English version for the school administration.

The second change I made in student assessment related to the frequency with which I communicated student progress to parents. For the elementary schools in the district where I work, report card conferences are held with parents only in November. Parents in this study, however, wanted informal conferences every 9 weeks.

A third change I made because of this study did not go into effect until the following year. Three of the families liked the idea of a checklist for learning about their children's progress, and three preferred my comments. One family thought the standard report card form was sufficient. On the basis of their ideas, I translated the district-approved checklist for math and literacy into Spanish. I then used this translated checklist instead of two pages of comments. Parents easily understood the Spanish checklist; it was more complete than the report card form alone and helped the parents understand more clearly what their children had learned.

Phase Four: Reflection and Modification

At the beginning of the study, my personal beliefs about reporting assessment to Latino parents were that the report card forms we used were not adequate to describe ESL learners, that the parents did not necessarily understand that their children were being compared with native-English-speaking children, and that parents needed more specific information. To address these concerns, I now develop individual comments and use checklists that more completely describe each child as a learner.

Suggestions from parents caused me to modify my teaching practices in four ways. The first three ways, as I noted above, relate to reporting grades: (a) write comments in Spanish for the parents and in English for the school administration, (b) have informal conferences with parents every grading period, and (c) develop checklists in Spanish and English that show what the child had learned in comparison to what was expected for first- and second-grade native-English speakers. The fourth change was possibly more subtle and overlaps both teaching practice and classroom environment. Because I became personally familiar with the parents, with their backgrounds, culture, and home lives, I was better prepared to connect home experiences with school experiences. For example, while discussing ecology and deserts with my students, I was able to say that Alex sees the Sonoran Desert and organ pipe cacti when he goes to visit his grandmother in Hermosillo and that Ana sees saguaros and ocotillos as in one of our classroom magazines when she goes to visit her grandparents in San Luis.

Phase Five: Description and Speculation

Parent collaboration and involvement were serendipitous by-products of my research. Given what I learned during this project, I am now investigating the process of building collaborative partnerships between Latino parents, me, and the school context. First, I am exploring the nature of the interaction between Latino parents and another teacher in my school. Second, I am examining home-school communication in one classroom by recording parents' perspectives of schools in the United States through daily school notes, formal conferences, informal meetings, and notes and letters written by parents to me. Finally, I am exploring how Latino parents' informational needs for their children's progress in school develop over time.

REFERENCES

Allen, J., Combs, J., Hendricks, M., Nash, P., & Wilson, S. (1988). Studying change: Teachers who become researchers. *Language Arts, 65*(4), 379–387.

Banks, J. (1991). Teaching multicultural literacy to teachers. *Teaching Education, 4*(1), 135–144.

Bennett, C. (1988, April). *The effects of a multicultural education course on preservice teachers' attitudes, knowledge, and behavior.* Paper presented at the Annual Meeting of the American Educational Research Association, New Orleans.

Bennett, C. (1990). *Comprehensive multicultural education: Theory and practice* (2nd ed.). Boston: Allyn & Bacon.

Bissex, G. L., & Bullock, R. H. (1987). *Seeing for ourselves: Case-study research by teachers of writing.* Portsmouth, NH: Heinemann.

Clandinin, J. (1985). Personal practical knowledge: A study of teachers' classroom images. *Curriculum Inquiry, 15*(4), 351–385.

Connelly, M., & Clandinin, J. (1990). On narrative method, personal philosophy, and narrative unities in the story of teaching. *Journal of Research in Science Teaching, 23*(4), 293–310.

Delpit, L. (1988). The silenced dialogue: Power and pedagogy in educating other people's children. *Harvard Educational Review, 58*(3), 280–298.

Evans, T., & Winograd, K. (1992, April). *The quality of experience of preservice teachers as they engage in an ill-defined action research task.* Paper presented at the Annual Meeting of the American Educational Research Association, San Francisco.

Fosnot, C. (1989). *Enquiring teachers enquiring learners: A constructivist approach for teaching.* New York: Teachers College Press.

Freire, P. (1972). *Pedagogy of the oppressed.* Auckland, New Zealand: Penguin Books.

Garibaldi, A. M. (1992). Preparing teachers for culturally diverse classrooms. In M. E. Dilworth (Ed.), *Diversity in teacher education: New expectations* (pp. 23–39). San Francisco: Jossey-Bass.

Gonzalez, V. (1993, April). *Using reflective teaching for changing in-service teachers' attitudes and increasing their cognitive-ethical development and academic knowledge in multicultural education.* Paper presented at the Annual Meeting of the American Educational Research Association, Atlanta.

Goodman, J. (1987). Factors in becoming a proactive elementary school teacher: A preliminary study of selected novices. *Journal of Education for Teaching, 13*(3), 207–227.

Grant, C., & Secada, W. (1990). Preparing teachers for diversity. In W. R. Houston (Ed.), *Handbook of research on teacher education* (pp. 403–422). New York: Macmillan.

Greene, M. (1978). *Landscapes of learning.* New York: Teachers College Press.

Heath, S. B. (1983). *Ways with words: Language, life, and work in communities and classrooms.* New York: Cambridge University Press.

Hunt, D. (1987). *Beginning with ourselves.* Cambridge, MA: Brookline Books.

Irvine, J. J. (1992). Making teacher education culturally responsive. In M. E. Dilworth (Ed.), *Diversity in teacher education: New expectations* (pp. 79–92). San Francisco: Jossey-Bass.

Kelly, G. (1970). A brief introduction to personal construct theory. In D. Bannister (Ed.), *Perspectives in personal construct theory* (pp. 1–29). New York: Academic Press.

Kelsay, K. (1991). When experience is the best teacher: The teacher as researcher. *Action in Teacher Education, 13*(1), 14–21.

Kemmis, S., & McTaggart, R. (1988). *The action research planner* (rev. 3rd ed.). Victoria, Australia: Deakin University Press.

Lather, P. (1986). Research as praxis. *Harvard Educational Review, 56*(3), 257–277.

Lather, P. (1991). *Getting smart: Feminist research and pedagogy with/in the postmodern.* New York: Routledge.

Lucas, T., Henze, R., & Donato, R. (1990). Promoting the success of Latino language-minority students: An exploratory study of six high schools. *Harvard Educational Review, 60*(3), 315–340.

Lytle, S., & Cochran-Smith, M. (1992). Teacher research as a way of knowing. *Harvard Educational Review, 62*(4), 447–474.

McKernan, J. (1988). Teacher as researcher: Paradigm and praxis. *Contemporary Education, 59*(3), 154–158.

Neisser, U. (1976). *Cognition and reality: Principles and implications of cognitive psychology.* New York: Freeman.

New, C., & Sleeter, C. (1993, April). *Preservice teachers' perspectives of diverse children: Implications for teacher education.* Paper presented at the Annual Meeting of the American Educational Research Association, Atlanta.

Nieto, S. (1992). *Affirming diversity: The sociopolitical context of multicultural education.* New York: Longman.

Noordhoff, K., & Kleinfeld, J. (1990). Shaping the rhetoric of reflection for multicultural settings. In R. Clift, W. R. Houston, & M. C. Pugash (Eds.), *Encouraging reflective practice in education: An analysis of issues and programs* (pp. 163–185). New York: Teachers College Press.

Oakley, A. (1981). Interviewing women: A contradiction in terms. In H. Roberts (Ed.), *Doing feminist research* (pp. 30–61). Boston: Routledge & Kegan Paul.

Rist, R. (1971). Student social class and teacher expectations: The self-fulfilling prophecy in ghetto education. *Harvard Educational Review, 40,* 411–451.

Schön, D. (1987). *Educating the reflective practitioner.* San Francisco: Jossey-Bass.

Shulman, L. (1987). Those who understand: Knowledge growth in teaching. *Educational Researcher, 15*(2), 4–14.

Spradley, J. (1979). *The ethnographic interview.* New York: Holt, Rinehart & Winston.

Storm, H. (1994). *Lightningbolt.* New York: Ballantine Books.

Strudler, N., & Powell, R. (1994). Preparing teacher leaders and change agents for technology in education. *Journal of Technology and Teacher Education, 1*(4), 393–408.

Zeichner, K. (1993, April). *Educating teachers for diversity.* Paper presented at the Annual Meeting of the American Educational Research Association, Atlanta.

Zeichner, K. (1994, April). *Action research and issues of equity and social justice in preservice teacher education.* Paper presented at the Annual Meeting of the American Educational Research Association, New Orleans.

Chapter 3

Examining Your Autobiography and Beliefs About Cultural Integration

Life experiences and background are obviously key ingredients of the person that we are, of our sense of self. To the degree that we invest our "self" in our teaching, experience and background therefore shape our practice.   (Goodson, 1991, p. 144)

Consider first your life story–the sort of account you might give if musing over how you got to be where you are, or if trying to make your past known to another.   (Gergen, 1991, p. 161)

INTRODUCTION

As you teach in classrooms, you bring your life experiences and personal background to your practice. With your life experiences come much of what you have learned socially and what you have become personally. This chapter's central premise, which follows from Goodson's (1991) comment above, is that your life experiences and personal background contribute in important ways to the kind of teacher you are,[1] to your teaching self,[2] and to the classroom environment you establish for your students.

Studies with both preservice and experienced teachers suggest that your life history shapes the beliefs and personal theories you have for your teaching.[3] If your life history has been limited primarily to monocultural experiences, you may have a limited sensitivity for teaching students with culturally diverse backgrounds.

Considering your life story (Gergen, 1991) helps you understand how your prior experiences contribute to your ability to effectively reach all students in multicultural classrooms. Examining your autobiography also helps you understand your cultural identity and clarify your cultural values.[4] Clarifying your values and exploring your cultural identity are essential first steps toward having successful classroom interactions with culturally diverse students.[5]

The purpose of this chapter is to help you discover how biography shapes your beliefs and practices for teaching culturally diverse students. In thinking deeply and critically about your biographical experiences both inside and outside school, you develop a greater awareness of how these experiences shape your classroom instruction. In this chapter, you also explore the biographical antecedents to your beliefs for teaching culturally diverse students and begin charting changes in these beliefs. This approach reflects the view expressed by Banks (1991) that teachers must be engaged in a proactive knowledge construction process that illuminates the degree to which their values and assumptions about culture align with those of their students.[6]

ACTIVITY 3.1 Thinking About Your Autobiography

Below are autobiographies by three prospective teachers: Amy, Jennifer, and Karrie. Amy and Jennifer lived in the same urban school district when they were growing up, but they attended different schools.[7] Karrie attended rural schools in a farming and ranching community in the Southwest. Amy and Karrie attended middle-class public schools; Jennifer attended upper middle-class private schools. The autobiographies[8] of Amy, Jennifer, and Karrie include salient educational experiences from primary to postsecondary school. They wrote about their social class structure (middle class), the value their families had for education, and the role school played in their lives. They also wrote about their experiences in school with other cultural groups.

As you read their autobiographies, think how your prior experiences are similar to and different from those of Amy, Jennifer, and Karrie. Think about how their autobiographies have provided them with different values for teaching. Consider also how your teaching beliefs and perspectives might differ from theirs for classrooms that contain a culturally diverse group of students. Use the questions in Figure 3–1 to help you gain insights from comparing the three autobiographies.

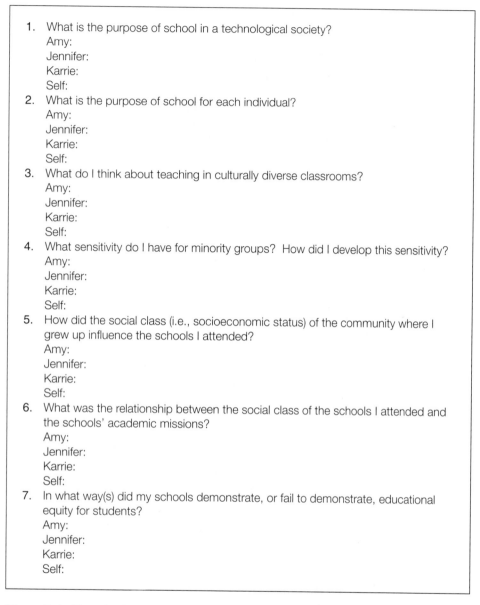

1. What is the purpose of school in a technological society?
    Amy:
    Jennifer:
    Karrie:
    Self:
2. What is the purpose of school for each individual?
    Amy:
    Jennifer:
    Karrie:
    Self:
3. What do I think about teaching in culturally diverse classrooms?
    Amy:
    Jennifer:
    Karrie:
    Self:
4. What sensitivity do I have for minority groups? How did I develop this sensitivity?
    Amy:
    Jennifer:
    Karrie:
    Self:
5. How did the social class (i.e., socioeconomic status) of the community where I grew up influence the schools I attended?
    Amy:
    Jennifer:
    Karrie:
    Self:
6. What was the relationship between the social class of the schools I attended and the schools' academic missions?
    Amy:
    Jennifer:
    Karrie:
    Self:
7. In what way(s) did my schools demonstrate, or fail to demonstrate, educational equity for students?
    Amy:
    Jennifer:
    Karrie:
    Self:

Figure 3–1   Thought diagram for exploring autobiography

Amy Owens

The first school I entered was Mt. Zion. It wasn't a real school building, but it was a preschool in a church. I don't remember much about attending there, but I do remember there being maybe 30 or 40 students. I remember taking naps every day. I was dropped off by my parents in the morning, and the baby-sitter would pick me up in the afternoon. It was a place for me to be while my parents were working.

I attended kindergarten at Matthew Sixth Grade Center (MSGC). It was a public school. Although MSGC had only sixth grade, kindergarten was there too. MSGC was about four houses down the street from where I lived, so I was able to walk to school while my mother watched me. In kindergarten there were maybe 15 students, and all of us were Black. The school was located in a Black neighborhood.

For first through fifth grades, I attended Rocky Elementary School. This was also a public school. It was located on the other side of town from where I lived. I had to get up early every morning to catch the bus for school. Everybody was being bused here, including both Blacks and Whites. It was kind of scary at first. I was a small child having to ride all the way across town with kids much bigger than I.

After attending Rocky Elementary (grades 1–5), I then returned to MSGC, where I finished sixth grade. When I attended MSGC in kindergarten, it was an all-Black school. But in sixth grade, it was mixed with minorities and Whites. It seemed like more Whites were being bused there than the number of Blacks who were attending at that time.

After sixth grade, I attended Park Junior High (PJH). I went there for the seventh through ninth grades. I made new friends but kept old friends too. I seemed to be going to school with some of the same kids I grew up with. By junior high, however, I was able to distinguish the housing project kids from everyone else. The project kids were rowdy and constantly getting into trouble. Most students at the PJH came from middle-class families.

I couldn't wait to get into high school; I attended Claire High School (CHS). I was an office aide, so I knew most of the staff too. I got along with everyone. After I became 16 years old, my friends and I were able to drive to school. My senior year was great.

My family had a big impact on my education. There are only four of us in my family. My father, Elemon, grew up in Tallulah, Louisiana. He graduated from high school and never went to college. He doesn't have a lot of book knowledge, but he does have street knowledge. Jessie, my mother, did go to college for a few years. She grew up in a small town called Delhi, Louisiana, about 25 miles from where my dad grew up. After my mother got pregnant with me, she never went back to school. Whenever I had a problem with my schoolwork, she would always help me out, especially in math. Maybe that's why I love math so much now.

My parents were very strict when I was in school. I had to show them every report card I got. They never gave out any money for my grades either. They thought that getting good grades was something I should do anyway. I remember in ninth grade I cried all the way home from school. I got my first C on my report card. My father said, "C is average, and you are above average."

In junior high and high school, we had student body officers, and in high school I was treasurer of the class. We had an organization called Human Relations. It was for everyone, but Blacks mostly participated in it. I played basketball for two years. There were scholarships for minorities, and I received an academic scholarship. I graduated with honors in the top percentage of my class.

School has played a major role in my life. Without school I believe I would be lost. I spent 5 days a week, approximately 6 hours a day there, not including extracurricular activities. School can play a big role in a person's life, but it's really up to the individual to make it work for him or her.

Throughout my life, I have seen and been around many ethnic groups in schools. As I think back, there wasn't much interaction between them. During recess or break, there was no interaction at all. Everyone remained in his or her own ethnic group. And if some did move outside their group, they were considered outcasts. I know most Black students thought that if another Black student didn't associate with them, it's because the person thought he or she was too good for them. During class, however, I don't think it could be avoided. It seemed as if once class started, we all became united. We would work together, get into groups with one another, or just talk with each other. The classroom was a place to put all prejudice aside and work together.

As I become a classroom teacher, I believe I have benefited from having these school experiences with ethnic groups. I know now it's best not to alienate anyone. My philosophy is for everyone to socialize with each other, in and out of the classroom. If I decide to put my students into groups, I'll make sure its interracial. Even though I know most children would try to get into groups with mostly their ethnic friends only, I'll be sure to mix them. Interacting with each other is something that should begin at an early age and continue throughout one's life. Not only as a teacher but as a person I think it is very important for everyone in this society to be able to get along.

Jennifer Gosse

I went to private Catholic schools for 11 years. During these years, I don't remember being around minorities in school. My school peers were White. I started first grade at a public school but then moved to St. Victor in the second grade. So I really don't have much of an idea what public schools are like.

I'm the daughter of a professional dancer and a police officer, so I got my share of ribbing at school from my friends about my parents. But usually this ribbing was nothing worse than my father being referred to as a "pig."

When I was in second grade, my mother opened a dance studio in connection with St. Victor. All of the little girls took classes; therefore, I was something of a leader in school because I excelled at dancing and my mom was the "boss." My sister, who is 5 years younger, also went to St. Victor. But whereas I maintained an A–B average, my sister struggled. After sixth grade, my sister was allowed to quit St. Victor and go to public school. Once in public school, my sister joined the band, the bowling team, cheerleading, and student council. These things weren't offered at St. Victor.

St. Victor prided itself on its reputation as the toughest grade school in [the school district]. The teachers were also known as the best in [the area]. At St. Victor there weren't any extracurricular activities unless you include attending church six times a week or attending the choir, which performed once a year for Christmas.

Basically, my mother's dance studio was the only thing close to an extracurricular activity at St. Victor. The emphasis at that school was strictly academic. There were many placement tests, IQ tests, and even national religion standardized tests. At our eighth-grade graduation from St. Victor, many awards were given for best science, best creative writing, and all-around students.

Money really wasn't an issue among students at St. Victor, and popularity was based largely on physical ability and "looks." However, my high school, St. Mary, was another story. I went to high school with some of the wealthiest teens in town. Money seemed to be everything in school. Of course, students who didn't have money also attended St. Mary High School, but the students who "ruled" the school were from very wealthy families. A few students who came from families with less money did manage to break the money barrier, usually by being the best athlete on one of the teams or by remaining friends with one of the rich kids from grade school. These exceptions were usually boys.

St. Victor and St. Mary were both small schools. Only 36 students were in my class at St. Victor, the same 36 from second to eighth grade. St. Mary had fewer than 200 students in all, so everyone knew everyone else. The teachers knew each student, and they knew the students' parents personally. Some of the teachers were impressed by some parents, but all-in-all in both schools I only saw a few instances of the teachers playing obvious favoritism to these students.

College was much different from high school. I went to [a mid-sized state university]. There seemed to be two kinds of students at college: those for an education, and those for sports. I fell into the sports division because I was on a ballet scholarship, but I also wanted an education. My degree was in physical education/ballet.

My father graduated from Oregon State University with a degree in forestry, and he is very book-smart. My parents were concerned about our education even before we were born. My father believes that getting a degree, any degree, is beneficial.

At St. Mary I begged my parents to allow me to transfer to a public school, but I was never allowed to transfer. Now I think I would enjoy teaching at a private school. And I think I know private schools, whereas I don't know anything about public schools. The students in private schools, on the whole, seem to put a higher value on education, maybe because most came from parents who were successful and made a lot of money and the students want to follow in their footsteps. Or maybe because the students just know how much money was being spent on their education and they felt pressured to perform as I did.

Throughout my early school years (K–8), I didn't have much experience with different ethnic groups. This is because I went to a strict Catholic school in the early 1970s. The only group I was around was the wealthy upper class Spanish who had a strong Catholic tradition.

In high school there was very limited contact with Black, Hispanic, or other ethnic groups, other than those minority students who were very wealthy, and there were very few of them. And those wealthy minority students weren't your typical kids off the street. In college I met many people of different races, and my roommate was a Black female. Unfortunately, we ended up having a falling out. I was in the athletic crowd, which at my college was dominated by Black students.

I am concerned that when I start teaching, I will act differently toward different, specifically Black, students. I don't think I'm prejudiced, but I think my upbringing will show my inexperience and awkwardness around different ethnic groups. I find that even now I'm clumsy when speaking with ethnically mixed groups, and I know they can sense it. I believe that the best place for me to teach would be a predominantly White Catholic high school like the one I attended. I wouldn't know the first thing about dealing with some of the problems that go on in today's public high school, which I largely blame on the ethnic mixtures. I don't want to hide from the ethnic problems, but I don't think I'm equipped to handle them.

Karrie Terrill

From kindergarten to my senior year in high school, I was in the same school district. The town was relatively small, with around 15,000 people. There was almost no diversity as far as ethnic groups were concerned. The majority of the students were from White middle-class families, which is where my family fit in. As an elementary student, I do not remember any other cultural or ethnic groups, other than White middle class. However, there probably were some Hispanic students and I just didn't notice.

My town had two elementary schools. One was composed of mostly middle-class students; the other was composed of mostly lower middle and lower class students. I attended the middle-class school, which could account for no minorities in my classes. I say this because Hensonville [not the real name] was and still is a very "Christian" town. In my elementary classes, I can remember saying a prayer before lunch every day. I am sure that some of the classes still do this today. Religion is a big part of the town, and no one seems to care if it was included in the school system. When I was in fourth grade, I remember a friend of mine telling me that she was Jewish and that she wanted that fact kept a secret. As far as I know, she was the only Jewish student in the school and the Christian environment never seemed to bother her.

Learning has always been a big part of my life. My family has several teachers in it, including my mother, aunt, great-aunt, and others. When I was in elementary school, my mother and father would spend time with me to make sure I was learning everything I possibly could. My father would spend hours at night listening to me read book after book and giving me practice on spelling tests. He would also check my homework to see whether I missed anything so that I could go back and correct it, but he never corrected it for me. My mother would make me go over papers that my teachers had handed back so that I would not forget anything. My parents had high expectations for all of their children. Instead of rewarding us for making A's, they expressed concern when we made B's. This school ethic of high standards followed me into my college years, and I am very thankful that my parents cared enough to push me to learn.

Academic competition was a big part of junior high and senior high. Students in the school district won many awards in various competitions. The town and the school were very proud of these accomplishments. In high school, we had the Renaissance Program. In this program, every student was issued an identification card with six sections at the bottom. At the end of every six weeks, a section was punched according to whether the A, B, or C honor rolls were made. A business in town then donated prizes and offered discounts according to how well one did in school. The better the grades, the better the prize and the bigger the discount. At the end of the year, a Renaissance reception was held at the school, and the students who had made the various honor rolls were recognized.

The years of school that most determined my enthusiasm for teaching were my last 2 years in high school. In these years, I took mostly honors courses, which were academically stimulating as well as beneficial to my motivation. The teacher who made the biggest impact on my life was Mrs. Fain. She was a very quiet teacher who was near retirement. I had her for Algebra II, trigonometry, and calculus. She expected her students to learn, and we did. She had an answer for every question and never seemed to lose her temper. The examples she used related to things we could understand. As a result of having her for a teacher, I learned more than I needed for entering college, and she inspired me to become a math teacher myself.

Because of supportive parents, a strong school system, and great teachers, I have always had an open mind toward education. For my own reasons, I do not want to teach in the same town that I grew up in, but I do want to teach in a town very similar to it. Teaching is something I have wanted to do for a long time. I hope I can have the same impact on my students as teachers like Mrs. Fain had on me.

ACTIVITY 3.2   Exploring Your Autobiography

The stories of Amy, Jennifer, and Karrie demonstrate how writing your autobiography can help you determine the relationship between life experiences and your teaching. The items below will help you begin constructing your autobiography: to think about how your personal history shapes your teaching "self" and, in turn, how this self influences your interaction with students. As you think carefully about the list of items, you will undoubtedly develop additional insights into your background that are not listed below. Be sure to record these too. For each of the items below, write how your own classroom instruction might be influenced.

Schools Attended

- Nature of the elementary schools you attended, including socioeconomic status (SES) of the schools
- Nature of the secondary schools you attended, including SES of the schools
- Significant positive and negative teacher role models in elementary and secondary schools, including ethnicity of these teachers
- Composition of student body, including cultural, racial, religious, academic, gender, and social class diversity

Family Values Toward Education

- Educational background of parents/guardians
- Educational background of grandparents
- Attitudes of parents/guardians toward education
- Attitudes of parents/guardians toward schooling
- Values that parents/guardians have for school and for education
- Support provided by parents/guardians for your schooling

Role of School in Your Life

- Significant positive school experiences
- Significant negative school experiences
- School as an academic experience
- School as a social experience
- School as a cultural experience
- School as a class (SES) experience
- School as a religious experience
- Function of school in your life
- Participation in peer group(s)
- Participation in extracurricular activities
- Cultural diversity of your peer group(s)
- Personal accomplishments in school

Community and Your School

- Nature of the communities where you lived when you attended elementary and secondary schools

- Relationship between the schools you attended and the community (or communities) where you lived
- Nature of the community where you now teach or where you now are doing classroom-based field experience work

Prior Teaching (Nonschool Teaching)

- Prior teaching experiences outside K–12 classrooms
- Experience with persons from other cultures in prior work and prior nonschool teaching

ACTIVITY 3.3   Writing Your Autobiography

Using the information and insights you recorded about yourself in Activities 3.1 and 3.2, write your autobiography. As you develop your autobiography, consider events that were most salient in shaping your beliefs about teaching in general and about teaching culturally diverse students in particular.

BELIEFS ABOUT INTEGRATION

Your prior experiences with family, community, peers, and social groups shaped your beliefs about other cultural groups. From these prior experiences, then, came your beliefs about cultural integration within the broader frameworks of school and society. ***Cultural integration*** is the process of blending persons with differing cultural backgrounds together in a common community. In this section of the chapter, you explore three models of social integration, determine how your alignment with these models is related to your biographical experiences, and then consider how your beliefs about integration may influence your interaction with students in the classroom.

Your personal views about integration have their roots in the experiences you've had with other cultural groups throughout your life. Because contemporary schools are being challenged with pluarlistic ideals unlike at any other time in history,[9] you need to be aware of how your personal views on integration influence your classroom instruction.[10]

Three approaches to cultural integration are described below: assimilation, pluralism, and suppression (see Bennett, 1990).

Assimilation

Assimilation occurs when minority groups are expected to (a) give up their original culture, (b) identify with the predominant Anglo-Western European culture, and (c) no longer identify themselves as distinct from the predominant culture.[11] Melting pot is a metaphor commonly used to describe cultural assimilation. Inherent in this metaphor is the belief that all people within specific geographical regions, regardless of race, ethnicity, or culture, should have the same values, customs, and beliefs. Nieto (1992) notes that cultural assimilation is a "model that maintains that differences need to be wiped out to form an amalgam" (p. 307). Nieto gives the name "anglo-conformity" to assimilation when Anglo-Western European ideals and values predominate the assimilation process and when minority cultures are expected to conform to White mainstream values and customs.[12]

Assimilation has been criticized for its failure to acknowledge and affirm the cultural ideals of minority groups.[13] Assimilation as a model for intercultural relationships in school classrooms is unable to accommodate the needs of culturally diverse students. Critics of assimilation argue that it contributes to the marginalization and silencing of some student groups. For example, Trueba, Jacobs, and Kirton (1990) conducted a study of Hmong students with limited English language proficiency in American classrooms. Teachers in this study held firmly to their own training and to their own mainstream cultural values in the classroom. Consequently, they required Hmong students to comply completely to the American cultural norms of classroom performance, which they communicated to Hmong students in the English language. Trueba et al. found that when the academic expectations the teachers had for these students were not met, the teachers

> passed judgments on the children's ability to learn and determined collectively with other resource staff that these children had learning disabilities. School personnel viewed these students as having low potential, performing at low levels of achievement, and giving clear signs of suffering learning disabilities, but neither teachers nor principal nor psychologist could explain the nature of the disability. (p. 75)

Hmong students in this study reported feelings of frustration, anxiety, and hopelessness with their classroom participation. Educators have become increasingly aware that traditional teaching practices requiring conformity to mainstream values (assimilation) are limited in their potential to meet the school-based needs of students like the Hmong children. Consequently, cultural pluralism has emerged as an alternative model for making school curriculum and classroom instruction more culturally sensitive.

Pluralism

Pluralism occurs in societies in which minority groups (a) retain many of their traditions (e.g., language, religion, social customs), (b) participate in aspects of the predominant culture (e.g., language, military service, federal laws), (c) identify with the nation as a whole, and (d) acknowledge and respect the individuality of other cultural groups.[14] In a culturally pluralistic society, the mainstream culture respects minority cultures, appreciates diversity, and encourages cultural identity. Metaphors typically used to depict cultural pluralism include salad bowl, tapestry, and great community.

In this book, we endorse the principles of cultural pluralism. Two aspects of cultural pluralism that are particularly important in this book are the affirmation of cultural identity in schools and classrooms and the acceptance of cultural differences. Affirming cultural identity and accepting cultural differences hold promise for making classroom interactions with students culturally responsive, academically sound, and more authentic. In a discussion of cultural pluralism, Maxine Greene (1993) notes,

> The more . . . authentic personal encounters can be [with other cultural groups], the less likely it will be that categorizing and distancing [these groups] will take place. People are [then] less likely to be treated instrumentally, to be made "other" by those around. (p. 13)

Suppression

Suppression, or segregation, the third model of social interaction, occurs when the dominant social group separates itself from minority groups in social places such as churches, schools, jobs, housing, and clubs. The dominant culture supporting suppression tends to view minority groups as a threat to traditional local and/or national values. Although legislation has tried to overcome separatist views related to suppression, some contemporary school practices, such as tracking, intelligence testing, and standardized testing, have been criticized as implicitly maintaining segregationist practices.[15]

ACTIVITY 3.4   Prior Interaction with Culturally Diverse Groups

To explore and describe your personal beliefs about social interaction (assimilation, pluralism, suppression) and to speculate about how these beliefs influence your classroom learning environment, reflect on your prior interactions with culturally diverse groups. Consider how your prior interactions contribute to or perhaps hinder your multicultural sensitivity. These activities will help you assess your level of readiness for teaching culturally diverse students.

Figure 3–2 contains a representative list of student groups. As you consider each group, determine your prior and present involvement with these groups. Place a check in the space that best represents your level of involvement. Compare your list with those of peers and colleagues.

Social Groups	Quantity of Interaction					
	Prior Experiences			Present Experiences		
	Always	Sometimes	Never	Always	Sometimes	Never
Asian*						
Black						
Hispanic**						
Jewish						
Native American						
White						

Figure 3–2   Quantity of personal interactions with student groups

* Cambodian, Chinese, Filipino, Indochinese, Japanese, Korean, Laotian, Vietnamese, and individuals from other Asian countries

** Cuban, Latino, Mexican American, Puerto Rican, and individuals from other Latin American countries

We do not want you to think of students as stereotypical members of selected cultural and ethnic groups as you complete Figure 3–2, nor do we want you to get the impression that checking off items on a list makes issues surrounding personal interactions with various student groups cut and dried. On the contrary, the act of putting checks on Figure 3–2 will enhance your awareness of just how complex personal and social interactions with culturally diverse groups other than your own can be.

Use Figure 3–3 to describe the nature of the personal interactions you have had and now have with each group. Think about how you have seen each group depicted in literature, film, and school textbooks. Consider whether the depiction reflects assimilation, pluralism, or suppression. Think about the depiction and determine whether it tends to stereotype members of various groups. Consider also how these depictions influence your views of social interaction.

BELIEFS ABOUT INTEGRATION IN THE SCHOOL CLASSROOM

Figures 3–2 and 3–3 helped you think about your prior and present experiences with cultural groups. To what degree have these experiences shaped your beliefs about diversity and molded your views of cultural integration in the classroom? Do you think multicultural classrooms should be melting pots (cultural assimilation) where stu-

Social Groups	Quality of Interaction
Asian* Personal Interaction: Literature/Film/Textbook:	
Black Personal Interaction: Literature/Film/Textbook:	
Hispanic** Personal Interaction: Literature/Film/Textbook:	
Jewish Personal Interaction: Literature/Film/Textbook:	
Native American Personal Interaction: Literature/Film/Textbook:	
White Personal Interaction: Literature/Film/Textbook:	

Figure 3–3   Quality of personal interactions with ethnic minority groups

* Cambodian, Chinese, Filipino, Indochinese, Japanese, Korean, Laotian, Vietnamese, and individuals from other Asian countries

** Cuban, Latino, Mexican American, Puerto Rican, and individuals from other Latin American countries

dents become part of a homogeneous classroom community with a unified culture and a common set of values? Do you believe that students in multicultural classrooms should resemble a tapestry (cultural pluralism) in which students become part of a classroom society but in which cultural identity is affirmed? Activity 3.5 will help you find answers for these questions.

ACTIVITY 3.5   Cultural Integration and Classroom Instruction

Think about the general strengths and limitations of assimilation, pluralism, and suppression for classroom instruction. Your responses should be based on four sources of information: (a) personal prior experiences in school, (b) awareness of other social and minority groups, (c) personal beliefs about the integration of minority groups into society, and (d) literature on cultural diversity and schooling. Use Figure 3–4 to write strengths and limitations of each model.

Now consider classroom learning environments that might characterize the models. In Figure 3–5, describe how each model influences specific classroom features. As an example, what curriculum materials would you use if you endorse the cultural assimilation model? How do these materials differ from those that reflect cultural pluralism or cultural suppression?

ACTIVITY 3.6   Personal Alignment with Integration Model

After completing Figures 3–4 and 3–5, determine the model with which you are most familiar. For which model were you able to describe most clearly the general strengths and limitations for classroom instruction (Figure 3–4)? Which of the models were you able to apply readily to

Integration Model	Classroom Instruction	
	Strengths	Limitations
Assimilation		
Pluralism		
Suppression		

Figure 3–4   General strengths and weaknesses of three integration models for classroom instruction

Classroom Feature	Integration Model		
	Assimilation	Pluralism	Suppression
Curriculum Materials			
Teaching Strategies			
Seating Arrangement			
Peer Tutoring			
Classroom Management			
Student Discipline			
Group Activities			
Classroom Environment			
Teaching Style			

Figure 3–5   Attributes of integration models for classroom instruction

features of classroom instruction (Figure 3–5)? Because the negative effects of cultural suppression, or segregation, have been clearly demonstrated historically, you may have been more aware of the negative effects of this model for classroom instruction. Consequently, you might be less familiar with how assimilation and pluralism actually influence classroom teaching, particularly if you live in an area such as Karrie Terrill's, whose autobiography was included earlier in this chapter and who attended schools that tended to be assimilationist in their orientation. To gain clarity on this influence, discuss these models further with peers, experienced teachers, and multicultural educators.

SUMMARY

Throughout this chapter, you reflected thoughtfully on many of your prior experiences. You explored the relationship between these experiences and your beliefs about teaching culturally diverse students. Our intention was not to prescribe a cultural integration model to you, but rather to allow you to explore the appropriateness of the beliefs you now hold for teaching in culturally diverse classrooms, to compare these beliefs with those held by your peers, and to begin restructuring any beliefs you have that might interfere with effective teaching for all students.

Through this personal journey, you became aware of how past experiences in school classrooms influence your present teaching strategies. You also increased your awareness of the many individual students you teach, of the interesting cultural stories being written by your students that collectively contribute to the narrative of your classroom teaching. Just as former teachers contributed in significantly memorable ways to your autobiography and to your beliefs about effective teaching, you are now contributing to your students' views of themselves as learners.

RESEARCH TOPICS

Topic 1: Biography and Classroom Instruction

Problem Posing

Throughout this chapter, we discussed the relationship between personal history and teaching culturally diverse students. From this discussion, we pose the question, What is the relationship between your autobiography, your beliefs about teaching, and your classroom instruction? To answer this question, consider how prior and present experiences inside and outside school influence your beliefs about instruction and your social interactions with students. Areas to focus on include preferred teaching strategies, teaching style, interaction with individual students academically and socially, and interaction with diverse groups and classroom management. Also consider how your self and your personality influence your classroom environment (e.g., how you organize your classroom, how you communicate expectations to students).

Exploration and Discovery

Methods for conducting this research project include biography, personal journal, peer observation, and discussion groups about prior experiences. Your autobiography can be a basis for connecting your preferred teaching practices to prior experiences. By collecting your ideas and reflections regularly in a personal journal, you can record the nature of your classroom instruction, or the nature of classroom instruction for another teacher if you are filling the role of classroom observer, and you can reflect on the quality and quantity of interactions you recorded with individual students and with groups of students. Be open and honest with yourself as you write in your journal about the feelings you have for teaching in culturally diverse classrooms.

For peer observation, invite a colleague or mentor teacher to observe your classroom instruction, especially your interactions with students. The feedback you receive from peer observations provides you with an outsider's view of your classroom environment. Discussion groups help you gain insight into the historical antecedents of your preferred teaching strategies. Taking part in discussion groups that focus on the relationship between autobiography and classroom teaching can illuminate how autobiography influences your social and academic interactions with students.

Reflection and Modification

Think about what you recorded as you explored and described the relationship between your autobiography and classroom instruction. Have you discovered particular beliefs, attitudes, feelings, and practices that you think need to be modified if you are to be effective in teaching all students in multicultural classrooms? List below specific areas relative to your beliefs and practices for teaching that you would like to modify or further refine.

1. _____

2. _____

3. _____

4. _____

Description and Speculation

Given what you have learned about the relationship between your autobiography and teaching culturally diverse students, what more would you like to know? You might consider, for example, focusing on your prior social and academic experiences as an elementary and secondary student and how these experiences influence your views, beliefs, attitudes, and willingness to teach all students. Write below several topics that can give you a deeper understanding for how autobiography influences your effectiveness in teaching all students in your classroom.

1. _____

2. _____

3. _____

4. _____

Topic 2: Cultural Integration in the Classroom

Problem Posing

In our discussion about integration of culturally diverse groups in school classrooms, we provided you with a framework for exploring your personal views about social integration. The activities in Figures 3–4 and 3–5 helped you examine your level of awareness for three models of social integration. You also considered the influence of these models on classroom instruction and determined your alignment with the models. To further examine your personal views about cultural integration, ask yourself, What relationship exists between my autobiography, my personal beliefs about integration, and the interaction I have with students in the classroom?

Exploration and Discovery

Using your autobiography as a framework, write a personal narrative about how your view of integration developed. Include key events in your life that influenced your beliefs about the integration model you endorse. As another strategy, maintain a personal journal over a portion of the school year about the quality of your interactions with cultural groups in your classroom. Making regular entries in the journal will help you reflect on how the integration model you align with most closely influences your interactions with students. In your journal, ask yourself, How do my interactions with specific cultural groups influence my instruction? Do I give preferential treatment to one group over another group? Which group or groups am I most comfortable teaching? How have my past experiences influenced the comfort I have in working with specific cultural groups? As you write in your journal, be sure to examine your beliefs about cultural diversity in school classrooms. Monitor these beliefs and determine how your beliefs change, if at all, during the study.

Reflection and Modification

Now that you have thought more critically about your views on cultural integration in the classroom, determine how your views influence your classroom instruction. Do you have any views or beliefs that interfere with your willingness and ability to reach all students in the classroom? Which of your beliefs need to be modified before you will be more effective in reaching all students? Write these beliefs below.

1. _____
2. _____
3. _____
4. _____

Description and Speculation

On the basis of what you discovered from this research, think about other studies you might conduct about cultural integration in schools and classrooms. Studies could include interviewing expert teachers about their views or examining school and classroom curriculum materials for appropriateness in culturally diverse classrooms (see Chapter 12). List below several topics you would like to explore further.

1. _____
2. _____
3. _____
4. _____

NOTES

1. Knowles, J. G. (1988, April). *Models for understanding preservice and beginning teachers' biographies: Illustrations from case studies.* Paper presented at the Annual Meeting of the American Educational Research Association, New Orleans.
2. Bullough, R. V., Knowles, J. G., & Crow, N. A. (1991). *Emerging as a teacher.* London: Routledge.
3. Hunt, D. (1987). *Beginning with ourselves.* Cambridge, MA: Brookline Books; Clandinin, D. J. (1985). Personal practical knowledge: A study of teachers' classroom images.

Curriculum Inquiry, 15, 361–385; Clandinin, J., & Connelly, M. (1992). Teacher as curriculum maker. In P. Jackson (Ed.), *Handbook of research on curriculum* (pp. 363–401). New York: Macmillan.

4. Banks, J. (1991). Teaching multicultural literacy to teachers. *Teaching Education, 4*(1), 135–144; Zeichner, K., & Melnick, S. (1993, April) *Studying the preparation of teachers for cultural diversity.* Paper presented at the Annual Meeting of the American Educational Research Association, Atlanta.

5. Gonzalez, V. (1993, April). *Using reflective teaching for changing in-service teachers' attitudes and increasing their cognitive-ethical development and academic knowledge in multicultural education.* Paper presented at the Annual Meeting of the American Educational Research Association, Atlanta.

6. Banks, J. (1991). Teaching multicultural literacy to teachers. *Teaching Education, 4*(1), 135–144.

7. This school district is in the desert Southwest and was the 14th largest school district in the country at the time this book was written. Real names for schools in the autobiographies have not been used.

8. These autobiographies were developed for a class assignment in a preservice teacher education program called Introduction to Secondary Education.

9. Greene, M. (1993). The passions of pluralism: Multiculturalism and the expanding community. *Educational Researcher, 22,* 13–18.

10. Nieto (1992) writes that society is at a new threshold of global history, where schools and their teachers are being challenged to accept a changing definition of humanity and consequently are adopting new views of cultural integration. This is especially true for teachers in geographical locations where cultural diversity has a significant influence on local communities. In these and other locations, minority voices are choosing no longer to be silenced by dominant cultures.

11. Bennett, C. (1990). *Comprehensive multicultural education: Theory and practice* (2nd ed.). Boston: Allyn & Bacon.

12. Robert Jiobu (1988, p. 6) also uses the notion of Anglo conformity to describe situations where the minority group loses its distinctiveness and becomes like the majority. See Jiobu, R. (1988). *Ethnicity and assimilation.* Albany: State University of New York Press.

13. See Greenbaum, W. (1974). America in search of a new ideal: An essay on the rise of pluralism. *Harvard Educational Review, 44*(3), 411–440.

14. Bennett, C. (1990). *Comprehensive multicultural education: Theory and practice* (2nd ed.). Boston: Allyn & Bacon.

15. See, for example, Persell, C. H. (1993). Social class and educational equality. In J. Banks & C. Banks (Eds.), *Multicultural education: Issues and perspectives* (2nd ed., pp. 71–89). Boston: Allyn & Bacon. See also Oakes, J. (1985). *Keeping track: How schools structure inequality.* New Haven: Yale University Press.

REFERENCES

Banks, J. (1991). Teaching multicultural literacy to teachers. *Teaching Education, 4*(1), 135–144.

Bennett, C. (1990). *Comprehensive multicultural education: Theory and practice* (2nd ed.). Boston: Allyn & Bacon.

Bullough, R. V., Knowles, J. G., & Crow, N. A. (1991). *Emerging as a teacher.* London: Routledge.

Clandinin, D. J. (1985). Personal practical knowledge: A study of teachers' classroom images. *Curriculum Inquiry, 15,* 361–385.

Clandinin, J., & Connelly, M. (1992). Teacher as curriculum maker. In P. Jackson (Ed.), *Handbook of research on curriculum* (pp. 363–401). New York: Macmillan.

Gergen, K. (1991). *The saturated self: Dilemmas of identity in contemporary life.* New York: Basic Books.

Gonzalez, V. (1993, April). *Using reflective teaching for changing in-service teachers' attitudes and increasing their cognitive-ethical development and academic knowledge in multicultural education.* Paper presented at the Annual Meeting of the American Educational Research Association, Atlanta.

Goodson, I. (1991). Teachers' lives and educational research. In I. F. Goodson & R. Walker (Eds.), *Biography, identity, and schooling: Episodes in educational research* (pp. 137–149). New York: Falmer Press.

Greenbaum, W. (1974). America in search of a new ideal: An essay on the rise of pluralism. *Harvard Educational Review, 44*(3), 411–440.

Greene, M. (1993). The passions of pluralism: Multiculturalism and the expanding community. *Educational Researcher, 22,* 13–18.

Hunt, D. (1987). *Beginning with ourselves.* Cambridge, MA: Brookline Books.

Jiobu, R. (1988). *Ethnicity and assimilation.* Albany: State University of New York Press.

Knowles, G. (1988, April). *Models for understanding preservice and beginning teachers' biographies: Illustrations from case studies.* Paper presented at the Annual Meeting of the American Educational Research Association, New Orleans.

Nieto, S. (1992). *Affirming diversity: The sociopolitical context of multicultural education.* White Plains, NY: Longman.

Oakes, J. (1985). *Keeping track: How schools structure inequality..* New Haven, CT: Yale University Press.

Persell, C. (1993). Social class and educational equality. In J. Banks & C. Banks (Eds.), *Multicultural education: Issues and perspectives* (2nd ed., pp. 71–89). Boston: Allyn & Bacon.

Trueba, H., Jacobs, L., & Kirton, E. (1990). *Cultural conflict and adaptation: The case of Hmong children in American society.* New York: Falmer Press.

Zeichner, K., & Melnick, S. (1993, April). *Studying the preparation of teachers for cultural diversity.* Paper presented at the Annual Meeting of the American Educational Research Association, Atlanta.

Chapter 4

Assessing Your Readiness for Teaching in Culturally Diverse Classrooms

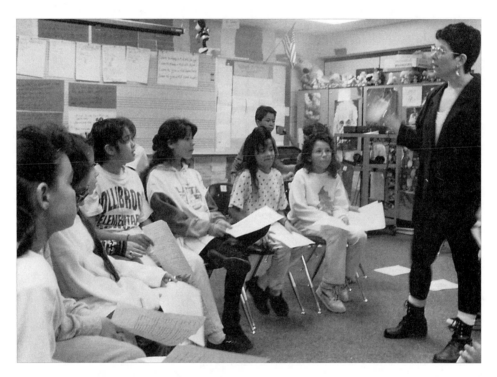

Jose Clarito is in my class. You might think he looks like he is Hispanic, but he's really Filipino. Another boy in my class that looks very Filipino is Mexican and Chinese. So, how do you get ready to teach that kind of cultural integration? You just have to get to know your kids, know who they are, know where they are from, know about their language, and acknowledge all that. Then you are ready to teach them, but not before.   (J. Phillips, 1993)[1]

The student teacher tried to identify the nationality of each child in the group, sometimes confusing nationality with ethnicity. To the Hmong children she said, "You're Laotian," to the Anglos she said, "You're American," and to the Latino students she said, "You're Mexican." There was an awkward silence since it showed her ignorance of the distinction of Hmong and Laotian ethnicity, and also offended some Mexican-American and Indochinese students who thought of themselves as American.   (Trueba, Jacobs, & Kirton, 1990, pp. 78–79)

INTRODUCTION

The idea of teacher readiness for contemporary classrooms requires each of us to rethink what we must know about teaching before we can reach students effectively. With an ever-increasing emphasis on technology and standardized curriculum, readiness is often defined by educators as knowing how to set in motion a series of routine and somewhat regimented learning experiences.[2] Knowing how to design and deliver carefully prepared lessons is, in fact, an important part of your teaching. Few educators would deny that. But an equally important part is getting to know the backgrounds of your students—not just knowing their names and how well they do in your class, but knowing their nationalities and how to tell the difference between their nationalities and ethnicities. Having this kind of understanding is no longer an option, as suggested above by Joannie Phillips; it is now central to classroom teaching everywhere. Without this understanding, without this multicultural readiness, you could easily offend some of your students without even knowing it and thus turn them off to even the best of your lessons (Trueba et al., 1990).

We have two purposes for this chapter. First, this chapter helps you understand the concept of readiness as it applies to teaching in today's multicultural classrooms and as it applies to being aware of the differing backgrounds of your students. As you consider the idea of readiness in the following pages, realize that increasing your readiness for teaching in a culturally diverse society helps you be more effective in meeting the varied needs of all your students.[3]

Second, this chapter helps you assess your own level of readiness for being a teacher in culturally diverse classrooms. Assessing your own readiness is an important step toward developing a culturally sensitive classroom curriculum and toward being prepared for rapid and sweeping shifts in student demographics that are changing local school populations.

TEACHER BACKGROUND AND MULTICULTURAL READINESS

Think about the notion of readiness more closely by exploring the relationship between your background and classroom teaching. To begin thinking about this, consider the following two stories of Anna Ramirez and Allen Hayes.

Anna Ramirez[4]

Anna is a first-generation U.S. citizen. Her parents immigrated to the United States from Latin America, and at home Anna's parents speak Spanish. The ESL program in Anna's high school helped her develop very good English-speaking skills during the first few years she was in the United States. Anna graduated from a high school in one of the large suburbs surrounding a major urban area. Her high school student body was comprised mostly of Asians and Hispanics, with a smaller percentage of newly immigrated Latinos. She earned a bachelor's degree in history from a city university and now wants to become an elementary school teacher. She has applied to a postbaccalaureate teacher licensure program at a nearby university. For the past two summers, Anna has returned to Latin America to visit relatives.

Allen Hayes

Allen was raised in a small community in the United States. The nearest large metropolitan area is a 3-hour drive from his home. Two generations of Allen's family have lived in this same community, and Allen graduated from the local high school. Allen, who graduated in the top 10% of his class, remembers that, during the last 2 years of high school, several Vietnamese families moved to town; until then, there were essentially no other social groups in the community except Whites. Most community members in Allen's hometown live in comfortable homes. Allen is now a junior in a private university in the same state, and he is majoring in secondary education. He wants to become a social studies teacher in his hometown, but he realizes that he might have to begin his teaching career in an urban area because social studies openings in his hometown probably won't occur for the next 5 or 6 years. During his senior year at the university, Allen wants to participate in a travel-abroad program to England. That will be his first trip out of the United States.

The biographies of Anna Ramirez and Allen Hayes raise many important questions regarding readiness for teaching in multicultural classrooms, just as the biographies of Amy, Jennifer, and Karrie did in the previous chapter. For example, given the biographies of Anna and Allen, which one might have greater sensitivity for customs, beliefs, values, and lifestyles of other cultural groups? Given that both Anna and Allen could begin their teaching careers in urban or suburban areas where schools will likely be culturally diverse, which one might be better prepared to interact with students socially, personally, and academically? What might happen to Anna if she gets a teaching job in Allen's hometown? What kind of cultural readiness might Anna need before she can teach effectively in Allen's former elementary school? What kind of cultural readiness might Allen need to teach in Anna's former high school?

If your prior schooling and life experiences align more with those of Allen Hayes than Anna Ramirez, then you may be faced with some pressing questions. Have you considered how cultural lifestyles frame the educational values of the students you teach? Have you determined how cultural diversity influences the way students interact with you in the classroom? Do you know about the cultural background of your students? Can you tell where your students' families are from, as Joannie Phillips does in her opening comment to this chapter?

WHY FOCUS ON READINESS?

Before you assess your own readiness for teaching students in culturally diverse classrooms, we ask you first to consider some important reasons to focus on multicultural readiness. From the many reasons that call for a consideration of this type of readiness, we selected four reasons that appear particularly salient: shifting student populations, shifting teacher populations, unintended cultural bias, and needs of local school districts.

Shifting Student Populations

In the preceding chapters, we mentioned that communities, once thought to be culturally singular and seemingly impervious to outside influences, have now become multicultural. For example, Mark Keppel High School (MKHS), a suburban high school near Los Angeles (see Chapter 6 for a discussion of Mark Keppel High School), in only two decades has had two major student body transformations. The student body changed from being predominantly White in the 1960s and early 1970s to mostly Hispanic in the 1970s and early 1980s. More recently, the student body at MKHS has been transformed into predominantly Asian. Differing languages, cultures, perspectives, and customs have become mainstream at MKHS and at other similar schools.

Transformations in student composition like that at MKHS have created the need for you to develop specialized skills for interacting with many types of social groups. You must now develop the same repertoire of skills that international officials develop; that is, you must be able to effectively communicate with students from many different cultural backgrounds.

Shifting Teacher Populations

The second reason to focus on multicultural readiness is shifting teacher populations. Economic uncertainty in some parts of the United States and economic growth in other parts have caused demographic shifts in populations during the past two decades. The obvious implication of these shifts is that teachers who were once accustomed to teaching students in one part of the country must now become acquainted with student cultures in perhaps entirely different locations. Consequently, teachers who were effective in one location may find themselves in other school contexts that challenge this effectiveness.

A case example of shifting demographies for teachers is seen in the recent dramatic growth of Clark County, Nevada, and the corresponding growth of its school district. Clark County is in southern Nevada and includes the Las Vegas metropolitan area, as well as several surrounding suburban and rural communities. In the late 1980s and early 1990s, the population of Las Vegas and the surrounding suburban areas grew at such a rate that, between 1990 and 1993, 41 new schools and 4,382 new teachers were added to the district. Approximately 67% of these new teachers were hired by Clark County School District (CCSD) recruiting officials out of Nevada.[5] Many teachers who have moved to Clark County from other parts of the country have had to adjust to a variety of student cultures in the local area. CCSD has responded to this influx by making multicultural education a top priority for all teachers.

Unintended Cultural Bias

Unintended cultural bias is the third reason to consider multicultural readiness. Whether new groups of students are moving into communities that were once stable, like the communities surrounding Mark Keppel High School, or whether you are moving to locations like Clark County, Nevada, that are having rapid growth, you must acquire skills for living and teaching around other cultures. Lacking these skills and lacking an awareness of the implications of cultural diversity on your instruction, you could perpetuate what Contreras and Lee (1990) call **unintentional cultural bias.** This kind of bias occurs in your classroom when you marginalize students socially and academically by not being sensitive to students' cultural styles of learning.

Unintended cultural bias causes you to interact with some students more effectively than other students, thus creating academic inequities in your classroom.[6] Because shifting student and teacher populations will continue well into the next century, the potential for unintended cultural bias will be continuously present. This potential is reflected in the comment made by Trueba et al. (1990): "In a matter of a few years entire school districts have changed their balance of ethnic minorities served, yet teachers and administrators have not been prepared for this change" (p. 134). The changes mentioned by Trueba et al. point to the need to develop a new form of classroom readiness, one that focuses on the relationship among student diversity, classroom curriculum, and your instruction. The need for this type of classroom readiness is highlighted by Mahan and Boyle (1981), who note, "Teachers who have previously been successful teaching in communities that are undergoing change are discovering that what had worked for them in the past no longer works. As a result, new [teaching] methods are needed" (p. 98).

By relating unintended cultural bias to your classroom, we do not want to give you the impression that schools are neutral and that teachers are thus in control of all possible bias. In fact, schools can give "permission" for bias through unequal funding and resources, differential climates, tracking, grouping, and any institutionalized behavior that, in effect, is biased toward certain students.

Local School Districts

The fourth reason to consider multicultural readiness is the needs of local school districts. As local teacher and student populations have changed with shifting demographies and as schools continue to become more culturally diverse, the needs of local school districts to hire teachers with multicultural teaching skills have also increased. Acknowledging this need, some school districts require prospective teachers to demonstrate a readiness for teaching in culturally diverse classrooms. For example, Bowen and Salsman (1979) reported that the Ann Arbor Public School System of Ann Arbor, Michigan, in an agreement between the school board and the local education association, began requiring student teachers to demonstrate appropriate teaching skills for culturally diverse classrooms. A document prepared by the school system stated:

> No student teacher shall be accepted by the Ann Arbor Schools unless he/she can demonstrate attitudes necessary to support and create the multi-ethnic curriculum. Each such student teacher must provide a document or transcript which reflects training in or evidence of substantive understanding of the multi-ethnic or minority experience.[7]

As student and teacher populations continue to shift and as the potential for un-intended cultural bias heightens, many local school districts and state education agencies must ensure that teachers have a substantive understanding of multicultural educational issues locally, nationally, and globally.

TEACHER QUALITIES FOR DEVELOPING MULTICULTURAL READINESS

Developing multicultural readiness for teaching in contemporary classrooms re-quires you to develop and refine certain personal qualities. These qualities include al-ternative flexible teaching, open-mindedness, whole-heartedness, responsibility, pa-tience, and perseverance.[8]

Alternative Flexible Teaching

The effective multicultural educators we interviewed (see Chapter 7) and the cultur-ally diverse schools we explored (see Chapter 6) to prepare sections of this book have strong desires to implement alternative flexible teaching and to create nontraditional classroom curricula.[9] Although the educators and school administrators we visited acknowledge the value of some traditional classroom practices and, in fact, use these practices when appropriate, they more often endorse nontraditional practices. Indeed, restructuring classroom instruction entirely to meet the needs of all students is endorsed and supported by staffs at these schools. As an example, staff at Brown Barge Middle School (BBMS) in Pensacola, Florida (see Chapter 6 for a discussion of Brown Barge Middle School), restructured the entire curriculum around conceptual themes (e.g., environment, ethnicity/tapestry). Consequently, teams of teachers at BBMS now develop integrated lessons around these themes, rather than around lessons found in school textbooks.

Open-Mindedness

Open-mindedness means being open to change. It also means being open to learn-ing about multicultural teaching strategies. Unfortunately, not all teachers are open to change, and they enter the classroom with inflexible notions of what and how to teach. Shifting student populations, however, are requiring a restructuring of both classroom teaching and school curricula. Being open to change allows you to alter teaching practices as warranted by student needs and by cultural learning styles.

Whole-Heartedness

Whole-heartedness is an enthusiastic willingness to try new instructional ap-proaches, to explore their value for your teaching, and to commit to using these ap-proaches over time. Even the most committed teachers from time to time lose "heart" in their teaching. They become disillusioned in trying yet another newly pre-scribed teaching strategy, including one that is termed "multicultural." In the face of ongoing daily pressures of classroom teaching, staying with old teaching habits, whether or not they work, is often much easier than making needful changes. With dedication and determination, however, you must be willing to openly explore multicultural teaching practices and consider their value for your students.

Responsibility

Responsibility refers to your willingness to accept the consequences of any new understandings you develop about multicultural teaching, including changing your beliefs about the kind of teaching strategies that are appropriate for your students. You also have a responsibility to give up your long-held beliefs about teaching if these beliefs are inappropriate for multicultural schools. Acknowledging the subjectivity of your beliefs about teaching is another step you must take before you can make changes that may be needed in your instructional practice.[10] That is, you must acknowledge that the teaching beliefs you have and that ultimately guide your classroom instruction are framed by the cultural values you acquired during your formative years as these values were influenced by race, class, and gender.

Patience and Perseverance

Two additional qualities you need for assessing and developing multicultural readiness are patience and perseverance. You should not expect to examine all of your beliefs about cultural diversity in school classrooms in only a few weeks. Nor should you assume that, after completing action-centered books like this one, you will automatically have a multicultural readiness for teaching in contemporary classrooms. Examining your personal beliefs about teaching culturally diverse students and then determining how well these beliefs align with the local student population is a process that may require many months of thoughtful reflection. Indeed, it is a process that needs to be an ongoing part of your professional development as a teacher.

The need for patience and perseverance was demonstrated in a study conducted by Sleeter (1992). Sleeter explored the influence of multicultural in-service education on experienced elementary classroom teachers. After teachers in this study participated in 14 all-day in-service sessions on multicultural education during an entire school year, they were yet in an early phase of developing an awareness of the issues and problems surrounding multicultural education. They had not reached the level of readiness at which they could actually develop new teaching skills based on this awareness. Studies such as this clarify the need to set realistic goals for yourself as you develop multicultural readiness.

TOWARD A DEFINITION OF READINESS

What exactly is multicultural readiness? How do you know when you've got it? How do you assess this kind of readiness? What awareness, knowledge, and understanding do you need before you are ready to deliver instruction effectively to culturally diverse classrooms? These questions highlight the complex issues surrounding the notion of readiness, especially when you realize two factors. First, questions relative to readiness lack clear, definitive answers. Second, these questions are context specific; that is, answers appropriate for one school may be ineffectual in another school where there are students from other cultural groups.

Readiness and Monocultural Schools

Further complicating the notion of readiness is the phenomenon of monocultural schools (e.g., mostly Latino schools, mostly White schools, mostly Native American schools). Karrie, whose biography is included in Chapter 3, attended one of these schools. Questions surrounding the type of readiness needed for these schools include, What kind of multicultural readiness is needed to teach students who are mostly one social/ethnic group? If you plan to teach or now teach in a school that is mostly monocultural, what strategies will you use to help your students understand how the content is related to a greater multicultural global society? Are you ready to help monocultural students understand their future role in a culturally diverse workplace? What kind of multicultural curriculum and instruction materials might you use to help you prepare students for such a workplace?

Readiness as Developmental Stages

Some staff developers in multicultural education view readiness as something that develops in stages.[11] Baker (1983), for example, discusses three stages: acquisition, development, and involvement. Grant and Melnick (1978) note that awareness, acceptance, and affirmation are stages to developing teacher readiness for culturally diverse classrooms. Another stage model is suggested by Burstein and Cabello (1989), who note that development of cultural readiness includes awareness, knowledge, acquisition of skills, application of skills, and self-reflection.

Although these stage models provide an important theoretical framework for staff development, on a very personal level the models are more limited. This limitation exists because students in one school may require you to demonstrate an altogether different kind of teacher readiness than students in another school. Our view of readiness is therefore a nonlinear, ongoing process, rather than a linear, hierarchical process.

Readiness as an Ongoing Process

Multicultural readiness for teaching as an ongoing process involves two types of knowledge: cultural knowledge (theoretical information about cultural lifestyles and cultural strengths) and experiential knowledge (practical information about multicultural classrooms).[12] As a multicultural educator engaged in an ongoing process of renewal, you are always acquiring new knowledge. Consequently, you are continuously enhancing your readiness for specific school settings. There is never a final stage of readiness for you to reach, but rather new insights to develop and new skills to acquire.

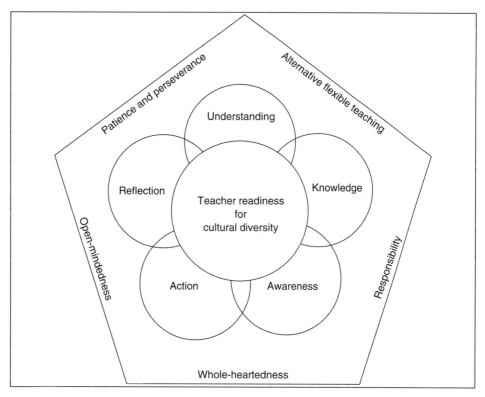

Figure 4–1 Attributes that foster readiness for teaching in culturally diverse classrooms

Five attributes comprise this view of readiness, as shown in Figure 4–1. Drawn from the work of Bennett, Niggle, and Stage (1991) and from Burstein and Cabello (1989), these attributes are

1. **awareness** of social and educational issues related to cultural diversity
2. **knowledge** of theory and research about multicultural education
3. **understanding** of how the interaction of culture, race, class, gender, and religion influences the educational values of your students, their parents, and the community
4. **reflection** on your own teaching beliefs and practices
5. **action** on classroom teaching based on awareness, knowledge, understanding, and reflection

These five attributes are continuously changing, continuously interacting with the personal teacher conditions we noted earlier, to provide you with a site-based readiness. In other words, teaching in entirely new schools where you are unfamiliar with student cultures requires a new understanding of student needs. Moving to a different school may also require a broadened awareness of cultural diversity, expanded knowledge about cultural groups, continuous reflection, and most likely new teaching actions.

ACTIVITIES FOR ASSESSING AND DEVELOPING READINESS

The following activities on multicultural readiness are intended to guide you through self-exploration of your beliefs, values, and predispositions for teaching all students. From this self-exploration, you should be able to determine areas in Figure 4–1 that you need to develop further.

Another purpose for the activities is to help you in your transformation to a multicultural teacher. Zeichner (1993) notes that developing a multicultural perspective involves a personal transformation and a professional transformation. **Personal transformation** occurs when you move away from a monocultural perspective to a multicultural, pluralistic perspective. **Professional transformation** occurs when you move away from culturally insensitive teaching to culturally sensitive teaching—that is, when you move away from teaching strategies designed for one culture to teaching strategies designed for multiple cultures. These transformations, which occur simultaneously, help you develop greater readiness for cultural diversity and help you move toward acquiring a multicultural perspective.

A final purpose for these activities is to help you determine whether you have an authentic readiness, not an altruistic readiness, for teaching in culturally diverse classrooms. Persons with only an altruistic readiness (readiness based on romanticized ideals, rather than on actual classroom practice) may become frustrated, feel helpless, and develop hostility toward students when they first encounter culturally diverse students in the rigor of daily teaching.[13]

ACTIVITY 4.1   Exploring Factors That Influence Readiness

This activity helps you examine factors that reportedly constrain and foster readiness. The factors[14] below are not intended to be exhaustive and complete, but rather provide you with a means to reflect on some areas you might need to refine as you develop your own readiness for teaching culturally diverse students.

Factors That Foster Readiness

The statements in Figure 4–2 represent factors that provide a basis for fostering your awareness, knowledge, and understanding of diversity issues. When you develop these kinds of factors in yourself, you then have a personal knowledge base for making classroom decisions about your teaching actions. For each statement in Figure 4–2, put a check in the space that best reflects your degree of alignment.

For factors you marked "no" or were unsure about, develop an action plan for enhancing your awareness and understanding of this area. For factors you marked "yes," summarize how you developed this quality.

Response			Item
Yes	No	Unsure	
____	____	____	1. I am comfortable teaching in culturally diverse classrooms with students who share different value systems.
____	____	____	2. I am comfortable conferencing with parents of diverse cultures.
____	____	____	3. I accept and affirm students' usage of nonstandard English.
____	____	____	4. I can explain how culture enhances students' learning of academic content.
____	____	____	5. I know how to design and implement lessons that are instructionally appropriate and academically challenging for all students.
____	____	____	6. I can develop strategies that engage all students in instruction and that help them express themselves confidently at school.
____	____	____	7. I can describe the historical antecedents to the marginalization of Black and Hispanic students at school.
____	____	____	8. I can identify subtle forms of racism, including unintended cultural bias, that might influence my own teaching.
____	____	____	9. I can explain how my autobiography influences the values and beliefs I hold for making classroom decisions about curriculum and instruction.
____	____	____	10. I am able to tailor instruction to the needs of all my students.
____	____	____	11. I am able to describe the relationship between local communities and schools in all economic and social areas, especially urban public schools where students are frequently disadvantaged.

Figure 4–2 Factors that foster readiness for teaching in culturally diverse schools

Factors That Constrain Readiness

Other reports indicate factors that may constrain your readiness for teaching culturally diverse students. These factors may lead you to develop strategies that lack the kind of cultural sensitivity needed to openly invite your students to engage meaningfully in your lessons. For each statement in Figure 4–3, put a check in the space that best reflects your degree of alignment with that factor. Remember that this activity is intended to enhance your readiness for teaching in culturally diverse classrooms by pinpointing areas that may constrain your

Response			Item
Yes	No	Unsure	
____	____	____	1. I prefer teaching students who share my social class and cultural background.
____	____	____	2. I believe that limited-English-proficiency (LEP) students need lower-level work.
____	____	____	3. I have limited cross-cultural experiences.
____	____	____	4. I believe that some minority groups, such as Blacks and Hispanics, may not be as capable of learning as other minority groups, such as Asians.
____	____	____	5. I'm unsure about the cultural qualities of social groups other than my own.
____	____	____	6. I believe that more problems than assets surround cultural diversity at school.
____	____	____	7. I have a limited understanding of the complex relationship among society, schools, and ethnicity.
____	____	____	8. I'm unsure how biases and stereotypes that I might have for other cultural groups could unintentionally influence my classroom instruction.
____	____	____	9. I would rather teach in monocultural school settings.
____	____	____	10. I have a limited understanding of how sociocultural and/or cognitive factors related to student diversity could influence my personal and academic relationship with students.

Figure 4–3   Factors that constrain readiness for teaching in culturally diverse schools

effectiveness to interact with students. Therefore, be honest and open with yourself as you respond to each statement.

For any statement you marked "yes" or were unsure about, develop an action plan for developing an understanding for how these factors might constrain student learning.

ACTIVITY 4.2   Examining Your Multicultural Education Experiences

This activity helps you examine the extent of your multicultural education experiences and determine any additional experiences you may need to strengthen your multicultural awareness. One assumption for this activity is that multicultural education experiences have an important influence on your multicultural readiness.

Figure 4–4 contains a list of questions to ask yourself about the educational experiences you have had during your teacher preparation. These questions were adapted from a study conducted by Grant (1981) on the multicultural educational experiences of students in one teacher preparation program.[15] As you read each question, put a check in the space that best describes your degree of alignment.

After you complete Figure 4–4, reflect carefully on the breadth and depth of multicultural experiences you have had. Determine which additional educational experiences, if any, you will need in order to develop your readiness.

ACTIVITY 4.3   Examining Your Stages of Ethnicity

This activity introduces you to the stages of ethnicity proposed by Banks (1991) and lets you assess your multicultural readiness relative to these stages. The stages of ethnicity proposed by Banks are shown in Figure 4–5. Although the stages appear to be mutually exclusive, Banks notes that the "division between the stages is blurred rather than sharp" (p. 66).

If you are at higher stages of ethnicity (e.g., Stage 5, Stage 6), you may have greater readiness for teaching in culturally diverse classrooms than if you are at lower stages of ethnicity.[16] Your potential for successful classroom teaching, however, is not based entirely on Banks's stages of ethnicity. You may be able to demonstrate excellent technical skills for teaching (e.g., planning lessons, writing objectives, developing materials) but still be at a lower stage of ethnicity. If you are at a lower stage, you need to broaden your awareness of other ethnic groups and deepen your understanding of your own ethnicity if you want to respond appropriately to persons in groups other than your own. You also need to consider how your limited sensitivity for ethnic groups, if any, may cause you to have unintended cultural bias.

To assess your alignment with the stages of ethnicity, examine the descriptors for each stage in Figure 4–5. Put a check mark next to those descriptors that you feel best align with your present state of ethnic awareness. You might check descriptors in several stages, in which case you overlap these stages. Consider how the stage you most closely align with influences your classroom instruction.

SUMMARY

Some educators see multicultural readiness as being little more than adding to their existing curriculum a few extra lessons that focus on racial issues. This chapter demonstrates, however, that multicultural readiness is more than merely knowing how to insert a few extra lessons into an existing curriculum. The kind of readiness we described is related to your curriculum decision making, including the ongoing interactions you have with students each day.

The activities in this chapter were intended to help you explore your own level of multicultural readiness and to determine which personal attributes you need to develop further. Rather than prescribe a stage model for developing readiness, specific personal attributes were suggested that can be continuously reshaped and broadened to align your multicultural readiness with the needs of students.

Response			Item
Much	Some	None	
_____	_____	_____	1. Do you know what multicultural education means?
_____	_____	_____	2. Have you completed any projects or activities that included aspects of multicultural education?
_____	_____	_____	3. Have you seen any school classroom environments with instruction that appeared to be multicultural?
_____	_____	_____	4. Have you received instruction on how to plan and implement multicultural lessons?
_____	_____	_____	5. In school classrooms you have observed, did you hear any mention of the contributions of people from various racial, cultural, and economic groups?
_____	_____	_____	6. Have you examined any school curriculum materials, including textbooks, for bias?
_____	_____	_____	7. Have you participated in any discussions that have focused on how to adapt different teaching strategies to the various learning styles of your students?
_____	_____	_____	8. Have you considered your role as a teacher in school-community relations?
_____	_____	_____	9. Have you examined any tests for cultural bias?
_____	_____	_____	10. Have you discussed the relationship between hidden curricula and unintended cultural bias?
_____	_____	_____	11. Have you completed any projects or activities that caused you to explore the relationship between instructional strategies and student self-esteem?
_____	_____	_____	12. Have you done any work outside formal university education or in-service workshops where you increased your awareness of multicultural education?
_____	_____	_____	13. Are you comfortable raising questions about multicultural issues (a) in groups of peers, (b) in your teaching, (c) in university or other formal educational settings?

Figure 4–4   Questions about the educational experiences you have had during your teacher preparation relative to multicultural education

Stage 1. Ethnic Psychological Captivity

_____ hold negative ideologies about own ethnic group
_____ voice negative beliefs about own ethnic group
_____ demonstrate ethnic self-rejection
_____ demonstrate ethnic low self-esteem
_____ avoid contact with other ethnic groups purposely
_____ strive aggressively to become highly culturally assimilated
_____ have intrapsychic conflict about own ethnic group

Stage 2. Ethnic Encapsulation

_____ show ethnic exclusiveness
_____ live voluntarily around own ethnic group
_____ participate primarily in own ethnic community
_____ believe own ethnic group is superior
_____ show low tolerance for other ethnic groups
_____ prefer to live around own ethnic groups

Stage 3. Ethnic Identity Clarification

_____ clarify personal attitudes about own ethnicity
_____ hold low or no intrapsychic conflict about own ethnic group
_____ voice positive attitudes about own ethnic group
_____ accept self as member of a specific ethnic group

Stage 4. Biethnicity

_____ hold a full and rich understanding of own ethnic identity
_____ demonstrate skills needed to participate positively and productively in own ethnic group
_____ demonstrate skills needed to participate positively and productively in another ethnic group
_____ desire to function effectively in two ethnic cultures

Stage 5. Multiethnicity

_____ demonstrate skills for functioning positively and productively in several ethnic sociocultural environments
_____ understand, appreciate, and share the values, symbols, and institutions of several ethnic cultures

Stage 6. Globalism and Global Competency

_____ hold skills, attitudes, and abilities needed to function in ethnic cultures within own and within other nations
_____ demonstrate a balance of ethnic, national, and global identifications
_____ internalize and act on the universalistic ethical values and principles of humankind

Figure 4-5   Characteristic features of the stages of ethnicity

Multicultural readiness is not easily reduced to a set of skills, nor is it attained in short-term educational experiences at universities or in-service workshops. Readiness for teaching culturally diverse students is tied to your own personal history, to your understanding of students' backgrounds, and to your ever-growing awareness of other cultures. Higher levels of readiness come from ongoing, thoughtful reflection on your own teaching. Just as we hold the view that all students in school classrooms are capable of attaining higher levels of learning, we also hold the view that all teachers are capable of attaining higher levels of multicultural readiness.

RESEARCH TOPIC

Topic: Teacher Readiness for Culturally Diverse Classrooms

Problem Posing

The emphasis throughout this chapter has been on developing readiness for teaching in contemporary school classrooms. Many questions surround the notion of readiness that make a clear definition for this concept problematic. Moreover, because different school contexts require teachers to have different kinds of cultural readiness, stage models that prescribe one set of skills for attaining higher levels of readiness are limited in generalizability. Like Sleeter (1992), we believe that readiness is not a set of skills, but rather is a worldview that requires ongoing transformation and realignment with new contexts. The schematic model in Figure 4–1 depicts personal attributes that reportedly foster multicultural readiness. These attributes should not, however, be viewed as fixed and static. They should be viewed as constantly changing as you continuously develop new insights into teaching culturally diverse students.

Two related questions are possible from our discussion of readiness as an ongoing and nonlinear process. First, how have experienced teachers in culturally diverse classrooms developed their readiness for meeting the needs of all their students? Second, are different kinds of readiness needed for teaching in schools that have differing cultures of students?

Exploration and Discovery

Suggested methods for conducting this research project on teacher readiness include teacher interviews and classroom observations. Conduct teacher interviews in two school sites. If possible, these sites should differ in student composition; for example, if one school contains students who are predominantly Hispanic, then the other school should contain predominantly Black, White, or Asian students. Locate in each of these schools at least one experienced teacher willing to be interviewed and to be observed during classroom instruction.

During these interviews, explore and record the teachers' views of multicultural readiness. Ask the teachers about formal and informal educational experiences that have contributed to their ability to communicate personally, socially, and academically with the students they now teach. Ask them whether they have taught in other school settings. Explore how their teaching strategies may have changed from one school to another. Inquire about the sensitivity the teachers have for the cultural backgrounds of their students. Determine whether or not the teachers alter their strategies to accommodate the needs of varying student cultural groups.

As you observe these teachers in the classroom, try to determine how their teaching styles are similar and how they are different. Consider how any differences you note might be influenced by cultural backgrounds of the students.

Reflection and Modification

In the interviews you conducted and in the classrooms you observed, did you discover any trends between the two teachers on how they developed their readiness for teaching their students? How did they describe multicultural readiness? What suggestions, if any, did they have for developing readiness for cultural diversity? What particular classroom strategies did you observe that appeared to be culturally sensitive? Record below the insights you developed about multicultural readiness from your interviews and observations.

1. _____

2. _____

3. _____

4. _____

What modifications have you made in your own beliefs about readiness for teaching in culturally diverse classrooms? After talking with experienced teachers and after completing the activities in this chapter, determine your own level of readiness. What specific areas in Figure 4–1 might you need to strengthen before you can more effectively reach all students and before you can be more attentive to the possibility of unintended cultural bias in your instruction?

Description and Speculation

Given what you learned from this research project, what more would you like to know about multicultural readiness? What additional research projects will deepen your understanding of readiness for teaching culturally diverse students? What additional reading might be helpful to broaden your understanding of readiness and to enhance your literacy of other cultures and their educational needs? Write below several research projects you might now undertake to extend your understanding of teacher readiness.

1. _____

2. _____

3. _____

4. _____

NOTES

1. Interview conducted with Joannie Phillips, October 28, 1993, at Las Vegas High School, Clark County School District, Las Vegas, Nevada. See further details about Joannie Phillips in Chapter 7.

2. See Apple, M. (1993). *Official knowledge: Democratic education in a conservative age.* New York: Routledge.

3. Developing this kind of readiness is complicated by personal biases and predispositions you may have for other cultures. This statement is supported by the study conducted by Patricia Larke: Larke, P. (1990). Cultural diversity awareness inventory. *Action in Teacher Education, 12*(3), 23–30.

4. Anna Ramirez and Allen Hayes are not real names for the characters depicted in these vignettes.

5. These figures were obtained in a telephone conversation with the assistant superintendent for personnel, Clark County School District, February 1994.

6. This is dramatically revealed in the study on cross-cultural communicative failures conducted by Jo Anne Kleifgen: Kleifgen, J.-A. (1988). Learning from student teachers' cross-cultural communicative failures. *Anthropology and Education Quarterly, 19,* 218–234.

7. Ann Arbor Public Schools and Ann Arbor Education Association. (1971–73). "Negotiation 3.625," *Master Agreement,* p. 70. Cited in Bowen, E., & Salsman, F. (1979). Integrating multiculturalism into a teacher-training program. *Journal of Negro Education, 48*(3), 390–395.

8. These qualities were derived from the work of John Dewey (1933) and Paulo Freire (1972).

9. Another well-known example of how one teacher implemented alternative flexible teaching to meet the needs of secondary students is the Jaime Escalante story. For an overview of the instructional practices of Jaime Escalante, see Escalante, J., & Dirmann, J. (1990). The Jaime Escalante math program. *Journal of Negro Education, 59,* 407–423.

10. The fallacy of approaching classroom teaching from an objective framework is discussed by Christine Sleeter (1992). She notes that some forms of multicultural education are grounded in the assumption that teachers who are predominantly White, middle class, and academically successful will approach cultural diversity in their classrooms in an objective fashion. Sleeter argues that this is not possible to do, that "people always frame questions and choose among analytical frameworks from a position that reflects their own values" (p. 38).

11. See Christine Sleeter's discussion of staff development: Sleeter, C. (1992). *Keepers of the American dream: A study of staff development and multicultural education.* Washington, DC: Falmer Press.

12. That a cultural knowledge base and experiential knowledge base are needed concurrently to foster readiness is supported by the work of Patricia Larke, Donna Wiseman, and Charmaine Bradley: Larke, P., Wiseman, D., & Bradley, C. (1990). The minority mentorship projects: Changing attitudes of preservice teachers for diverse classrooms. *Action in Teacher Education, 12*(3), 5–11.

13. Two recent case reports suggest that idealized, altruistic motives for teaching in culturally diverse settings can be detrimental to teacher success and to student learning. See York, D. (1993, April). *Cultural alienation in a culturally diverse classroom: Evidence from an ethnographic case study.* Paper presented at the Annual Meeting of the American Educational Research Association, Atlanta. See also Birrell, J. (1993, April). *The influence of ethnic encapsulation on a beginning teacher's cultural sensitivity: A case study.* Paper presented at the Annual Meeting of the American Educational Research Association, Atlanta.

14. The factors included in this activity were compiled from Avery and Walker (1993); Fine (1987); Fuller and Ahler (1987); Grant (1981); Haberman (1991); Heath (1983); Kleifgen (1988); Larke (1990); Larke, Wiseman, and Bradley (1990); Moll (1988); Reed and Simon (1991); Ross and Smith (1992); Tippeconnic (1983); and Trent (1990). We also considered the items contained in the Cultural Diversity Awareness Inventory developed by Gertrude Henry (1985).

15. Carl Grant (1981) developed an interview protocol to study the perspectives that preservice teachers had for the multicultural preparation they were given by their teacher education programs. We have adapted the questions here to help you examine the extent of your own multicultural preparation. See Grant, C. (1981). Education that is multicultural and teacher preparation: An examination from the perspectives of preservice students. *Journal of Educational Research, 75*(2), 95–101.

16. See the case study on ethnic encapsulation conducted by James Birrell (1993).

REFERENCES

Ann Arbor Public Schools and Ann Arbor Education Association. (1971–73). "Negotiation 3.625," *Master Agreement.*

Apple, M. (1993). *Official knowledge: Democratic education in a conservative age.* New York: Routledge.

Avery, P., & Walker, C. (1993). Prospective teachers' perceptions of ethnic and gender differences in academic achievement. *Journal of Teacher Education, 44*(1), 27–37.

Baker, G. C. (1983). *Planning and organizing for multicultural instruction.* Reading, MA: Addison-Wesley.

Banks, J. (1991). *Teaching strategies for ethnic studies* (5th ed.). Boston: Allyn & Bacon.

Bennett, C., Niggle, T., & Stage, F. (1991). Preservice multicultural teacher education: Predictors of student readiness. *Teaching and Teacher Education, 6*(3), 243–254.

Birrell, J. (1993, April). *The influence of ethnic encapsulation on a beginning teacher's cultural sensitivity: A case study.* Paper presented at the Annual Meeting of the American Educational Research Association, Atlanta.

Bowen, E., & Salsman, F. (1979). Integrating multiculturalism into a teacher-training program. *Journal of Negro Education, 48*(3), 390–395.

Burstein, N., & Cabello, B. (1989). Preparing teachers to work with culturally diverse students: A teacher education model. *Journal of Teacher Education, 40*(5), 9–16.

Contreras, A., & Lee, O. (1990). Differential treatment of students by middle school science teachers: Unintended cultural bias. *Science Education, 74*(4), 433–444.

Dewey, J. (1933). *How we think.* Boston: D. C. Heath.

Escalante, J., & Dirmann, J. (1990). The Jaime Escalante math program. *Journal of Negro Education, 59,* 407–423.

Fine, M. (1987). Silencing in public schools. *Language Arts, 64*(2), 157–174.

Freire, P. (1972). *Pedagogy of the oppressed.* London: Penguin Books.

Fuller, M-L., & Ahler, J. (1987). Multicultural education and the monocultural student: A case study. *Action in Teacher Education, 9*(3), 33–41.

Grant, C. (1981). Education that is multicultural and teacher preparation: An examination from the perspectives of preservice students. *Journal of Educational Research, 75*(2), 95–101.

Grant, C. A., & Melnick, S. L. (1978). Multicultural perspectives of curriculum development and their relationship to in-service education. In R. A. Edelfelt & E. B. Smith (Eds.), *Breakaway to multi-dimensional approaches: Integrating curriculum development and in-service education* (pp. 81–100). Washington, DC: Association of Teacher Educators.

Haberman, M. (1991). Can cultural awareness be taught in teacher education programs? *Teaching Education, 4*(1), 25–31.

Heath, S. (1983). *Ways with words: Language, life, and work in communities and classrooms.* New York: Cambridge University Press.

Henry, G. (1985). *Cultural diversity awareness inventory.* Hampton, VA: Hampton University Mainstreaming Outreach Services.

Kleifgen, J-A. (1988). Learning from student teachers' cross-cultural communicative failures. *Anthropology and Education Quarterly, 19,* 218–234.

Larke, P. (1990). Cultural diversity awareness inventory. *Action in Teacher Education, 12*(3), 23–30.

Larke, P., Wiseman, D., & Bradley, C. (1990). The minority mentorship projects: Changing attitudes of preservice teachers for diverse classrooms. *Action in Teacher Education, 12*(3), 5–11.

Mahan, J., & Boyle, V. (1981). Multicultural teacher preparation: An attitudinal survey. *Educational Research Quarterly, 6*(3), 97–103.

Moll, L. (1988). Some key issues in teaching Latino students. *Language Arts, 65*(5), 465–473.

Reed, D. F., & Simon, D. J. (1991). Preparing teachers for urban schools: Suggestions from historically black institutions. *Action in Teacher Education, 13*(2), 30–35.

Ross, D. D., & Smith, W. (1992). Understanding preservice teachers' perspectives on diversity. *Journal of Teacher Education, 43*(2), 94–103.

Sleeter, C. (1992). *Keepers of the American dream: A study of staff development and multicultural education.* Washington, DC: Falmer Press.

Tippeconnic, J. W. (1983). Training teachers of American Indian students. *Peabody Journal of Education, 61*(1), 6–15.

Trent, W. (1990). Race and ethnicity in the teacher education curriculum. *Teachers College Record, 91*(3), 361–369.

Trueba, H., Jacobs, L., & Kirton, E. (1990). *Cultural conflict and adaptation: The case of Hmong children in American society.* New York: Falmer Press.

York, D. (1993, April). *Cultural alienation in a culturally diverse classroom: Evidence from an ethnographic case study.* Paper presented at the Annual Meeting of the American Educational Research Association, Atlanta.

Zeichner, K. (1993, April). *Educating teachers for cultural diversity.* Paper presented at the Annual Meeting of the American Educational Research Association, Atlanta.

Chapter 5

Using Multicultural Concepts in Diverse Settings

It befalls to me, as someone who so awkwardly carried the label, to question it now, its juxtaposition of terms–minority student. For me there is no way to say it with grace. I say it rather with irony sharpened by self-pity. I say it with anger. It is a term that should never have been painted on me. One that I was wrong to accept. (Rodriguez, 1982, p. 143)

We will not be recommending that beginning teachers try to learn details about the cultures of different groups. . . . It is impossible because there may be too many cultures represented in the classroom; it is dangerous because limited knowledge can lead to stereotypes that impede learning. (Cazden & Mehan, 1989, p. 47)

INTRODUCTION

As you interact in school with a variety of learners, you soon realize that some of them reflect your particular lifestyle and others do not. At times you may feel unable to reach learners who are culturally different from you. These are students who perhaps express thoughts and behaviors you just cannot relate to. In this chapter, our objective is to help you better understand why you may not feel comfortable teaching in culturally diverse classrooms, to describe what you need to do to feel secure and at ease, and to convince you that, regardless of your background, you can be a highly successful teacher in classrooms of diverse learners. Many teachers comment that diversity is not a part of their lives, but we believe it is a part of each of us and should be recognized and viewed as a valuable asset in the classroom.

We address anxieties you may have about cultural pluralism by providing you with a historical look at America's pluralism, describing some of the terms employed in the area of multicultural education; identifying racial groups commonly associated with the phrase **multicultural education** and suggesting a rationale for the inclusion of other groups; and defining key concepts related to cultural diversity. We also outline strategies you might employ to better understand and use the diversity you may find in your classroom, and we encourage you to build on these strategies so that you will become a highly successful teacher for all students.

How do you become culturally sensitive? As we mentioned in Chapters 3 and 4, one way is for you to look closely at yourself and at your autobiography, striving for a better understanding of who you are and why you selected teaching as a profession. Another way equally important is to acquire a broad cultural understanding of the students you teach and to help them understand their opportunities in a pluralistic society. Culturally sensitive teachers understand the need to prepare students to live in a nation and world that is culturally diverse.

CULTURAL DIVERSITY AND TODAY'S TEACHERS

Why the stress on cultural diversity? We listened to you! Typically, when preservice teachers exit a teacher education program and are asked to identify program weaknesses and strengths, many cite a lack of experiences in the area of cultural diversity and therefore do not feel qualified to assume a teaching position in a school or classroom characterized as culturally diverse. Why do beginning teachers make these statements? First, many do not see themselves as culturally different. Second, they mistakenly associate the term *diversity* with people of color and believe that only teachers of minority background have the experiences to address issues of diversity. And, when introduced to the concept of diversity in professional classes, they do not see its value in becoming an effective teacher; that is, they have not been able to translate theory (the idea) into practice (its usefulness in the classroom).[1]

Before describing cultural diversity and America's learners, we should take a look at who is entering the teaching profession. As we mentioned earlier, the students who are enrolled in colleges and universities and who have selected teaching as a major are predominantly White, female, and middle class. In preservice courses, they describe the suburban cities or rural towns where they have grown up as culturally homogeneous, and their social acquaintances as predominantly White, as are the friends of their parents. Their college peers and friends also are, for the most part, identified as White. A few state, though mistakenly, that they do not have a culture because they are White and have no ethnic affiliation![2]

That many prospective teachers enter college and admit to having had little contact with minorities or other individuals who label themselves ethnic Americans is true. It is also true that what they know about members of these groups and the concept of cultural diversity is what they have gleaned from watching television, what they have heard from their peers, and what they have read in school assignments. A few confess that their first contact with a minority person was when they entered college. When asked to define cultural diversity, many describe it as an educational approach that has something to do with minorities who do not perform well in school, particularly African Americans. Some are hostile toward the concept, viewing it as an attempt to advantage minorities over others. A few believe that cultural diversity has no role to play in the classroom.

Is this an accurate characterization of today's beginning teachers? Somewhat. However, that today's preservice teachers lack diversity is *not true*. Regardless of where you grew up, you have experienced diversity; it may not have included people of color or recent immigrants. You might not have seen "racial, gender, and religious" diversity because you were not asked to see the world from these perspectives and were not helped to think in those terms. In your home community, issues dealing with race and gender may not have surfaced sufficiently to warrant a view of the world through these lenses. And in those few occasions when it did, diversity was usually associated with "problems" the community experienced, rather than with beneficial contributions made by cultural groups.

To most beginning teachers, the world is White and has a particular sameness. They are virtually unable to see the diversity that surrounds them in their home communities. They are unaware that many suburban and rural communities in the United States are inhabited by a variety of individuals: the poor and the wealthy; workers and the unemployed; Catholics, Protestants, and a variety of non-Christians; country club members and those belonging to no formal social organizations; those living in extended family structures and those in nuclear family units; long-term residents and new arrivals. This is diversity, but to the beginning teacher, it is just "middle-class America," which, of course, it is not.

Most beginning teachers also are unaware that all communities are in a constant state of change. Some communities, as a result of recent immigration and emigration patterns, are changing faster than others as residents move within and out of their communities and as newcomers gravitate to these areas (see the discussion of Mark Keppel High School in Chapter 6). For example, as a result of greater employment opportunities, more and more minorities are opting to live in suburban America. In addition, as new immigrants (e.g., Russian Jews, Colombians, Chinese, Haitians) arrive, they, too, seek locations where employment is a possibility and homes are available. Although many are attracted to the cities, as were previous immigrants, a significant number have turned to the suburbs, and some have relocated in rural areas. Communities that a decade ago characterized themselves as homogeneous are now culturally diverse.[3]

Many preservice teachers move from homogeneous home communities and become members of more culturally diverse communities, including colleges or universities. Here they interact with people from all over the world. And as they attempt to find their place in this new environment, they join old and new clubs and associations, enroll in a variety of classes, change majors more than once, and learn to become citizens of the world. Given their comments as they exit teacher education programs, however, many prospective teachers insulate themselves by refusing to acknowledge the cultural diversity in their lives and by associating with other preservice teachers who behave in a similar fashion. Perhaps many "justify" this insulation by believing that they will return to their "homogeneous" home communities to teach.[4]

The above statements are not meant to be critical of prospective teachers but are merely presented to offer you a general description of the pool of candidates choosing teaching as a profession. In this chapter, we attempt to sensitize you with general understandings about diversity and to help you see that diversity exists within each of us, in our neighborhoods, in the United States, and in the global community. And as you reflect on these basic understandings, you will realize that only you—the individual, the teacher—have the power to ensure that you leave your teacher preparation program with the fundamental knowledge and skills to begin teaching in America's culturally pluralistic classrooms. Once you have come to accept cultural diversity as a valuable concept, you will make use of this "new" way of looking at the world to prepare your students to live in a world community that is culturally diverse.

ACTIVITY 5.1   Who Are You?

Many teachers describe themselves as "similar to other persons in their professional teacher education classes." Although we do not claim to know what this phrase really means, we do believe that you are sending us an important message when you describe yourself in this manner. We believe that you are telling us you do not wish to describe yourself or to explore issues related to race and culture.

In this exercise, we challenge this position by having you explore the unique qualities you possess as an individual and the common experiences you share with other human beings. Our intent is to illustrate to you that you are different from and similar to your colleagues. And it is our intent to have you view your unique and shared experiences as positive attributes. We hope that what you learn from this exercise will carry over into your field experiences as you observe classrooms and student teach.

Working individually, use some of the questions listed below to develop a composite of yourself. Then, working with a small group of colleagues, develop a composite that describes your group. Share your personal and small group composites with a larger group of colleagues and as a larger group attempt to construct a comprehensive composite. Finally, initiate a discussion that focuses on two issues: (1) How important are differences in better understanding an individual? and (2) What experiences do members of your group share as individuals and teachers, and how important are these experiences in the classroom?

Questions

1. Who are you (name)?
2. What is your major course of study? Minor?
3. What was (is) your favorite class in college? Least favorite? Why?
4. How much time do you spend on your work each week?
5. How did you pay for school (loan, scholarship, working)?
6. Where do you live (dorm, apartment, home, with relatives)?
7. With whom do you share your life?
8. Were you a member of a fraternity or sorority?
9. What did you like most about your college community? Least?
10. What do you do for entertainment? When do you do it (e.g., evenings, weekdays)?
11. Where do you work? How many hours a week do you work? What do you like most and least about your job?
12. If you could go somewhere special this weekend, where would you go?
13. What pets do you have, if any?
14. How many close friends do you have? How do you choose your friends?
15. Is your closest friend male or female?
16. Are you married?
17. How would you describe yourself (race, ethnic background, lifestyle, gender)?
18. How would you describe the community where you grew up?
19. If you lived in an ethnically diverse neighborhood, how would you describe relations among the residents?
20. In what area of the country did you grow up?
21. Have you returned to your home community, or do you plan to return to your home, to teach?
22. What is your religious affiliation? What role does religion play in your life?
23. How would you describe your family's economic background?
24. How many times has your family moved?
25. How many brothers and sisters do you have?
26. How would you describe your role in your family?
27. How old were your parents when you were born?
28. How close does your family live to your extended family (e.g., grandparents, aunts)?
29. How often did you see your grandparents as a child? Now?
30. How old were your grandparents when your parents were born?

DEFINING MULTICULTURAL EDUCATION

Let's familiarize you with the concept of multicultural education. One way to begin is to offer you a definition. Multicultural education already has many definitions, so rather than create another, we employ a definition that one of us (Garcia) developed elsewhere:

> A layered concept that includes not only the experiences of particular individuals and groups but also their shared interests and relationships, which, in turn, are embedded in the interconnectedness of all peoples of the world. In its full complexity, then, multiculturalism implies the cultivation of a global view of human affairs. Paradoxically, perhaps, this expanded view of multiculturalism places primary emphasis on the individual and on the importance of individual decisions regarding all issues concerning the welfare of humankind. (Garcia & Pugh, 1992, p. 218)*

Although our definition does not mention *you,* we do want to reinforce the importance of a popular saying: "To understand who you are, you must understand others; to understand others, you must understand who you are." When you know who you are and who your students are, then you are able to promote a greater recognition and respect for cultural diversity in your classroom. Our interest is in promoting a definition of multicultural education that focuses on "shared interests and relationships" at all levels: local, regional, national, and global. We want you and your students to gain an understanding of yourselves and others as human beings who have a stake and a responsibility in the welfare of humankind; that is, we want you and your students to see that we are all connected. For example, what I do or what my neighbors do affects others. My behavior as a teacher affects the behavior of students in a classroom. My actions and the actions of my students outside the classroom also affect others. My decision to purchase products manufactured in places other than the United States affects more than one economy. The decision of the United States government to support the North American Free Trade Agreement (NAFTA) also affects my life and the lives of millions of other people. In short, as human beings living on this planet, all of us must learn to become responsible citizens—accountable for our actions and understanding of the actions of others.

Notice that we employ a definition that makes no reference to particular groups, but rather it focuses on individual responsibility and a global view of human affairs. As we discuss our definition in greater detail, you will find that, in most cases, we believe that ideas should guide multicultural education. The ideas selected are dictated by individual needs, the needs of students, and the needs of a school and community; ideas guide behavior in the classroom. To the classroom teacher, some of the following are

---

* The definition we use here focuses primarily on the individual; this focus aligns with the overall intent of this book, which is to help you examine, refine, and, where necessary, reconstruct your personal practical philosophy for teaching culturally diverse students. We acknowledge the comments made by one of the initial reviewers of this chapter, however, who suggested that the definition we use in this book privileges the individual. This reviewer noted, "The definition of multicultural education used in this chapter privileges the individual, which I find important but problematic. While I too believe in the importance of individual action, any definition that does not address notions of power, oppression, the systematic, institutionalized 'isms' that plague our nation and world, and the need for collective action will lead teachers to believe that individuals can change structures. While an individual teacher can alter what happens in his or her classroom, significant educational change takes more than that. Therefore, any definition of multicultural education maintains the importance of the individual but also acknowledges relationships of power, institutionalized 'isms' and collective action."

examples of needs: (a) gaining a better understanding of the students in a classroom, (b) identifying and infusing material in the classroom to better promote cultural diversity, and (c) gaining a better understanding of the greater school community by volunteering to serve on school committees aimed at involving more parents in the formal education of their children. We believe that multicultural education is teachers promoting intellectual ideas because they enhance learning in the classroom. We also believe that teachers are intellectual beings capable of identifying these ideas and implementing a course of action that addresses these school and classroom needs.

Once you accept cultural diversity as a legitimate concept, you will begin to see its value in the classroom. In all probability, you may begin by using material other than the textbook to promote a multicultural curriculum. You may even include material to provide students with multiple perspectives to issues and events. You may learn more about your students to better meet their needs—learning styles, communication modes, and methods of assessment. In short, you will gain the knowledge and skills that will identify you as someone who is becoming an outstanding teacher prepared to teach all students.

In the next three sections of this chapter, we provide a brief history of cultural pluralism in the United States. We believe that you need to become familiar with its early beginnings to better understand recent developments in the area. Although we provide a broad survey of cultural pluralism, we focus on the status of minorities in public education. We believe that multicultural education is essential in assisting minorities who are experiencing difficulties in the classroom. Our intent in providing this historical background is to help you understand and become sensitive to the growing need for multicultural education among all learners.

CULTURAL PLURALISM AT THE TURN OF THE TWENTIETH CENTURY

In the late 1700s, the framers of the Constitution focused on political democratic pluralism. "Their concern was with building and maintaining a nation of one dominant culture from the many political and economic factions represented in the original thirteen states" (Appleton, 1983, p. 3). In this period, the predominant culture in America was British. Although cultural diversity existed in the colonies (religious diversity, individual rights), its influence in early American history was secondary to the forces that led to the colonies rebelling against the Crown and creating the United States of America. The country's early leaders acknowledged cultural diversity (e.g., Germans, Scotch-Irish, Welsh, Irish), but when individuals from these groups initiated actions that were seen as a threat to nationalism, they were quickly quashed. The term **cultural diversity,** however, was not employed when discussing the life experiences of slaves, free African Americans, and Native Americans.

The early history of the Germans is perhaps one of the better examples of nationalism winning over cultural diversity. In the late 1700s, the Germans had to contend with Benjamin Franklin, who took it upon himself to rid the Germans of their "supposedly inferior, non-English customs that might eventually dominate Pennsylvania and Germanize us instead of Anglifying them" (Weaver, 1970, p. 47).

A century later, White Americans, alarmed by the large influx of German immigrants, foiled attempts by this group to establish a "New Germany" in Missouri.[5] Within a few generations, most Germans had assimilated into mainstream American culture.

This one example is not meant to suggest that immigrants passively gave up their old ways to become Americans. On the contrary, there are numerous examples of immigrants resisting the calls of America's leaders that they cast off their native skins. As Seller (1977) reminds us, "Three important institutions limited change and preserved European traditions: the ethnic family, the ethnic church, and the ethnic school" (p. 22). The Dutch, "with one of the best developed school systems in seventeenth century Europe, were successful in establishing ethnic schools in colonial America" (p. 5). In the 19th century, when Irish parents viewed public schools with suspicion or learned of the mistreatment of their children at the hands of Protestant teachers, they turned to their religious leaders and the Catholic Church and created parochial schools, a social maneuver that allowed them to resist Anglo-Saxon conformity, further formalize their ties with the Catholic Church, and reinforce their spiritual ties with their faith.

At the turn of the 20th century, the debate among educational leaders centered on two major ideologies: Americanization/Anglo-Saxon conformity and cultural pluralism. Whereas the Americanization process required immigrants to give up their old ways and to assimilate into the dominant Anglo-Saxon culture, the ideal of cultural pluralism denied the supremacy of Anglo-Saxon culture and rejected the demand that immigrant cultures melt and fuse to create an original American.[6] Horace Kallen, an early 20th-century philosopher and writer, was the first to call for a new theoretical and practical approach to the relationship of the dominant society and the ethnic groups (Krug, 1977). Although the cultural pluralism theory was popular among some, especially those who found the Americanization process a dehumanizing experience, it was not a theory that was embraced by most of America's educational leaders.[7]

Educational leaders, however, did not establish the educational agenda for the 20th century. Rather, economic and political forces outside the public schools—specifically, industrialization and the Nativist movement—established the educational agenda. As immigrants entered the United States, urbanization increased, aided by the industrialization of the Northwest and key cities in the Midwest. With the growth of cities came a need for a labor force that was sufficiently educated to perform the tasks required in the factories that dotted the Eastern seaboard and parts of the Midwest. As the cities swelled in populations, so did the social problems. Not only was a gap noticeable between the wealthy and the poor, but crime also increased, as did alcoholism. According to Tozer, Violas, and Senese (1993), "the unprecedented flow of immigrants with different ethnic and religious backgrounds helped turn nineteenth-century schools into socialization factories where it was hoped, American values could be instilled into a diverse population" (p. 49).

Nativism, a national movement that surfaced in the 19th century, was a major political force at the turn of the century. The movement was composed of a number of Americans, many of whom felt left behind in the industrialization of the nation. To the nativists, the root of many of their problems was the immigrants. The immigrants, with "their odd dress, unintelligible languages, and odd behaviors," were seen as a threat to 19th-century American life. To whip up support against anyone who, in their eyes, was "foreign," the nativists employed jingoistic and racial arguments. Some of the leaders were not above using physical force to keep the immigrants "in their place." At the turn of the century, with Europe about to embroil itself in a war and the United States slowly being drawn into this foray, nativists campaigned to limit the flow of immigrants, particularly those from Eastern and Western Europe. The Nativist movement gained sufficient strength at the turn of the century to solicit support from organized labor and key politicians. As the Nativist movement became a viable political force, it was "aided and abetted by the so-called Americanization Movement, whose adherents wished to quickly and forcibly assimilate the millions of new immigrants into the mainstream of American society" (Appleton, 1983, p. 4).

As these two forces gained in intensity, educational leaders opted for "Anglo conformity as the ideology that would strongly shape American education to this day" (Appleton, 1983, p. 5). Perhaps to placate the multiculturalists and to gain greater acceptance of this ideology, educators disguised the movement by referring to it as "the melting pot" process. The name comes from the popular play *The Melting Pot,* which was staged at the turn of the century in New York City. As a result, educational leaders described what was happening to the millions of immigrants from Eastern and Southern Europe in more "humanizing" terms: "All ethnic differences would amalgamate and a novel person would emerge from this new ethnic synthesis" (Banks, 1975, p. 3). There was little doubt, however, that Anglo conformity (Americanization programs) was the established policy of schools.

In their eagerness to Americanize immigrants and their children, educators played down attempts that promoted a recognition of cultural differences. In school the language of instruction was English, the teachers were Anglo Americans, and the curriculum reflected the views of the Anglo American majority. To further reinforce this particular ideology, some teachers resorted to denigrating immigrant cultural patterns and traditions. Those students who exhibited a reluctance to accept this school environment or who were unwilling to give up their ethnic heritage were systematically pushed out of schools.

Americanization programs were urban endeavors aimed at the children of immigrants and other White Americans. African Americans and American Indians were not part of the grand experiment. Moreover, they were considered inassimilable. (Hispanics—namely, Mexicans and Puerto Ricans—were yet to make their mark on U.S. history.) Pinkney (1969) summarizes the education of African Americans at this time:

> In the decade following the Civil War, when most [African Americans] lived on farms, few of their children were enrolled in school. Those who were enrolled attended for only short periods. The schools were overcrowded and the buildings were dilapidated . . . The situation improved little with the turn of the century. It is reported that only 58 percent of the [African American] children between the ages of 6 and 14 were enrolled in school as late as 1912. (p. 73)

For American Indians, the situation was no better. According to Van Til (1974),

> On the reservations there was always ambivalence as to whether education should absorb [the American Indian] into the American majority patterns or respect his civilization and identity. The vacillation between opposing poles of thought was accompanied by the growth of a large governmental bureaucracy, the Bureau of Indian Affairs (BIA). (p. 296)

The BIA adopted the Anglo conformity ideology and began establishing "Indian Schools" on remote areas of some reservations. These self-contained facilities isolated American Indians from their families and tribes, ignored the students' cultural traditions, and forced them to "dress and act like Americans." Acting American meant gaining training in the "arts and crafts, farming, and animal husbandry" (Rice & Krout, 1991, p. 69). Many students refused to leave their homes and enroll in these schools; some who enrolled left after only a few weeks of schooling. For many the BIA schools were a dismal failure.

CULTURAL PLURALISM IN THE FIRST HALF OF THE TWENTIETH CENTURY

Although public education expanded during this time period, little occurred in the area of cultural pluralism. Anglo conformity continued to be the prevailing ideology, and although some White Americans may have put up some resistance, it was not strong enough to draw national attention or reach the ears of educational activists. In general, the educational system continued as it had at the turn of the century. The ethnic composition of the teachers and administrators changed somewhat, but the curriculum—formal and hidden—remained Anglocentric.

When African Americans moved into the North and Mexicans into the Southwest and their numbers remained relatively small, they enrolled in public schools with White Americans and were provided opportunities for success similar to those of their White peers. A few were able to overcome overt and subtle obstacles and to advance their station in life. A small but significant number of African Americans living in the North and South, for example, were able to enroll in the few black colleges and universities found in the South (e.g., Fisk, Howard, Morehouse, and Talladega). Many who graduated from these schools returned to their segregated communities and assumed leadership roles. In 1896 the *Plessy v. Ferguson* Supreme Court decision legalized segregation and dealt a death blow to any efforts aimed at integrating society. Segregation became an "American way of life." In the North, African Americans replaced the Irish, Italian, and Jewish immigrants who had left the urban ghettos; and a "Mexican side of town" became a fixture in many Southwestern towns and cities as the population of indigenous Mexican Americans grew and as Mexicans escaped the political turmoil in their country and sought greater economic opportunities in the United States.

As the African and Mexican American student populations increased in public education—segregated and "integrated" schools—officials developed curricula that again reflected the groups' status in society. Between 1920 and 1950, most of the segregated schools were African American or Mexican. Those schools that were "integrated" were segregated by the curricula offered to the students. Not surprisingly, in both instances, educators developed curricula that prepared minority students for vocational and low-skilled job opportunities. In these schools and classrooms, the language of instruction was English and the curriculum was Anglocentric.

With the expansion of public education and the inclusion of greater numbers of minority youths into the system, "dropout" rates for African Americans and Mexican Americans increased to levels considered unacceptable to educators. To "explain away" the groups' poor school performances, educators developed "position statements." These statements surfaced in the early part of the 20th century as psychologists were developing IQ tests and as many Americans were examining phrenology and other "scientific" approaches that posited the superiority of the "Nordic race" (see Chapter 9 for a further discussion of standardized IQ tests). The "genetic deficit" position held that African American and Mexican American students did not possess the intellectual tools to succeed in school. Subscribers to this position were reluctant to divert school resources to improve instructional programs for children who were perceived as incapable of profiting from them. According to Armstrong, Henson, and Savage (1993), the other popular position statement was called "cultural deficit":

> Those who subscribed to this argument contended that poor school performance could be blamed on the failure of minority-group children's parents to provide an intellectually stimulating home atmosphere that prepared the learners for the expectations of the school. The cultural deficit view seemed to allow schools a way out when confronted with statistics revealing high dropout rates and other evidence of mediocre levels of school performance on the part of minority-group learners. This position permitted blame for these dismal statistics to be placed on learners' homes rather than the school. (p. 191)

Although it is true that, in the first half of the 20th century, public education did little for minorities, a small number of educators whom we label activists did attempt to place the groups' concerns on the national educational agenda. These activists saw the limitations of schools, particularly the practices of tracking and differentiated curricula. They were aware that minorities were not graduating from high schools, entering college, and effectively competing with White Americans for blue- and white-collar jobs. These activists pointed out that discriminatory treatment toward minorities also affected nonminorities:

> (1) segregated educational facilities promoted a two-tiered society and did little to advance intergroup relations; (2) ignoring the needs of minorities forced the group out of education and heightened the probability that such individuals could become liabilities rather than assets to society. In short, the schools minorities attended provided them with a second class education. (Garcia, 1984b, p. 25)

CULTURAL PLURALISM IN THE SECOND HALF OF THE TWENTIETH CENTURY

A number of events occurred between 1945 and 1990 that identified cultural pluralism as a major force in education. However, the terms employed to describe cultural diversity and the definitions of multicultural education that evolved during these decades were different from the definition we use in this book. These terms and definitions suggest a logical evolution in the area of multicultural education. Whether it was cultural pluralism as described by Horace Kallen or educational reform in the early 1990s, educators remain focused on the central question: How can we best provide a quality education for all learners?

In the 1940s, after serving overseas, African American soldiers returned home to find that their communities remained segregated. They had fought to "make the world safe for democracy" but returned home to find that democracy remained an elusive goal in their own country. In the South, the world was divided into two parts—White and Black—and the White part always seemed the more advantaged. Many African Americans rejected this second-class citizenship and joined organizations such as the National Association for the Advancement of Colored People (NAACP) and began to work to change America. These individuals laid the groundwork for the tumultuous changes that would occur in the next two decades.

In the early 1950s, the federal government enacted the G.I. Bill, a program that provided returning soldiers with financial resources to continue their formal education. Thousands of veterans, mostly men, opted for this program and went on to college. Because lack of finances was one reason that many African Americans and Mexican Americans did not go on to college, the G.I. Bill provided an excellent opportunity. Many minorities took advantage of the program, graduated from college, went on to graduate school, and became the teachers, doctors, and lawyers of the 1950s and 1960s. Some of these individuals would become major contributors to the 1960s Civil Rights movement by organizing their communities and directing them toward constructive ends.

It is difficult to point to one event as the catalyst, but perhaps the case of *Brown v. Board of Education* (of Topeka, Kansas) served as a rallying point. *Brown vs. Board of Education* "declared that segregation was inherently unequal and a denial of equal protection under the Fourteenth Amendment. The decision forced educators to find methods of desegregating America's schools" (Garcia, 1984b, p. 25). The federal government stepped in to help educators deal with the changes that were about to confront the schools. Title IV of the 1964 Civil Rights Act authorized the establishment of short-term training institutes that included familiarizing teachers with the culture and history of African Americans. In 1965 the Elementary and Secondary Education Act provided educators with financial assistance to help meet the needs of America's minority groups.

In the 1960s, Hispanic (Chicano) students (we define these terms in the next two sections of this chapter) in the Los Angeles area boycotted their classes to protest the lack of a relevant curriculum, the absence of Hispanic role models, and teachers and staff who exhibited little concern for their well-being. They were joined by parents and social activists as they marched to the Los Angeles Board of Education to have their protests heard. In other parts of the country, similar walkouts occurred as many African American, Mexican American, and Native American communities expressed their discontent with the status quo. Also in the 1960s, social activists attacked institutions of higher learning, particularly schools of education, for their insensitivity at meeting the needs of minorities. Specifically, these activists called for courses that addressed the needs of minorities and the hiring of minority faculty and staff. Multicultural education was about to be reborn.[8]

An important point to remember is that, in the 1960s, attempts to bring about change in schools were not initiated by the educational community but by those ill-served by it. Social activists (minorities who had returned home from the war to segregated communities, others who had taken advantage of the G.I. Bill, and a small core of White educators), students, and parents were the first to publicly attack the schools. And although initially the focus was on the plight of African Americans, the movement gained momentum to embrace other groups. Social activists, along with students and parents who lobbied for change in schools and who led the marches and demonstrations of the 1960s and 1970s, were catalysts for the passage of federal acts and laws designed to help underserved groups gain greater access to schools and other societal institutions.

From 1970 to 1990, a number of forces have influenced the evolution of multicultural education. Perhaps the most salient is the significant increase of immigrants, particularly those from Latin America and Asia. Many of these immigrants have found jobs and homes in urban areas, but as we mentioned elsewhere, they also have been attracted to the opportunities available in suburban America. As a result, many "all-White communities" have begun to experience diversity firsthand. Today, suburban communities outside Chicago, San Francisco, Houston, Boston, and elsewhere are attempting to provide the offspring of recent immigrants from Greece, Russia, Lebanon, China, Colombia, and El Salvador with a multicultural school environment. This influx of recent immigrants and the migration of African Americans and Hispanics from urban centers have changed the educational agenda of many suburban schools. The discussion in many suburban school districts has begun to lean toward such issues as bilingual education, a multicultural curriculum, building a diverse faculty and staff, promoting better intergroup relations, and learning strategies for conflict resolution.

Another major force is the increase in minority populations. The African American, Native American, and Hispanic populations are increasing significantly. In some instances, these increases are outdistancing the White population. In 1990 the median age of African Americans was 28.1, and was 32.9 for all races; the median age for Whites was 34.4. In 1992 the average size of a Hispanic family was 3.81 people; for African Americans, 3.43; and for all families, 3.17; for the White population it was 3.11. Projections are for the figures for minorities to continue to increase. Today, minorities are majority student populations in many of America's major cities (e.g., Washington, DC; Oakland; Los Angeles); urban schools that were once culturally mixed are now predominantly African American or Hispanic or Asian American. In Chicago's northern (e.g., Highland Park, Fort Sheridan) and western (e.g., Norridge,

Franklin Park, Melrose Park) suburbs, migration has led to major changes resulting in communities with significant African American and Hispanic populations.[9] Mark Keppel High School (MKHS) in Alhambra, California, shows similar patterns for Asian students (see discussion of MKHS in Chapter 6).

Another trend is that minorities continue to perform poorly in public schools, particularly African American and Hispanic students in urban areas. The reasons for this poor performance are complex. Certainly, any discussion of this issue should include an examination of school organization, curriculum, school funding, parental involvement, community environments, and a number of other issues. No matter how the discussion is framed, however, schools, for the most part, are not meeting the educational needs of minority learners. Urban educators are aware of this phenomenon and continue to look for methods of improving schools.

Other developments that surfaced in the 1980s and aimed at improving schools in general but that also seem to be directed at better addressing the needs of America's culturally diverse population are educational reform, national curriculums, standards in the disciplines, teacher performance in the classroom, and trends in assessment. What will be interesting as educators pursue these issues is the value placed on cultural pluralism as an intellectual idea and meeting the educational needs of culturally diverse students. Today, educators across the nation acknowledge ethnic differences and describe schools as "celebrating diversity." And although politicians and society in general have accepted the notion of cultural diversity, voices are calling for restrictions on immigration and schools that offer a curriculum that places a high value on a common history and culture.[10]

Teacher educators who are involved with the schools are aware of changing demographics and changes occurring in society and schools throughout the country. Continued involvement with the schools has convinced us of the need for teachers who are culturally sensitive and prepared to teach in diverse settings. Moreover, our belief in cultural diversity continues to be reinforced when we visit schools and speak with classroom teachers, principals, personnel directors, students, and parents. In the decades ahead, the need for teachers who are culturally sensitive, academically prepared, and committed to cultural diversity will increase as educators attempt to enhance the quality of education they provide to all learners.

ACTIVITY 5.2   Labeling Process

This activity helps you reflect on and examine how students can be negatively labeled at school. In our extensive experience with all social classes of schools, with both preservice and in-service teachers, and with schools in various locations (urban, suburban, rural), we see labeling as a constant and severe problem. Little improvement has been made in the conceptualization of IQ, ability groups, racial and cultural groups, and other groups susceptible to stereotyping and discrimination at school. As a preservice teacher or student teacher, you might feel pressured into silence about this topic, perhaps because your more experienced cooperating teacher in the classroom is evaluating you—if not explicitly, then implicitly—on your proficiency to use existing strategies and norms, not on your ability to openly question and change the status quo. As an experienced or beginning teacher, you might feel similar pressure from supervisors who evaluate your teaching. Regardless of the professional circumstances, you must learn to deal successfully with the politics of your teaching while also being a strong advocate for your students. Lacking this commitment, you could very well perpetuate existing practices that are discriminatory to some students regardless of how unintentional this discrimination might be. The following brief scenario helps you consider the very subtle kind of unintended discrimination that often occurs in school classrooms.

Scenario

It's late October, and you are about to begin your 5th week of teaching. In the late morning of the 1st day of the week, you hear a knock at your classroom door. The principal greets you, accompanied by three learners he describes as "Hispanics." The students, he states, are from a family that moved into the neighborhood last week. The principal leaves your room and wishes you well with the three students.

As the principal walks out of the classroom and down the hall, what thoughts run through your mind? Why did the principal describe the students as "Hispanics"? What does the term *Hispanic* mean to you? Are you totally perplexed by the use of such terms as *Hispanics, African Americans,* and *minorities* to describe representatives from these groups?

Return to the opening quotation of this chapter. Why do you think Richard Rodriguez is so bitter about being labeled a minority student? What are your thoughts about descriptions of students that refer to their racial/ethnic background, gender, and social economic background?

What information should you gather about your students to better understand them and to meet their educational needs? List this information below. Share the list with your colleagues. Be prepared to provide a rationale for the collection of particular information.

1. _____

2. _____

3. _____

4. _____

5. _____

6. _____

A REVIEW OF TERMS AND DEFINITIONS

What is meant by the term **multicultural education**? What are the goals of multicultural education? What term should you use, for example, when discussing the experiences of African Americans? Many preservice and in-service teachers raise these questions in their professional classes as they seek answers to questions about cultural diversity. In the preceding pages, we provided you a historical look at cultural pluralism. If you have reviewed the history of education, you may have reached the conclusion that multicultural education is similar to other movements (e.g., special education, testing, ability grouping) in education: It did not "happen," but rather evolved over time. For example, the overall goal of special education is to provide a quality education for a group of learners that historically has been marginalized. Similar to advocates of multicultural education, advocates of special education have had to lobby aggressively to change public education. Review its history to gauge its progress: Did special education exist at the turn of the 20th century? How was it defined by educators? What was special education in the 1950s? What is it today? Has the evolution of special education resulted in greater accessibility of educational resources to a greater cross section of society's youths? Multicultural education began at the turn of the 20th century in the writings of Horace Kallen and evolved to what it is today. Similar to special education, its goal is to ensure that all learners are provided with the educational resources that allow students the opportunity to reach their intellectual potential.

Perhaps another way of looking at these changes is to review the definition of multicultural education we provided you on page 88. What changes, if any, have occurred over the last three decades to suggest that multicultural education is a new way of looking at education, is beneficial to all teachers, and when properly implemented, is an approach that will equip students to live in a culturally diverse society and a global community?

It is important to note that the evolution of multicultural education is as much immersed in education as it is in politics. (The same can be said of other educational movements.) Some of the terms described in this chapter originated in the clashes between social activists (outside education) and professional educators. Others surfaced as more and more educators began to pay greater attention to groups that historically have been underserved by public education.

The terms we selected and presented in this chapter are those we consider crucial in gaining an understanding of multicultural education. They are not presented in alphabetical order, but in their order of appearance on the political and educational scenes. In some cases, we borrowed definitions from other authors who have written in the area of multicultural education; in other instances, we developed our own definitions. You will assuredly discover alternative definitions and alternative views on multicultural education. What is important as you listen to these definitions and views is that you think critically about them before adopting one that aligns with your specific needs.

CONTEMPORARY TERMS AND DEFINITIONS

In the early 1960s, when activists, students, and parents gained a foothold in public education, multicultural education was defined as *minority education*—addressing the "deficits" of African American, Mexican American, and Native American students; the educational approaches developed during this time period emphasized changing the learners, not the schools. Not surprisingly, such terms as *culturally dis-*

advantaged and *culturally deprived* were used to describe the groups. When the argument surfaced that minorities were not culturally "disadvantaged" or "deprived," educators used the term *different* to describe the groups. This was an important concession on the part of educators because it meant the discussion was about to shift from students' genetic and cultural backgrounds to an objective look at the culture of minority groups and an examination of schools. In the mid-1960s, educators took a broader and more comprehensive look at schools and addressed some of the following questions: How can we incorporate students' cultures into day-to-day school experiences? What educational practices limit students' participation in school? What preparation should be required of teachers who assume positions in schools where the majority student population is minority?

In this chapter and in other parts of this book, we use the terms **ethnic** and **minority** to refer to particular groups. According to Banks (1975) an **ethnic group** (e.g., Irish, Jewish, Italian American) "shares a common sense of values, behavior patterns, culture traits, and a sense of peoplehood" (p. 13). A **minority group** also shares a sense of peoplehood, but unlike ethnic groups, it has "unique physical and/or cultural characteristics which enable persons who belong to dominant ethnic groups to easily identify [them and] treat them in a discriminatory fashion" (p. 13). According to Banks, these differences between ethnic and minority groups are crucial in gaining an understanding of each and the interactions among the groups:

> While a Polish American immigrant can Anglicize his or her name, acquire Anglo-American cultural traits, and move into almost any White neighborhood without evoking much animosity, no matter how culturally assimilated an [African] American becomes, his or her skin color remains a social stigma of immense importance to most members of White ethnic groups. (p. 13)

In addition to being highly distinguishable, a significant number of minorities reside in urban and rural ghettos, disproportionately occupy the lower socioeconomic classes, and are the victims of an inordinate number of acts of racism.

In the early 1960s, *minority groups* referred to African Americans, Mexican Americans, Native Americans, Chinese Americans, Japanese Americans, and Puerto Ricans. In the context of schools, they are referred to as minorities because individuals from these groups have not performed well in school and/or the history of the group includes an inordinate number of acts of racism by members of the dominant society.

As we identify the minority groups, it is important to discuss the labels used to describe them. Historically, others (the dominant society) have defined minority groups, and occasionally the terms employed have been disparaging. In most instances, the terms have been inadequate to describe the groups and the diversity within them. Minorities have always spoken out against this labeling process. Although it appears that no label would satisfy all, many minorities would prefer to label themselves. For example, the shift in terms—*Black American, Afro American, African American*—represents an attempt by African Americans to seek self-identity and identity as a group. As leaders of the group search for a label and appropriate descriptors, they contextualize their discussion in Africa (continent of origin), skin color (black), and their experiences in the United States (low socioeconomic status, contributions to the American experience, acts of racism).

How does one identify 20 million Hispanics? Besides *Hispanic,* other terms used by members of this group and the educational community are *Latino/Latina* and *Latin American.* In the 1950s, though, the common term was *Mexican American* because Mexican immigrants and their descendants were the most numerous of the groups in the United States. In the 1960s, the terms used were *Mexican American, Puerto Rican,* and *Cuban American.* During this decade, some Mexican Americans identified *Chicano* as the term they preferred to be called. According to Nieto (1992):

> Chicano . . . was a decidedly self-affirming and political term reflecting the unique culture and realities of urban, economically oppressed Mexican Americans in U.S. society. Its use in the recent past, however, seems to have been abandoned by many segments of the community, and the more descriptive but less political term Mexican Americans appears to be back in common use. . . . **Mexican,** on the other hand, is used generally to refer to those who are the first generation to come from Mexico. (p. 15)

Today, an estimated 20 million Hispanics reside in the United States. Although most are Mexican Americans, Puerto Ricans, and Cuban Americans, there are significant numbers of Colombians, El Salvadorans, Ecuadorans, and others. As additional immigrants arrive from South America, activists in each group are searching for an appropriate "umbrella" label. In all probability, they will not succeed; there is too much variability within the group and among the subgroups for one label to correctly identify 20 million people.

A focus on minorities also led to an emphasis on societal forces that were seen as having limited the groups' opportunities in society. In public school or college classrooms, discussions of minority experiences focused on particular school practices (e.g., tracking, Anglocentric curriculum, nonminority teaching force) and historical incidents (e.g., slavery, Mexican War, Jim Crow laws, Chinese exclusions acts, relocation of American Indians on reservations). These discussions invariably led to broader discussions of the American experience and the forces of *racism, prejudice, discrimination,* and *stereotyping:*

- *Racism:* the belief that the inherited physical characteristics of a racial group strongly influence social behaviors as well as psychological and intellectual characteristics; the belief that some racial groups are inherently superior and others are inherently inferior[11]
- *Prejudice:* a set of rigid and unfavorable attitudes toward a particular group or groups that is formed in disregard of facts[12]
- *Discrimination:* differential behavior toward a stigmatized group[13]
- *Stereotypes:* predispositions and general attitudes and impressions of particular groups; crystallized descriptions of groups allowing for little variability

ACTIVITY 5.3   Stereotypes

Stereotypical content and images a teacher may hold of a group, whether positive or negative, have no place in the classroom. Stereotypes are unproductive because they are unrealistic portrayals of groups and individuals. Stereotypes

- are crystallized descriptions allowing for little variability
- limit variability by ignoring individual differences and assigning highly exaggerated characteristics to all members of the groups
- are too superficial to describe human behavior adequately
- are used to perpetuate the image of the problem-oriented minorities
- are used to explain and justify the status of minorities in society

Return for a moment to the second chapter opening quotation, by Cazden and Mehan (1989). Reflect carefully on the statement, "limited knowledge can lead to stereotypes that impede learning." What safeguards will you follow to ensure that the information you gather about your students does not lead you toward stereotypical thinking?

Listed below are some examples of stereotypes that have been heard in teachers' workshops and at local, state, and national conferences:

- "Don't worry about the Asian American students, they'll do well in your classroom."
- "Female students are naturally better than boys in English, foreign languages, and journalism."
- "Jewish American students perform well in school because they are gifted and talented in the academic areas."

Select a group (racial, ethnic, cultural, lifestyle, gender) and identify one or more stereotypes usually associated with the group. Attempt to identify the origins of those stereotypes by gaining additional information on the group. In your research, examine the group's socioeconomic status, geographical location in the United States, particular positions it holds on various issues, length of residence in the United States, intergroup relations, and other information that may help dispel these stereotype(s). As you report your findings to colleagues, focus on the dangers of stereotypes and discuss what teachers can do to minimize stereotypical thinking.

ADDITIONAL TERMS AND CONCEPTS

In the mid-1960s, with the publication of *The Other America* (Harrington, 1962) and the many federal initiatives that surfaced from President Lyndon Johnson's Great Society, **minority** was expanded to include the poor—Appalachian Whites and others. As the list of oppressed peoples grew, White ethnic groups (e.g., Italian Americans, Jewish Americans, Irish Americans) also argued for inclusion because they, too, are victims of stereotyping, prejudice, and discrimination. Today, the term *people of color* is employed by educators and social scientists to differentiate minority groups of the early 1960s from other groups that have embraced the phrase.

When social scientists and educators began to reach for broader conceptualizations of the minority experience that included more than the traditional minority groups, they adopted *multiethnic education,* a phrase that described approaches and strategies the schools were using to provide for minorities and the study of the history of minority groups. In the mid- and late 1960s, colleges and universities saw a proliferation of programs that focused on individual groups: Black/Afro-American, Native American, Chicano, Italian, and Jewish American studies. Some colleges and universities developed Ethnic Studies Departments that approached the study of ethnicity by examining the history of a number of groups and by focusing on the experiences they share in common. Although a few high schools developed minority studies courses, in general the more fruitful efforts centered on infusing a multiethnic perspective to social studies classes. In the middle and elementary grades, multiethnic education was often interpreted as the study of holidays and foods. In fact, you might have been exposed to this approach, in which case you might be saying to yourself, "What's wrong with focusing only on a few foods or talking about an ethnic holiday or two?" The food-and-holiday phenomenon and the thought that underlies it are dangerously naive. When such cultural attributes as holidays and foods are the only dimensions you highlight about specific ethnic groups for your students, you accomplish little more than deepening negative stereotypes that your students may already have for targeted groups. The holiday-and-food phenomenon, which has been inappropriately used for many years, could be made more acceptable if it becomes part of a much larger, sustained effort to incorporate students' cultures into classroom and school curricula, as described, for example, by Banks (1975, 1994).

In the 1970s, educators began to use the term *culturally different* to describe other groups that were being identified as ill-served by the schools and deserving of inclusion in the multiethnic movement. *Culturally different* referred to female students, students in special education, students with religious differences, and other cultural differences. In short, it referred to those who experienced difficulties with school culture and believed that their academic needs were not being met because they were different and the schools were not accommodating to their needs. Today, some educators use the term *at risk* in a rather loose manner to describe these students. *At risk* has now become so widely accepted that educators use it as a catch-all phrase. At every level and in almost every school situation, educators use the notion of at risk too glibly, talking about this student group or that student group or about whole school populations as being at risk. The stereotyping associated with this practice is further associated with a set of misconceptions: At-risk students are viewed as needing low-level instruction, being members of mostly non-White ethnic groups, living in dysfunctional homes, causing discipline problems, and being hard to manage. Out of these misconceptions has emerged the belief that all at-risk students need watered-down education replete with lower standards and lower expectations. Interestingly, this whole at-risk phenomenon has occurred in the absence of a carefully constructed, shared definition for "at riskness." Today, the term continues to be bantered around politically by school and government officials in order to secure federal funding or to qualify for special programs, thus deepening stereotypical images that educators and the public hold for selected students and schools.

As the list of culturally different learners increased, educators settled on the term **multicultural education** to describe what was happening in education. Because the term is inclusive, rather than exclusive, educators like Hernandez (1989) have borrowed more than one definition to explain this form of education: (1) a perspective that recognizes (a) the political, social, and economic realities that individuals experience in culturally diverse and complex human encounters; and (b) the importance of culture, race, sexuality and gender, ethnicity, religion, socioeconomic status, and exceptionalities in the educational process . . . ; (2) ". . . a multidisciplinary educational program that provides multiple learning environments matching the academic, social, and linguistic needs of students" (p. 4).[14] Although initially most advocates of multicultural education focused on national concerns, today many have broadened their horizons to also include global issues.

The definition of multicultural education we provide also looks at issues from a human perspective and suggests that connections exist between local and global issues. Similar to Hernandez (1989), we, too, focus on the importance of the individual. And perhaps similar to other multicultural educators, we trust you to make the proper educational choices that lead to all students succeeding in school and to leaving public schools with a strong understanding of the culturally pluralistic nature of American society and the world community.

MULTICULTURAL EDUCATION: WHAT DO I DO NOW?

Many educators ask the same question: What can I do to promote multicultural principles in my classroom? Our response to this question is to have you reflect on your professional education classes: Did you read about multicultural education? Did you participate in classroom activities? Did you see multicultural principles being practiced in your field experiences? Invariably, students have read the material, participated in class discussion, and performed well in education courses when asked to demonstrate their understanding of multicultural education.

However, the question What can I do to promote multicultural principles in my classroom? persists because theory has not translated into classroom practice. Preservice and in-service teachers who ask this question are able to provide a textbook answer when queried but have not internalized the principles of multicultural education; they are unable to practice theory. As a result, they resort to their preconceived notions of multicultural education or mimic the approaches of teachers who may have a distorted understanding of this field of education. When they find these approaches failing, preservice teachers are quick to place blame on their teacher preparation program for their inadequacies; experienced teachers are quick to blame a lack of in-service workshops or an overburdened schedule.

We don't want you to follow this pattern! We want you to be successful in your classroom teaching. To be successful, you must assume responsibility for becoming a culturally sensitive teacher—that is, for knowing when your personal biases and stereotypes and those of your school impede the learning process for your students, and for knowing the effect that labeling has on students, particularly labeling that creates a negative view of students.

NOTES

1. See Garcia, J., & Pugh, S. L. (1992). Multicultural education in teacher preparation programs: A political or an educational concept? *Phi Delta Kappan, 74*(3), 214–219.

2. See the yearbook published under the sponsorship of the Association of Teacher Educators for an excellent and contemporary look at the present status of teacher education in the United States: O'Hair, M. J., & Odell, S. J. (Eds.). (1993). *Diversity and teaching: Teacher education yearbook I.* Ft. Worth, TX: Harcourt Brace Jovanovich.

3. For a look at recent changes in America's population, see the special issue of *Time:* The new faces of America: How immigrants are shaping the world's first multicultural society. (1993, Fall). *Time, 142* [Special issue].

4. See Garcia, J., & Pugh, S. L. (1992). Multicultural education in teacher preparation programs: A political or an educational concept? *Phi Delta Kappan, 74*(3), 214–219; O'Hair, M. J., & Odell, S. J. (Eds.). (1993). *Diversity and teaching: Teacher education yearbook I.* Ft. Worth, TX: Harcourt Brace Jovanovich; and Zeichner, K. (1993, April). *Educating teachers for cultural diversity.* Paper presented at the Annual Meeting of the American Educational Research Association, Atlanta.

5. Hawgood, J. A. (1970). The attempt to found a new Germany in Missouri. In L. Dinnerstein & F. C. Jaher (Eds.), *The aliens: A history of ethnic minorities in America* (pp. 125–141). New York: Meredith Corporation.

6. See Garcia, J. (1984a). Multicultural teacher education. *Texas Tech Journal of Education, 11*(3), 5–10.

7. See Krug, M. M. (1977). Cultural pluralism: Its origins and aftermath. *Journal of Teacher Education, 28*(3), 5–10.

8. See Garcia, J., & Pugh, S. L. (1992). Multicultural education in teacher preparation programs: A political or an educational concept? *Phi Delta Kappan, 74*(3), 214–219.

9. See Famighetti, R. (Ed.). (1994). *The world almanac and the book of facts 1994.* Mahwah, NJ: Funk & Wagnalls Corporation, p. 423; U.S. Department of Commerce. (1993). *Statistical abstract of the United States 1993* (113 ed.). Washington, DC: Government Printing Office, p. 61; The new faces of America: How immigrants are shaping the world's first multicultural society. (1993, Fall). *Time, 142* [Special issue]; see also articles (e.g., Goering, L. [1994, September 5]. Franklin Park's goal is to age gracefully. *Chicago Tribune,* p. 6) that appear periodically in major U.S. newspapers.

10. See Hirsch, E. D., Jr. (1987). *Cultural literacy: What every American needs to know.* Boston: Houghton Mifflin; Ravitch, D. (1991). A culture in common. *Educational Leadership, 49*(4), 8–11; Schlesinger, A. M., Jr. (1982). *The disuniting of Americans.* New York: Norton.

11. Hernandez, H. (1989). *Multicultural education: A teacher's guide to content and process.* New York: Merrill/Macmillan, p. 30.

12. Banks, J. A. (1975). *Teaching strategies for ethnic studies.* Boston: Allyn & Bacon, p. 69.

13. Banks, J. A. (1975). *Teaching strategies for ethnic studies.* Boston: Allyn & Bacon, p. 69.

14. Hernandez (1989, p. 4) builds on the definitions from the National Council for the Accreditation of Teacher Education and from Robert H. Suzuki in developing her own definition of multicultural education. This appears to be a common approach among educators writing in this area.

REFERENCES

Appleton, N. (1983). *Cultural pluralism in education: Theoretical foundations.* New York: Longman.

Armstrong, D. G., Henson, K. T., & Savage, T. V. (1993). *Education: An introduction* (4th ed.). New York: Macmillan.

Banks, J. A. (1975). *Teaching strategies for ethnic studies.* Boston: Allyn & Bacon.

Banks, J. A. (1994). *Multiethnic education: Theory and practice* (3rd ed.). Boston: Allyn & Bacon.

Cazden, C., & Mehan, H. (1989). Principles from sociology and anthropology: Context, code, classroom, and culture. In M. C. Reynolds (Ed.), *Knowledge base for the beginning teacher* (pp. 47-57). New York: Pergamon Press.

Famighetti, R. (Ed.). (1994). *The world almanac and book of facts 1994.* Mahwah, NJ: Funk & Wagnalls Corporation.

Garcia, J. (1984a). Multicultural teacher education. *Texas Tech Journal of Education, 11*(3), 5–10.

Garcia, J. (1984b). Multicultural teacher education: Past, present, and future. *Texas Tech Journal of Education, 11*(1), 13-29.

Garcia, J., & Pugh, S. L. (1992). Multicultural education in teacher preparation programs: A political or an educational concept? *Phi Delta Kappan, 74*(3), 214-219.

Goering, L. (1994, September 5). Franklin Park's goal is to age gracefully. *Chicago Tribune,* p. 6.

Harrington, M. (1962). *The other America: Poverty in the United States.* Baltimore: Penguin Books.

Hawgood, J. A. (1970). The attempt to found a new Germany in Missouri. In L. Dinnerstein & F. C. Jaher (Eds.), *The aliens: A history of ethnic minorities in America* (pp. 125–141). New York: Meredith Corporation.

Hernandez, H. (1989). *Multicultural education: A teacher's guide to content and process.* New York: Merrill/Macmillan.

Hirsch, E. D., Jr. (1987). *Cultural literacy: What every American needs to know.* Boston: Houghton Mifflin.

Krug, M. M. (1977). Cultural pluralism: Its origins and aftermath. *Journal of Teacher Education, 28*(3), 5-10.

Liebman, L. (Ed.). (1982). *Ethnic relations in America.* Englewood Cliffs, NJ: Prentice Hall.

The new faces of America: How immigrants are shaping the world's first multicultural society. (1993, Fall). *Time, 142* [Special issue].

Nieto, S. (1992). *Affirming diversity: The sociopolitical context of multicultural education.* New York: Longman.

O'Hair, M. J., & Odell, S. J. (Eds.). (1993). *Diversity and teaching: Teacher education yearbook I.* Ft. Worth, TX: Harcourt Brace Jovanovich.

Pinkney, A. (1969). *Black Americans.* Englewood Cliffs, NJ: Prentice Hall.

Ravitch, D. (1991). A culture in common. *Educational Leadership, 49*(4), 8–11.

Rice, A. S., & Krout, J. A. (1991). *United States history from 1865* (20th ed.). New York: Harper Perennial.

Rodriguez, R. (1982). *Hunger of memory: The education of Richard Rodriguez.* Boston: David R. Godine.

Schlesinger, A. M., Jr. (1982). *The disuniting of Americans.* New York: Norton.

Seller, M. (1977). *To seek America: A history of ethnic life in the United States.* Englewood, NJ: Jerome S. Ozer.

Tozer, S. E., Violas, P. C., & Senese, G. (1993). *School and society: Educational practice as social expression.* New York: McGraw-Hill.

U.S. Department of Commerce. (1993). *Statistical abstract of the United States 1993* (113th ed.). Washington DC: Government Printing Office.

Van Til, W. (1974). *Education: A beginning* (2nd ed.). Boston: Houghton Mifflin.

Weaver, G. (1970). Benjamin Franklin and the Pennsylvania Germans. In L. Dinnerstein & F. C. Jaher (Eds.), *The aliens: A history of ethnic minorities in America* (pp. 47–64). New York: Meredith Corporation.

Zeichner, K. (1993, April). *Educating teachers for cultural diversity.* Paper presented at the Annual Meeting of the American Educational Research Association, Atlanta.

PART II

Conducting Field Experience

Chapter 6

Examining Culturally Diverse Schools

Carefully conducted study visits to effective institutions can help one to develop a vision of the possible while providing structural and process models. For these and other reasons, effort must be made to locate, describe, and analyze living examples of success. (Carter & Chatfield, 1986, p. 230)

CONTEMPORARY SCHOOLS AND THEIR STUDENTS

Standing at the doorsteps of most schools across the United States, you will see students from all nationalities entering the building. You might see a non-English-speaking Latino student who recently arrived in the United States entering the building near a bilingual Hispanic student who was raised in the United States. You might see a newly arrived Hmong student with very little formal schooling entering the building next to a Chinese student who attended a private school in Hong Kong and who can speak two languages—Mandarin and English. And if you listen closely to parents taking their children to school early in the morning, you'll hear them talk to each other in the various languages they speak at home. This kind of cultural and linguistic diversity is now commonplace in U.S. schools[1] and will continue to increase well into the next century.[2]

Cultural diversity is not the only factor that is changing the nature of students today. Another significant factor is the global assimilation of technology. The same culturally and linguistically diverse students we noted above who enter the school building each morning live in a world of videos, television, portable stereos, earphones, and computers. These info-driven students are saturated by new technologies.[3]

Although students have become culturally diverse and technology oriented, most schools have changed little.[4] They are essentially driven by a model of schooling that was developed at the turn of the 20th century.[5] And many of these schools are still guided by White middle-class values[6] despite the increase in student cultural diversity.[7] The current mismatch between culturally diverse students in contemporary society and the schools they attend should therefore be no surprise to you.

How can teaching practices be revised in light of how our society has changed so that you as an educator can begin to close the gap between culturally diverse students and schools and to reunite schools with multicultural society?[8] Examining actual learning environments of multicultural schools can help you examine these questions more closely. In this chapter, you will read about three selected multicultural schools in the United States. In various ways, staffs at these schools are closing the gap between students and society. To do this, they have institutionalized change. They recognize that long-term stability and monoethnic values, two symbols of the past, constrain effective teaching in today's society. They also acknowledge that students of the mainstream culture can be full participants in the building of pluralistic America.[9] Staffs at the schools we visited use the positive aspects of social change (e.g., cultural diversity, linguistic diversity) to build new programs that are culturally sensitive. Paquette (1991) believes that positive aspects of social change should be central foci for school change. Paquette notes,

> If, as nations and peoples, we are no longer who we once were, if, for the most part, we no longer earn our living in anything like the old ways, why shouldn't our schools both reflect and purposefully encourage the positive aspects of such social change—both in what they teach and how they are organized? (p. 174)

MULTICULTURAL SCHOOLS: EXPLORING VISIONS OF THE POSSIBLE[10]

The three schools described in this chapter are, by selected standards, successful multicultural learning environments.[11] The schools we visited were

Hollibrook Elementary School
Spring Branch Independent School District
Houston, Texas

Brown Barge Middle School
Escambia County School District
Pensacola, Florida

Mark Keppel High School
Alhambra School District
Alhambra, California

To explore what was happening in these schools, we visited each for 5 days.[12] We examined as much of the school contexts as we could during each site visit.[13] By engaging in this process, we followed the suggestion of Carter and Chatfield (1986), who indicate that educators need to "locate, describe, and analyze living examples of success" so that they can "develop a vision of the possible" (p. 230) for contemporary multicultural schooling.

At each school site, we observed classroom teaching and attended after-school activities for teachers and students. We visited the teachers' workrooms at various times and observed special teacher and student meetings. We watched students before school and at lunch as they interacted socially in various parts of the schools, including the cafeterias. And as much as time permitted, we "hung around" the campuses to get a sense of the school environments. We conducted formal and informal interviews with teachers, school administrators, district administrators, counselors, students, and other staff. We taped and transcribed all formal interviews. We examined classroom curriculum materials and studied school policy statements. We also conducted case studies of one teacher at each school site. These case studies are reported in the next chapter.

As we compared and contrasted the three schools, we developed a set of themes that link the schools together in important ways. These themes shed light on how staff at selected schools deal with the reality of cultural and linguistic diversity. Before discussing these themes, we provide an overview of each school site. Tables 6–1 and 6–2 present summaries of student and teacher demographics of the schools.

Hollibrook Elementary School[14]

Locality. Hollibrook Elementary School (HES) is located in one of the changing communities in the northwest area of Houston. As part of the Spring Branch Independent School District (SBISD), HES and the surrounding community have

Table 6–1   1993–94 demographics of students at three school sites

Student Features	Schools		
	HES*	BBMS**	MKHS†
Total students (%)	938	522	2541
Student ethnicity (%)			
Asian	3.4	6.5	61.0
Hispanic and Latino	82.2	0.7	31.0
Black	2.3	27.7	0.003
White	12.1	64.3	4.0
Native American	0.0	0.5	0.0
Other	0.0	0.0	4.0
LEP†† students (%)	71.4	0.0	45.7
English language only students (n)	15.5	95.6	12.0
Economically disadvantaged students (%)ǁ	85.8	33.0	62.0
Nationalities of students (n)	16‡	7‡‡	31§
Languages spoken by students (n)	10§§	12¶	22¶¶

  * HES = Hollibrook Elementary School, Houston, Texas

 ** BBMS = Brown Barge Middle School, Pensacola, Florida

  † MKHS = Mark Keppel High school, Alhambra, California

 †† LEP = limited English proficiency

  ‡ Cambodia, China, Egypt, El Salvador, Guatemala, Honduras, India, Japan, Korea, Mexico, Nicaragua, Pakistan, Panama, Saudi Arabia, U.S.A., Vietnam

‡‡ Argentina, Canada, China, Korea, Philippines, U.S.A.

  § Brazil, Burma, Cambodia, China, Denmark, Ecuador, El Salvador, France, Germany, Guatemala, Hong Kong, India, Indonesia, Japan, Korea, Laos, Malaysia, Mexico, Nicaragua, Peru, Philippines, Poland, Puerto Rico, Romania, Russia, Singapore, Taiwan, Thailand, U.S.A., Venezuela, Vietnam

§§ Arabic, Cambodian, Chinese, Egyptian, English, Japanese, Korean, Spanish, Urdu, Vietnamese

  ¶ Cambodian, English, Filipino, Greek, Italian, Korean, Mandarin, Portuguese, Spanish, Swedish, Tagalog, Vietnamese

¶¶ Arabic, Burmese, Cambodian, Cantonese, Chao Chou, Chinese, Chiu Chow, English, Indonesia, Japanese, Korean, Lao, Mandarin, Polish, Portuguese, Punjabi, Russian, Spanish, Tagalog, Taiwanese, Thai, Vietnamese

 ǁ Determined by eligibility for free or reduced lunch at school

undergone a major cultural transformation during the past few years. At one time, HES had mostly White students and the area surrounding HES was predominantly a White community. At the present time, the school has mostly Hispanic and Latino students and the area surrounding HES has been transformed into a community of Hispanic, Latino, and White citizens. At the beginning of the 1993–94 school year, HES had 938 students; 82.2% were Hispanic and Latino.

HES is characterized by school officials as economically disadvantaged. Several government-subsidized low-income apartment complexes immediately adjacent to the school have become a refuge for new immigrant workers from Mexico and Central America. Approximately 90% of HES students qualify for free and reduced

Table 6-2   1993–94 demographics of professional staff at three school sites

Staff Features	Schools		
	HES[*]	BBMS[**]	MKHS[†]
Professional Staff (n)			
Teachers	55	26	99[††]
Campus Administrators	3	2	7
Educational Aides (n)	12	2	15
Professional Staff (%)			
Asian	3.0	0.0	11.6
Hispanic	10.9	0.0	20.0
Black	10.3	10.7	0.0
White	75.8	85.7	66.6
Native American	0.0	3.5	0.9
Other	0.0	0.0	0.9
Professional Staff Bilingual (%)	47.2	14.0	41.5[‡]
Counseling Staff (n)			
Asian	0	0	2[‡‡]
Hispanic	2	0	3
Black	0	0	0
White	1	0	1
Counseling Staff Bilingual (n)	2	0	5

  [*] HES = Hollibrook Elementary School, Houston, Texas

 [**] BBMS = Brown Barge Middle School, Pensacola, Florida

  [†] MKHS = Mark Keppel High School, Alhambra, California

 [††] Figure does not include four hourly teachers (1 Chinese, 1 Japanese, 1 Hispanic, 1 White)

  [‡] Spanish, Mandarin, Cantonese, English, French, German, Armenian

 [‡‡] Vietnamese and Chinese (Mandarin)

meals. And many children living in the apartment complexes next to the school share single apartments with several families, especially newly immigrated families. After talking with Roy Ford, the principal of HES, we learned that street gangs and drugs are prevalent in the HES area, which is an ongoing concern of HES faculty, the school administration, and parents in the community.

School Context.   The Hispanic and Latino student population of HES consists of Mexican Americans, Mexicans, Colombians, Hondurans, and other groups. Other HES students were born in Vietnam, Pakistan, Egypt, Cambodia, China, India, Saudi Arabia, Japan, and Korea. English is not the native language for over 85% of the students. Because of the large Spanish-speaking population in the area, announcements that school staff send home to parents are in both English and Spanish. And signs posted on school doors and hallways are bilingual. This bicultural feature has a profound influence on the HES learning environment, which includes an extensive K–3 bilingual program and an ESL program for Grades 4 and 5.

Another important feature of the school is the parent center. The center is intended to help parents feel like part of the school. This perception is especially important for newly immigrated Spanish-speaking parents who lack confidence to talk with teachers about their children. Parents come to the center as volunteers to help prepare materials for the classrooms. When we visited the center, we found most of the signs and materials on the walls to be in Spanish, and the spoken language in the center was Spanish. Because many parents are unable to afford baby-sitters, parents are invited to bring their infants and small children with them to the center.

The HES school building was constructed in the 1950s and has been renovated several times. The most recent renovations (cafeteria, library, new classrooms) reflect the suggestions of HES teachers and administrators. The school has many computers, and students receive instruction on computers in both English and Spanish.

An overarching framework for the school is what has become known as the Accelerated Schools Program. In the late 1980s, HES became an accelerated school.[15] Since that time, HES has decreased its student annual turnover rate from 87% in 1988–89 to 38% in 1992–93. At the time of our visit to the school, the HES attendance rate had increased to 97%. In the 1989–90 academic year, 83% of HES's third-grade students who had limited English proficiency (LEP) passed the TEAMS reading and writing tests, compared with 28% prior to the implementation of the accelerated school model.

Brown Barge Middle School[16]

Locality. Brown Barge Middle School (BBMS) is in Pensacola, Florida, a small city in the Florida panhandle that has a population of approximately 59,000. In 1992–93, Escambia County, Florida, which contains Pensacola, had 43,658 students; 63% of these were White, 32% were Black, and 5% were classified as "other." The ethnicity of students in Escambia County is relatively stable, although new immigrants are moving to the area from Central America and Cuba. The stability of student ethnicity and of the local community was one of the reasons we visited BBMS. From this stability, we assumed that the learning environment at BBMS would be influenced by deeply ingrained racial tension between Black students and White students. One reason for visiting BBMS was to explore how BBMS was dealing with this challenge.

Because BBMS is a magnet school for technology, it draws students from the entire school district and from all social classes. We learned from the principal, Ms. Camille Barr, that school staff deal frequently with racial tension among students and between students and teachers. Unlike at HES, linguistic diversity at BBMS is not a deciding factor in the school environment or the curriculum (see Table 6–1).

School Context. One hardly notices BBMS when one drives into Pensacola on Interstate 110. The school is an old, somewhat inconspicuous building just off the interstate on the north side of the city. When one walks into the school building, however, the older appearance of the school falls away; one witnesses, just as we did, a restructured schooling experience unlike any other anyone has had either as a teacher or as a student. BBMS transcends traditional school contexts entirely; it is a completely engaging learning experience for every student who attends there and for every teacher who teaches there.

Two particularly striking features of BBMS characterize its learning environment. The first feature is its integrated curriculum.[17] Teams of teachers work together to plan 12-week curriculum units around specific themes. Examples of these themes are environment, weather, and art motifs. Each theme is called a "stream," and a large group of students is assigned to one stream for each 12-week unit. Interestingly, one of the streams taught each year, and the stream we specifically sought to observe, is called American Tapestries. In this stream, students deal directly with issues of culture, race, ethnicity, and diversity. All lessons, activities, projects, and content (e.g., math, social studies, English) are based on ethnicity issues.[18]

The second striking feature of BBMS is its multiplicity of new technologies. BBMS received a federal grant of $5.6 million during a 2-year period to develop a magnet school for technology. It also received a curriculum waiver from the Florida Department of Education. With this funding and with curricular leeway provided by the waiver, principal Camille Barr and her faculty developed an innovative school curriculum based on educational equity. The curriculum is also based on the premise that *all students are gifted and talented in specific ways.* Every BBMS student, therefore, is expected to achieve at high levels.

Each team of teachers at BBMS sets their own daily schedule for students, creates and selects instructional materials (traditional textbooks are not part of the BBMS curriculum), and designs field trips, major projects, and group work for the students. Unlike recent curricular reform efforts that have tried to toughen academic standards without addressing cultural conflicts within the classroom (see Erickson, 1984), the BBMS curriculum accomplishes this. School staff changed the content and the delivery of instruction while focusing extensively on the social relations between teachers and students. An overarching goal for BBMS is to create a learning environment where students and teachers work collaboratively to attain higher order thinking and then to apply these skills to the students' personal lives outside the school.

The curriculum at BBMS is so nontraditional in process and product that all students admitted to school must complete a 12-week Orientation Stream. In this stream, BBMS students learn to work cooperatively in groups, where they become accustomed to working productively without the pressures of competition found in traditional school settings and where they learn necessary technology skills to complete assignments and projects.

Specific qualities of BBMS that collectively characterize its uniqueness include a noncompetitive environment (e.g., no athletic teams or intramural activities, no grades, no traditional yearbook), removal of standardized test scores for ranking students, use of alternative assessment strategies, and use of global theme-based stream issues for teaching content. The BBMS curriculum is also needs based; that is, the stream topics were selected after students and their parents indicated what their greatest needs were for learning.

Mark Keppel High School[19]

Locality. Mark Keppel High School (MKHS), which is in the Alhambra School District, is uniquely located on the corners of four suburban communities. These communities, only a few minutes east of downtown Los Angeles on Interstate 10, are Alhambra, Monterey Park, Rosemead, and San Gabriel. Students from these communities, along with students on permit from other communities, attend MKHS. At the time of our site visit, MKHS had 2,541 students; almost 96% of these students were classified as ethnic minorities (see Table 6–1).

The communities that depend on MKHS to educate their youths are highly variable in social class, language, culture, and ethnicity. For example, Monterey Park is known as "Little Taipei."[20] Each day, dozens of new immigrants from Asia arrive in Monterey Park, including those from China, Japan, Vietnam, Cambodia, and Laos. Adjacent to Monterey Park is Rosemead, a community comprised primarily of Hispanics (50%) and a lesser number of Asians (33%).

During the past 30 years, several cultural transformations have occurred in the communities surrounding MKHS. In only three decades, Monterey Park, for example, has gone from primarily White to primarily Hispanic and then to mostly Asian. Consequently, MKHS has undergone several cultural changes, and now school faculty accept change as a way of life.

School Context. At MKHS cultural and linguistic diversity is not an abstract construct in a book on multicultural education; it is a daily reality. Teachers at MKHS must be accustomed to working around multiple cultures and must be sensitive to the needs of students who have limited English proficiency (LEP). Only 12% of MKHS students speak English as a first language. At the time of our visit, 55% of MKHS students were designated as new immigrants. In the 1993–94 school year, 61% of MKHS students were Asian (e.g., from China, Japan, Hong Kong, Vietnam, Cambodia, Laos, Korea, Thailand, Burma); 31% were Hispanic and Latino (e.g., from Brazil, Ecuador, Costa Rica, El Salvador, Guatemala, Mexico, Nicaragua, Puerto Rico, Venezuela). Approximately 22 languages were spoken by MKHS students (see Table 6–1); most linguistic diversity was represented by speakers of Spanish, Cantonese, Vietnamese, and Mandarin.

In our interactions with the staff at MKHS (administrators, counselors, teachers, classified personnel), it became clear that the diversity we encountered is considered to be a strength of the school. Numerous attempts are made in the school to affirm students, cultures, and languages. For example, the Spanish bilingual program at MKHS includes college preparatory strands in mathematics and social science. It also includes advanced placement courses in Spanish language and Spanish literature. And any announcements sent home to parents are in English, Cantonese, Mandarin, and Spanish.

Forty teachers at the school are bilingual; they speak Spanish, Mandarin, Cantonese, French, German, and Armenian. Most school counselors are bilingual, including one who speaks Vietnamese. And many of the support staff speak several languages, including Vietnamese.

Although we have spent much effort here to characterize the cultural and linguistic diversity at MKHS, the school also focuses continuously on improving the academic program for students. Linda Maryott, the Assistant Principal (AP) for Instruction at MKHS, is leading a schoolwide restructuring effort that will make language, technology, and cooperative learning central to instruction at MKHS.

SHARED FEATURES OF CULTURALLY DIVERSE SCHOOLS

As we gathered information on the schools, we discovered that they shared certain features. These features, which we call "themes," are described in this section. Although we identified many important themes, four were particularly salient at all schools: (a) living the experience of cultural diversity, (b) creating an equitable learning environment, (c) institutionalizing change, and (d) affirming cultural and linguistic diversity.

Living the Experience of Cultural Diversity

Individuals at HES, BBMS, and MKHS live each school day with cultural and linguistic diversity. Importantly, the administrators at the schools encourage teachers to affirm this cultural and linguistic diversity. During our site visits, we discovered that educators who live with and affirm cultural diversity on a daily basis have special challenges. These include (a) building trust and respect within a culturally diverse school, (b) creating cross-cultural harmony, and (c) developing a shared vision for teaching culturally and linguistically diverse students.

Building Trust and Respect.   Personnel at all three schools strive to build a climate of trust and respect. One strategy they use to build this climate is cooperative group learning. The Spanish-speaking and English-speaking students at HES work together in diads and triads to learn each other's languages. The Orientation Stream at BBMS helps students learn how to work productively in groups to complete projects.

A strategy that school staff use to build trust between home and school is to continuously include parents in school activities, especially parents with limited English proficiency. The parent center at HES, which we briefly described above, is one example of this effort. As another example, Roy Ford, principal of HES, organized English as a second language (ESL) classes in the evening at HES for Spanish-speaking members of the community, including parents of HES students. He also organized Spanish as a second language (SSL) classes for English-speaking community members. Ford believes that these classes foster trust between school personnel and the community.

Building trust and respect at these schools is not always an easy job. Regardless of the effort that staff at these schools make to build a trusting school climate for students, prejudice surfaces within the schools. Camille Barr, principal of BBMS, reported this to us on the first day of our visit to the school:

I'm very upset that we're losing a Black student today who is one of our most outstanding children. She feels discriminated against here [at BBMS] in a lot of different ways, so she is going back to the other middle school from where she came. She feels discriminated against by kids and by a couple of teachers.

Creating Cross-Cultural Harmony. Although all school staffs strove for a trustful and respectful atmosphere, they were fully aware of the racial tensions inherent in multicultural settings. Linda Maryott (MKHS) noted,

When visitors come onto our campus, they perceive our students as respectful and harmonious. However, the racial problems are deep seated. If something happens that gets the campus into a major problem, then some of the issues of racism and diversity come out. For 90 % of the time, those issues are underneath. We're very cognizant of it. We are attempting to address it.

MKHS is striving for cross-cultural harmony by creating and implementing a new year-long course for students called Conflict Resolution. The course will be for identified on-campus student leaders of traditional and nontraditional groups, including leaders of local street gangs. The purpose of the course is twofold: (a) to understand how personal and cultural characteristics may be misunderstood and lead to conflict and (b) to develop conflict mediation skills that will help these group leaders resolve conflict in a nonviolent manner.

As another example of cross-cultural harmony, the American Tapestries Stream at BBMS includes activities and projects that focus on global humanitarianism and cultural strengths. Bias, prejudice, and humane actions are topics that students learn about on a regular basis.

Fostering a Shared Vision. Living the reality of cultural diversity requires teachers and administrators to share a vision for attaining student success; each school we visited works toward building a shared vision among faculty and students. Teachers are instrumental in developing their schools' mission statements and are participating actively by restructuring activities.

A subtle, yet essential aspect of the schools, shared visions is a genuine caring attitude toward students from educators we observed and interviewed. We interpreted the caring we observed to be taken to another level in these schools because the teachers at HES, BBMS, and MKHS are in environments that demand a high level of caring for students whose needs are extraordinary. This pervasive caring provides an unspoken framework for the educational ideals of each school.

Creating an Equitable Learning Environment

A second theme shared by the schools is that of creating an equitable learning environment. Camille Barr (BBMS) told us, "All children can realize their full potential if you give them all the best of what you have to offer." The curriculum and instruction at BBMS invite all students to take part in the very best the school offers them. In school environments where many cultures meet and mingle every moment of the school day, where a high percentage of students do not speak English as a first language (e.g., HES, MKHS), and where there are multiple values for learning, creating equitable opportunities where every student can receive the best instruction is exceedingly challenging.[21]

The teachers we observed at HES, BBMS, and MKHS exhibit an ability to create equitable learning environments in their classrooms. They are sensitive to the needs of students from various cultures and are aware how culture influences learning. The teachers also exhibit an understanding for how to bring hundreds of students representing dozens of cultures together harmoniously under one roof. The sensitivity and awareness these teachers exhibit cause them to implement classroom instruction that is progressive, innovative, and creative.

In striving to establish equitable learning experiences, the teachers encounter two notable challenges: (a) providing equal opportunities for student involvement in school and (b) having the freedom to create instruction that aligns with student needs.

Providing Equal Opportunities.   Giving students equal opportunities to learn and equal opportunities to participate in school activities that are personally meaningful and culturally appropriate requires a school-specific sensitivity. This kind of sensitivity is not found in textbooks or derived from predetermined curricular frameworks, but rather is found in the daily experiences of students at school. At MKHS this sensitivity is translated into school experiences that, according to Linda Maryott, are "based on student needs and community needs." Linda noted,

> We include in our curricular offerings Folklorico and Chinese Dance classes, as well as a Chinese Music class. In addition, primary language development classes in Mandarin and Spanish are offered to the "native speakers" of these languages. If staffing permitted, we would also offer courses in Cantonese and Vietnamese. We feel that, by offering these classes, we validate the importance of our ethnic communities and offer all our students the opportunity to become multiculturally literate. Courses in dance and music are open to all students, and "nonnative speakers" are encouraged to become bilingual by offering Spanish and Mandarin to all interested students.

We discovered another example of equitable learning at BBMS. Tracking has been eliminated entirely from BBMS; students are heterogeneously grouped for projects and classroom activities. Because one third of the BBMS students have been identified as high achievers, the heterogeneous groups provide significant opportunities for students with various academic abilities to work cooperatively in peer-tutoring groups.

Giving Instructional Autonomy to Teachers.   The second challenge for creating an equitable learning environment at each school is for school and district administrators to give teachers high levels of autonomy. The teachers we observed have been given considerable freedom by their administrators to create and implement lessons that are sensitive to the needs of students. For example, Rudy Chavez, the principal at MKHS, noted, "One of the things that makes this school work is the fact that the teachers in their classrooms are able to do what they were hired to do, and that is teach."

At BBMS, where teachers have leeway to vary from the district's prescribed curriculum and where the principal, Camille Barr, expects innovative classroom activities, all teachers demonstrate highly creative lessons. Rather than use textbooks to develop their lessons, teachers at BBMS create their own classroom curriculum. Topics are selected from those suggested by students and their parents. Working together in teams, then, BBMS teachers decide instructional goals, select appropriate materials, create instructional activities, and become proactive learners with their students. The teachers reflect on and revise their instruction throughout each 12-week unit.

Institutionalizing Change

The third theme shared by the schools is the institutionalization of change. Many political and bureaucratic factors mitigate against change in schools; consequently, school curriculum and classroom instruction may remain the same for many years regardless of societal changes that surround the school. Strommen and Lincoln (1992) summarize this perhaps most clearly:

> We have allowed our schools to remain in the past, while our children have been born in the future. The result is a mismatch of learner and education. But it is not the children who are mismatched to the schools; the schools are mismatched to the children. Only by revising educational practice in light of how our culture has changed can we close this gap and reunite our schools with our children and the rest of society. (p. 475)

One factor that often mitigates against school change is a seemingly endless number of new instructional approaches that teachers are asked to implement. One educational trend after another can make teachers hesitant to adopt yet another educational innovation suggested by an enthusiastic administrator or college professor. In contemporary society, however, knowledge that was once viewed to be stable and reliable now changes almost overnight. And varying cultures, once disparate and remote, have converged to create a global community. Broad changes like these are putting pressure on school staffs everywhere to modify their curricula and instruction, not just with an instructional strategy or two but with schoolwide curricular and instructional reform. Although not every school staff reacts to these pressures in a positive way, staff at the three schools we visited are responding positively by acknowledging change as a necessary quality in order to accommodate the needs of students and parents.

Change at Hollibrook Elementary School.   When old practices of schooling at HES weren't effective for a new population of mostly Hispanic students, administrators and faculty sought alternative practices. By restructuring their school around the accelerated schools model, all teachers began rethinking their own instruction and what school should do for students. Teachers at HES now are working together to create instruction that is sensitive to the needs of their students. Teachers used the instructional autonomy they were given to try out new instructional strategies. HES teachers have been encouraged to use their professional wisdom and personal teaching knowledge to create learning experiences that effectively help students be successful at school.

Trying innovative teaching strategies not found in other schools and not documented in textbooks requires HES teachers to take risks. This risk taking is supported by Principal Roy Ford. As an example, when we visited HES, we observed two teachers—Lyn Williams and Jill Crawford—use a unique and innovative peer-teaching strategy with their students. Regarding this strategy, Ford noted,

> It's a risk to teach like that because this is extra instruction for the students. It goes beyond what the state normally expects teachers to cover. Lyn [Williams] and Jill [Crawford] put kids who aren't speaking English or Spanish very well into cooperative groups. So the kids teach other the language. Lyn and Jill are encouraging bilingualism in the kids. They take a risk when they do that. And I support that kind of risk entirely because it means we're trying to meet the needs of our kids. We're trying to give LEP students the language skills they need to get by outside of school, and we're trying to help our English-speaking kids be able to communicate better with the Hispanic community inside and outside of school.

Change at Brown Barge Middle School.   The changes made at BBMS to prepare students for contemporary society are unique in process and product. The standard curriculum that most middle schools use (curriculum divided into discrete subjects) and the traditional school day (discrete periods) have been restructured entirely. In place of these things is a theme-based, fully integrated curriculum. Teachers who specialize in specific subject areas (e.g., social studies, English, science) work together in teams to prepare student activities and projects around themes. There are no standard textbooks; there is no traditional teaching practice. At BBMS teachers and students learn content together; they actively negotiate curriculum and instruction during their social interactions in group study.[22] This type of instruction, which reflects the transformative education discussed by Doll (1993), makes BBMS teachers exemplary role models for learning and places them in a nonauthoritarian role as teachers.

A consequence of the curriculum restructuring at BBMS has been the emergence of instruction that we interpreted to be culturally sensitive. This instruction is a function of focusing extensively on students' needs. Camille Barr noted,

> We teach kids, not content. Our constituents are our children and their parents. And we have to be sensitive to what their needs are. I think we are truly one of the few schools in the country that operate their schools based entirely on what their kids have identified as their needs. And culturally sensitive issues come out of that. The topics we teach come from the bottom up. By this I mean they come from children and parents. The only topics we have in our curriculum have been determined this way.

Change at Mark Keppel High School.   At MKHS the curriculum is in many ways standard for a high school setting. The state requirements for California and the

Alhambra School District put limitations on the kinds of innovations that administrators at MKHS would like teachers to implement. Not standard at MKHS, however, is the rich diversity of student cultures.[23] In responding to this diversity, staff at MKHS have altered instruction in subtle ways; the teachers continuously redesign their instruction to accommodate ongoing cultural changes in the local communities. Consequently, some of the academic courses at MKHS and the extracurricular activities are specific to the needs of students.

School instruction at MKHS, like that at HES, is culturally congruent with patterns of social relationships found in home and community life (see Erickson, 1984). Modifications and additions to the MKHS curriculum are attempts to align instruction more closely with students' cultural backgrounds. Core courses required for graduation are offered in Spanish, and students have opportunities to participate in extracurricular activities that align with their cultural needs. Anthony Ortega, Assistant Principal for Activities at MKHS, explained:

> In addition to the many other activities we offer students, we have some clubs that are associated with ethnicity. We have the Asian-American Club. We have the Friendship Club, which is a Chinese Club, and we have ALAS, which is our Latin-American group. Some of our students are recent arrivals [in the U.S.], but yet they feel part of the school because they take part in clubs and in overall school activities. In terms of our athletic program, we were one of the first schools, at least in this area, to offer badminton, which is a sport very popular in Asian countries. And we've been extremely successful in that program.

As we took a self-guided tour of the MKHS campus during our visit, we noticed several large banners hanging on the gymnasium wall. The banners were presented to MKHS for being district champions in badminton.

Constraints to Change.   Each of these schools is engaged in various forms of change. Each is struggling to redefine itself locally in the midst of profound global transformations. And each is struggling to redefine the purpose of schooling for a nation that has become increasingly pluralistic and technological. By traditional standards, the instructional risks that staff at these schools are taking could be considered progressive. The schools we visited, however, are reflective of a new social order, and with this social order, educational risks like the kinds being taken at these schools are no longer an option; they are a pressing imperative.

Although the schools are progressive in their methods, in their intentions, and in their assessment of student learning, they still exist within the traditional bureaucracy of local school districts and state departments of education. Consequently, local and state officials require these schools to assess their students with traditional forms of assessment (e.g., standardized testing), thus comparing the schools we visited with other schools that have more traditional instruction. The instructional risks being taken at HES, BBMS, and MKHS to enhance instruction for culturally diverse students depart from traditional instruction and from traditional strategies of assessing student learning. It is not clear, therefore, whether traditional forms of school evaluation can be used to appropriately compare HES, BBMS, and MKHS with more traditional schools. Nevertheless, we found HES and BBMS in particular to be criticized by district and state officials for not comparing more favorably on standardized tests with other schools in the district. Although we found excitement, high levels of enthusiasm, and innovative thinking among teachers in all three schools, we also found these same teachers to be frustrated and disappointed for not being acknowledged more favorably for the long hours of creative work they spend implementing culturally sensitive instruction and for being inappropriately compared with teachers at schools with more traditional curriculum and instruction.

The frustration that teachers felt from being constrained by traditional standards for school evaluation was especially noticeable at BBMS. Teachers and students at BBMS engage in a genuine dialogue in both oral and written modalities, what Cummins (1986) calls the "reciprocal interaction model of teaching." All teachers at BBMS demonstrated careful guidance of student learning in a democratic, collaborative learning context. Learning factual information at BBMS is entirely secondary to developing higher level thinking and decision-making skills. Yet, factual information and lower level thinking skills are essential components of traditional standardized tests. Traditional forms of school assessment, therefore, are mismatched to the curriculum at BBMS.

Similar constraints have been imposed on HES and MKHS. Yet, students' personal, social, and academic needs in these schools surpass what most schools have experienced in the past. The schools we observed are changing their curricula and instruction to better meet the needs of their students; to move their instructional practices into the 21st century, however, district and state guidelines, in addition to traditional assessment strategies, are constraining their progress.

Affirming Cultural and Linguistic Diversity

Affirming Cultural Diversity.
The educators in the three schools we studied view cultural diversity as a strength of their students. They also believe that students' cultural backgrounds must be part of their school learning environments, including the content taught to students. Linda Maryott (MKHS) noted,

> To improve instruction for culturally and ethnically diverse students, our schools, teachers, and educational system must promote education that relates your field of expertise to the culture or country of the students with whom you're working. This validates that the students are important as persons, that their culture is important, that their country is important.

Debra Blair, dean of students at MKHS, reported,

> The MKHS staff has tremendous concern for our students. They go out of their way to reach out to the diverse cultures, and they are concerned about preserving the culture.

About the cultural backgrounds of students, Roy Ford (HES) said,

> You have to value what the kids bring to school. You have to value their backgrounds. Once you understand the family network in a culture and interact with that culture, you can be successful in the classroom. How can you be successful if you don't understand their culture? When a student comes into this school, his or her culture and related beliefs are deeply ingrained, and when the student goes home every day, the culture gets ingrained again. You have to understand all that to teach here [at HES] so you won't give the students a negative learning experience.

Affirming students' cultural diversity means knowing how to develop culturally relevant instruction. It means knowing how culture and ethnicity can pose special academic problems for some cultural groups. Mary Ellen DeSantos, the bilingual coordinator for the Alhambra School District, spoke with us about achievement differences among students. She noted,

> Surrounding the school [MKHS] is a large Vietnamese population and a large Chinese population, both Mandarin and Cantonese. We have a Latino population from Central America, and we have a large Hispanic community. In school what you see are the Asians achieving at much higher levels than the Latinos, Hispanics, and newly immigrated Vietnamese, who have little formal schooling. This is a concern of the district right now, a concern of the school board, and a concern of the superintendent.

Regarding teaching challenge for LEP students, Linda Maryott (MKHS) noted,

> As a teacher, you need to adjust to the various learning styles in your classroom. An LEP student who is mainstreamed into sheltered or regular classes is a student who has the cognitive ability but needs the teacher to take into account the learning style that will bring out his or her cognitive ability. Whether teachers have LEP, special education, high performance, or average students in their classes, teachers need to reflect on teaching methodology, materials used in the class, and assessment techniques and modify these as needed to bring out the best there is in the student.

Affirming Linguistic Diversity.   Educators at all schools view linguistic diversity as a strength of their students; they seek to incorporate student languages into classroom instruction as much as possible. Roy Ford (HES), who told us he is not bilingual, tells the Spanish-speaking children in his school who are becoming bilingual, "You are smarter than me because you know two languages and I only know one." Debra Blair, Dean of Students at MKHS, has LEP students come into her office. The way she and her staff work with students indicates the school's willingness to acknowledge students' languages and cultures. Debra Blair reported,

> In our office, we have students come in who speak different languages. Many of these students are just beginning to learn English. We have translators for these students. In the attendance office, there are many people who can assist the students in different

languages. So we reach out to students to assist them as they communicate to us in their language.

Linda Maryott (MKHS), who is in charge of instruction at the school, is a proponent of bilingual programs. From our formal and informal conversations with Linda and from our observations of her in several meetings with teachers and other administrators, we soon realized that she is a valuable change agent for MKHS. Linda, who is bilingual in Spanish and English, is a proponent of bilingual education programs. Linda is in charge of school restructuring for MKHS, and she wants bilingualism to become a central part of the school's curriculum. She noted,

> One of my goals for part of our restructuring is to see our kids graduate as bilingual students and have that as a seal on their diploma. I have always felt that one of the assets our kids bring to us is another language, and students who are bilingual can't do anything but help our economy and society. So I would like to see our school recognize bilingualism as an academic skill.

That HES,[24] BBMS, and MKHS are immersed in linguistic and cultural diversity is very clear. That the staffs choose to see these forms of diversity as strengths reflects their willingness to adapt to the needs of their students. These staffs are reacting proactively and positively to the educational demands of their local communities and to the educational needs of contemporary society, but not without taking risks. The changes being made in these schools are similar to the changes that all staffs must consider.

A final note must be made about changing instruction in schools where there is a long-standing tradition of direct instruction, where transmitting content is preferred over molding content to students' needs. Clearly, not every school will be like the three schools we describe in this chapter; we purposely depicted visions of the possible. Moreover, HES, BBMS, and MKHS certainly have had their share of difficult challenges in becoming institutions noted for culturally sensitive educational innovations. Yet, we believe, along with Ernst, Statzner, and Trueba (1994), that focusing on successful educational endeavors can serve as a beacon, a guiding light to others who wish to move forward but who need possibilities for taking the first step.

You might be fortunate to teach in a school like those depicted in this chapter, where you are encouraged to try innovative classroom strategies. Or, you might soon teach or are already teaching in a school that is more traditional, where instructional and curricular conformity to district and/or state educational mandates is expected, even demanded. Moving away from such standards—that is, teaching in a less traditional manner—could be professionally dangerous for you and result in serious criticisms and overly critical evaluations of your teaching. You might be in a school, for example, where staff are adverse to pluralistic educational ideologies or where the school board has taken a stand against bilingualism. In Chapter 8, we discuss more about teaching in schools where cultural diversity is not necessarily a true part of the school curriculum.

SUMMARY

Sufficient information exists today to guide the development of schools and classroom practices that successfully reach all students. The question, then, is not whether educators are capable of reaching all students, but whether educators want to reach all students. Educators at the three multicultural schools we visited very clearly want to reach every one of their students. With rare exception, the administrators, teachers, counselors, and other staff we interviewed have a collective vision for doing this. To transform this vision into educational reality, the schools are redefining their roles relative to student and community needs. Rather than reproduce the cultural relations of the wider society (e.g., some cultural groups are dominated by other cultural groups), these schools are establishing new relations in their effort to affirm cultural and linguistic diversity.

Students at Hollibrook Elementary School, Brown Barge Middle School, and Mark Keppel High School are empowered by their learning environments, not disabled by language, ethnicity, or culture. To empower students, the schools restructured the content, purpose, and organization of their curricula and instruction;[25] the schools have been transformed into cooperative, democratic institutions where students, parents, and teachers have voices in curriculum decision making.[26]

The schools we visited embrace change as an ongoing and needful educational process for students in today's society. The changes being made in the schools are creating a learning environment where student cultures are compatible with school curriculum and instruction. Cultural compatibility in contemporary society, according to Vogt, Jordan, and Tharp (1987), is a credible explanation for school success, whereas cultural incompatibility is one explanation for school failure. Trueba, Jacobs, and Kilton (1990) note that the purpose of creating culturally compatible learning environments is to break the cycle of stress, poor performance, and school failure that many minority students now experience. This cycle is being broken at the schools we visited.

The relationship between ethnicity and educational disadvantage is inseparable from our social structure (Hannan, 1982). School staffs that lack this awareness are unprepared to confront discrimination and inequality inside and outside the classroom. These same staffs are unprepared to help their students deal with the realities of a culturally diverse society. Staffs at the three schools we studied have a clear understanding of the forces that constrain educational equality. The curricular and instructional changes they are making reflect this understanding.

The most powerful, and perhaps the most valuable, part of the schools we explored is their staffs' attempts to develop a humanitarian perspective in their students. Students in these schools participate in learning activities centered on human dignity, equality, and personal worth. If we, as educators in the 21st century, are to develop schools that meet the academic and social needs of culturally diverse students while simultaneously preparing them to live in harmony, to develop mutual respect, and to pose and solve crucial societal problems, the educational practices now in place at HES, BBMS, and MKHS must become mainstream education in our society.

ACTIVITY 6.1 Locality and Context of Selected Schools

Our site visits helped us become personally familiar with the interesting dynamics of cultural diversity at three schools. This activity is intended to help you develop a better understanding of such schools by exploring a selected school's location and context. Select a grade level (elementary school, middle school, high school) and a school that are best suited to inform your teaching. By making observations of the school (or by talking with school officials), compile the information requested in Figures 6–1, 6–2, and 6–3. Figure 6–1 helps you organize demographic information on the school's community. Figures 6–2 and 6–3 help you compile information on the school's learning environment. Notice that the figures have two columns to record information. For Activity 6.1, use the column "Multicultural School" to record the information you gather.

From the information you gathered, what can you conclude about the cultural diversity in the school's community? Compare and contrast the locality and context of the school you studied with those of the three schools we studied. How are the schools alike? How are they different? Do you consider the school you examined to be culturally diverse? Why or why not? Do you think the curriculum and instruction are culturally sensitive? Why or why not? In addition to the demographic data you gathered while filling in the figures, answer these questions about the school you explored:

1. How does the school's curriculum reflect the cultural diversity of the students?
2. Does the school have any special extracurricular programs for culturally diverse students (e.g., Association for Latin American Students)?
3. Does the school place value on languages and cultures?

	Schools	
Community Features	Multicultural School	Your School
Total population		
SES (lower, middle, upper)		
Community ethnicity		
Asian		
Hispanic		
Latino		
Black		
White		
Native American		
Other		
Nationalities		
Languages spoken		
Economically disadvantaged citizens (%)		
Religions practiced		

Figure 6–1 Information about community

	Schools	
Student Features	**Multicultural School**	**Your School**
Total students		
Community ethnicity		
Asian		
Hispanic and Latino		
Black		
White		
Native American		
Other		
LEP students		
English-language-only students		
Economically disadvantaged students		
Number of nationalities		
Number of languages spoken by students		

Figure 6–2   Demographics of students

	Schools	
Staff Features	**Multicultural School**	**Your School**
Professional staff		
Teachers		
Campus administrators		
Educational aides		
Professional staff		
Asian		
Hispanic		
Black		
White		
Native American		
Other		
Professional staff bilingual		
Counseling staff		
Asian		
Hispanic		
Black		
White		
Native American		
Other		
Counseling staff bilingual		

Figure 6–3   Demographics of professional staff

4. Are all students expected to achieve at high levels?
5. What kind of staff development is available for teachers to become sensitive to the needs of culturally diverse students, especially new immigrants who have limited English proficiency?
6. Does the school have a high level of parental involvement?
7. To what extent do teachers' and students' cultural backgrounds align?

ACTIVITY 6.2   Locality and Context of Your Prior Schools

In this activity, you will extend the information you used to develop your educational autobiography in Chapter 3. Reflect on the schools you described in your autobiography. Although several years may have passed since you were in a K–12 school, try to gather as much information as you can on one of your former schools. Use the column "Your School" in Figures 6–1, 6–2, and 6–3 to record this information. Then answer the questions in Activity 6.1 for this school.

RESEARCH TOPIC

Features of Multicultural Schools: A Case Study
Problem Posing

This research topic is designed to help you explore features of multicultural schools. The case studies we conducted of HES, BBMS, and MKHS can serve as frameworks for how to explore the school you select for your case study. From an analysis of three school sites in the United States (HES, BBMS, and MKHS), you saw how these schools are similar in important ways. We did not determine the themes that link the schools together (see Figure 6–4) prior to studying the schools; rather, the themes emerged during our exploration of the school sites. The themes, therefore, are specific to these schools. Consequently, use caution when generalizing these themes to all schools because they were generated from only three schools. Because they were salient features of all three schools, however, and because they were found at all three grade levels (elementary, middle, and high school), you can use these themes as one basis for exploring other multicultural schools and for comparing newly explored schools with the successful ones described in this chapter.

When we began our case studies of each school, we initially asked five questions. You may use these same questions to begin your case study.

1. In what way is the school culturally diverse?
2. What features of the school contribute to its success as a multicultural learning environment?
3. What factors constrain the success of a school that is characterized as culturally diverse?
4. How does the school prepare its students for living in contemporary multicultural society?

Living the Experience of Cultural Diversity

_____ Building trust and respect

_____ Incorporating learners' cultures

_____ Creating cross-cultural harmony

_____ Fostering a shared vision

Creating an Equitable Learning Environment

_____ Providing equal educational opportunities for all students

_____ Giving instructional autonomy to teachers

Institutionalizing Change

_____ Embracing change as an ongoing process

_____ Making changes at the school site

_____ Overcoming constraints to change

Affirming Cultural and Linguistic Diversity

_____ Affirming cultural diversity

_____ Affirming linguistic diversity

_____ Infusing the curriculum with cultural diversity

Figure 6–4   Shared features of three multicultural schools (Hollibrook Elementary School, Brown Barge Middle School, Mark Keppel High School)

5. How does the school meet the academic and social needs of all students, especially those who are newly arrived immigrants and who have limited English proficiency?

Exploration and Discovery

In Activity 6.1, you began gathering information on a particular school site. Use this same site to conduct your case study. After getting permission from school officials to conduct the case study, explore the multicultural dimensions of the school. You may use methods similar to those we used when we explored HES, BBMS, and MKHS. These methods include observing specific aspects of the school, interviewing professional staff, interviewing students, and reviewing school documents. To help you better understand how we conducted our case studies, we have included a detailed account in Appendix A of this chapter. Although you might not be able to gather the same quantity and quality of information we gathered, try to get as much information as you can.

Your observations of the school can be formal and informal. Make formal observations of classroom teaching, after-school activities for students, and any special

Yes	No	Some	
____	____	____	1. Does the school build trust and respect among students and teachers?
____	____	____	2. Does the school incorporate students' cultures into the learning environment?
____	____	____	3. Does the school create cross-cultural harmony?
____	____	____	4. Does the school foster a shared vision for teaching culturally diverse students among faculty and students?
____	____	____	5. Does the school provide equal educational opportunities for all students?
____	____	____	6. Do teachers have autonomy to create and implement instruction that is sensitive to the specific needs of their culturally diverse students?
____	____	____	7. Does the school embrace change as an ongoing process to meet the educational needs of a changing society?
____	____	____	8. Is the school making changes in curriculum and instruction to accommodate changes in students' cultural backgrounds and related needs?
____	____	____	9. What political and/or bureaucratic constraints, if any, keep the school from making needed changes in curriculum and instruction?
____	____	____	10. Is the school overcoming constraints to change?
____	____	____	11. Does the school accommodate cultural diversity?
____	____	____	12. Does the school accommodate linguistic diversity?

Figure 6–5. Questions to ask about schools in contemporary society

workshops for teachers. Make informal observations of the school by "hanging around" the campus as much as school officials will allow during your study. These informal observations are valuable in giving you a sense of the school environment and insight into the daily life at the school.

Conduct interviews with various educators, including principals, assistant principals, deans, counselors, and classroom teachers. Where possible, interview students of various cultural groups. To understand the instructional goals of the school, review school documents, including district and classroom curriculum materials. District and school mission statements, usually contained in formal documents, help you understand the district's mission relative to cultural diversity.

The questions in Figure 6–5 can guide your observations and interviews. The questions were derived from the shared features of the three schools described in this chapter. By using these questions, you will be able to compare and contrast your studied school with Hollibrook Elementary School, Brown Barge Middle School, and Mark Keppel High School. You may also use the checklist in Appendix B of this chapter to explore your selected school. We used this checklist as part of our criteria for selecting the three schools. It is a modification of the criteria developed by Lucas, Henze, and Donato (1990) from their study of successful Latino high schools. As another framework for your observations, you may use, for example, the curriculum guidelines for multicultural education recommended by the National Council for Social Studies (National Council for Social Studies, 1992). Or, you may use the eight characteristics of multicultural schools suggested by Banks (1994, p. 11).

Reflection and Modification

From your case study, what salient features, or themes, did you discover about the school's learning environment. How is the school you studied similar to the schools described in this chapter? How is your school different from these schools? Did you find evidence of the themes suggested in Figure 6–4? What additional themes did you find that are not in Figure 6–4? List these themes below.

1. _____
2. _____
3. _____

From studying the schools in this chapter and from conducting your own case study, what modifications have you made in your beliefs about multicultural learning environments? Think about your ability and your willingness to teach in multicultural learning environments like HES, BBMS, and MKHS. In Chapter 4, you assessed your readiness for teaching in multicultural schools. Is your level of readiness sufficient to begin teaching in schools—for example, like MKHS—that are richly diverse and contain many student cultures?

To complete your case study, develop a report on the school you studied. The format used to describe the schools in this chapter can be a framework for developing your report. Include a section that appraises the school for its ability to meet the academic and social needs of all students. Also include a section that describes how your views of multicultural schools were modified, if at all, as you conducted the case study.

Description and Speculation

We assume that conducting a case study of an actual school helped you gain new insights into multicultural schools. From what you learned in this research project, describe additional projects that will further broaden your awareness and understanding of multicultural school learning environments.

1. _____
2. _____
3. _____

NOTES

1. Trueba, H. (1989). *Raising silent voices: Educating the linguistic minorities for the 21st century.* New York: Newbury House. See also Byrnes, D., & Cortez, D. (1992). Language diversity in the classroom. In D. Byrnes & G. Kiger (Eds.), *Common bonds: Anti-bias teaching in a diverse society* (pp. 71–85). Wheaton, MD: Association for Childhood Education International.

2. Pallas, A., Natriello, G., & McDill, E. (1989). The changing nature of the disadvantaged population: Current dimensions and future trends. *Educational Researcher, 18*(5), 16–22. See also Trueba, H. (1989). *Raising silent voices: Educating linguistic minorities for the 21st century.* New York: Newbury House.

3. See Gergen, K. (1991). *The saturated self: Dilemmas of identity in contemporary life.* New York: Basic Books.

4. Strommen, E., & Lincoln, B. (1992). Constructivism, technology, and the future of classroom learning. *Education and Urban Society, 24*(4), 466–476.

5. See Doll, W. (1993). *A post-modern perspective on curriculum.* New York: Teachers College Press; Kliebard, H. (1987). *The struggle for the American curriculum 1893–1958.* New York: Routledge & Kegan Paul.

6. We are not suggesting that White middle-class values are inherently bad or negative. As the diversity of students increases and as values from other ethnic groups begin to predominate school learning environments, however, other cultural values need to be considered in both curriculum and instruction. Studies indicate that, in culturally diverse schools where White middle-class values guide curricular and instructional practices and where linguistic differences are viewed as detriments rather than strengths, ethnic and cultural groups other than middle-class Whites experience frustration, anxiety, and learning difficulties (e.g., Cummins, 1986; Erickson, 1984; Gibson, 1988; Kalantzis, Cope, Noble, & Poynting, 1990; Kleifgen, 1988; Suarez-Orozco, 1987; Trueba, Jacobs, & Kirton, 1990; Villegas, 1988).

7. For discussions about the White middle-class nature of modern schools, see Fine, M. (1991). *Framing dropouts: Notes on the politics of an urban public high school.* New York: SUNY Press; Greenbaum, W. (1974). America in search of a new ideal: An essay on the rise of pluralism. *Harvard Educational Review, 44*(3), 411–440; Hollins, R. (1990). Debunking the myth of a monolithic White American culture: Or, moving toward cultural inclusion. *American Behavioral Scientist, 34*(2), 201–209; Stedman, L. (1987). It's time we changed the effective schools formula. *Phi Delta Kappan, 69,* 215–224.

8. Strommen, E., & Lincoln, B. (1992). Constructivism, technology, and the future of classroom learning. *Education and Urban Society, 24*(4), 466–476.

9. See Howard, G. (1993). Whites in multicultural education: Rethinking our role. *Phi Delta Kappan, 75,* 36–41. See also Garcia, J., & Pugh, S. (1992). Multicultural education in teacher preparation programs: A political or an educational concept? *Phi Delta Kappan, 74,* 214–219; Garcia, J. (1993). A commentary on increasing minority faculty representation in schools of education. *The Educational Forum, 57,* 420–429.

10. See the edited issue of *Anthropology and Education Quarterly, 25*(3) (Ernst, Statzner, & Trueba, 1994), which contains a series of articles on how teachers and culturally diverse students negotiate learning environments to attain success in student learning.

11. See Appendix B of this chapter for the criteria we used to identify and select these schools.

12. See Appendix A of this chapter for an account of the methods we used to explore each school.

13. We gratefully acknowledge Dr. Porter Troutman for his assistance in helping us conduct the site visits to all schools.

14. We visited Hollibrook Elementary School in November 1993. A more complete overview of the school is provided by McCarthy, J., & Still, S. (1993). Hollibrook accelerated elementary school. In J. Murphy & P. Hollinger (Eds.), *Restructuring schools: Learning from ongoing efforts*. Newbury Park, CA: Corwin Press. We are grateful to Dr. McCarthy, assistant director of the Accelerated Schools Project and Associate Professor at University of Nevada at Las Vegas, for providing us with background information of HES.

15. The Accelerated Schools Program was introduced by Henry Levin of Stanford University and now consists of a network of schools across the country. For an overview of the Accelerated Schools Program, see Levin, H. M. (1987). New schools for disadvantaged students. In Chief State School Officers (Eds.), *School success for students at risk* (pp. 209–225). Orlando, FL: Harcourt Brace Jovanovich.

16. We visited Brown Barge Middle School in October 1993. We are grateful to Dr. Tom Dickinson, Associate Professor of Education at Indiana State University and former editor of the National Middle School Association, for suggesting Brown Barge as one of the schools for our site visits.

17. The BBMS curriculum is outlined in a document prepared by the faculty and administrators of BBMS. See Brown Barge Middle School. (1993). *Middle school curriculum restructuring: A curriculum project of Brown Barge Middle School*. Pensacola, FL: Author [Available for a fee from Brown Barge Middle School, 151 East Fairfield Drive, Pensacola, FL 32503]. For additional information on middle school integrated curricula, see Beane, J. (1993). Problems and possibilities for an integrative curriculum. *Middle School Journal, 25*(1), 18–23.

18. Prior to, during, and after our visit to BBMS, we reviewed closely the school's curriculum guidelines and other materials. We compared our insights and observations of the school and examined transcripts from interviews we conducted at the school. We compared this information to current writings on multicultural education and to recent calls for curriculum reform. From these comparisons, we found the curriculum and instruction at BBMS to align almost entirely with Banks's (1994) characteristics of a multicultural school. We also discovered BBMS to exemplify the transformation and social action approaches to curriculum reform suggested by Banks (p. 25); that is, specific parts of the BBMS curriculum have been reformed to enable students to view concepts, issues, events, and themes from the perspective of diverse ethnic and cultural groups (the transformation approach to curriculum reform). During our site visit, we observed students engaged in activities and group projects during which they made decisions on important social issues and reflected on these issues in important ways (social action approach to curriculum reform). As another means to appraise the unique qualities of the BBMS curriculum, we compared it to the *Curriculum Guidelines for Multicultural Education* prepared by the National Council for Social Studies (National Council for Social Studies, 1992). BBMS strongly aligned with most of the guidelines, and in certain instances moved beyond them.

19. We visited Mark Keppel High School in December 1993.

20. For additional reading on the city of Monterey Park, see Horton, J. (1992). The politics of diversity in Monterey Park, California. In L. Lamphere (Ed.), *Structuring diversity: Ethnographic perspectives on the new immigration* (pp. 215–245). Chicago: University of Chicago Press.

21. As Trueba et al. (1990) note, "Creating a more suitable environment for learning in a school characterized by cultural diversity is not an easy task" (p. 132).

22. See Doll, W. (1993). *A post-modern perspective on curriculum*. New York: Teachers College Press; Gadamer, H. (1975). *Truth and method*. New York: Seabury Press; Gergen, K. (1991). *The saturated self: Dilemmas of identity in contemporary life*. New York: Basic Books.

23. Other areas in southern California and in other parts of the country, particularly large urban areas, have similar cultural diversity. Nationally, however, student cultural diversity is less extensive than at schools like MKHS.

24. See Cummins, J. (1986). Empowering minority students: A framework for intervention. *Harvard Educational Review, 56*(1), 18–36.

25. See Hollins, E. R., & Spencer, K. (1990). Restructuring schools for cultural inclusion: Changing the schooling process for African American youngsters. *Journal of Education, 17*(2), 89–100.

26. Hannan, B. (1982). The multicultural school: Or schools in search of their culture. In G. Dow (Ed.), *Teacher learning* (pp. 79–110). Boston: Routledge & Kegan Paul.

APPENDIX A   *Strategies for Selecting Schools and Conducting Case Studies*
Purposes for Visiting Schools

1. To explore the multicultural learning environments of each school
2. To determine how the school's staff meet the academic and social needs of a culturally diverse student population
3. To gain a deeper understanding of the relationships among school administration, faculty, students, and the community
4. To explore site-based staff development for diversity issues
5. To observe strategies that selected teachers use to accommodate cultural diversity in their classrooms
6. To determine how the school negotiates curriculum and instruction with culturally diverse students

Strategies for Selecting Schools

Initial Criteria for Selection.   In selecting schools for case studies, we did not rely exclusively on an academic analysis of student performance based on traditional assessment standards (e.g., SAT scores). Although helpful, these standards alone do not provide a deeper, more comprehensive understanding of the sociological factors in the school that influence student success (Eckert, 1989). An overreliance on academic achievement, according to Cummins (1986), keeps educators from attending to the relationship between teachers and minority students and between schools and minority communities (see also Hollins & Spencer, 1990; Stedman, 1987). Patthey-Chavez (1993) notes,

> By focusing so much on achievement, academic analysis rarely addresses the arena—the institution called school—within which discontinuities between [cultural groups] . . . are negotiated and resolved on a daily basis. (p. 34)

For the schools we studied, we wanted to explore how students from various cultures negotiate discontinuities in curriculum and instruction. We assumed that studying this negotiation process would give us a deeper understanding of how and why schools are successful in meeting the needs of culturally diverse student populations. This understanding better prepares us to interpret more traditional academic analyses of the schools.

By looking at the schools' negotiation processes for curriculum and instruction, we quite naturally focused on social processes; that is, we focused on the social interactions between educators and students and between schools and their communities. Eckert (1989) and Fine (1991) note that the social processes of schools contribute as much to school success as effort or aptitude of students (see also Patthey-Chavez, 1993).

Additional criteria for selecting schools were provided by Lucas et al. (1990), who developed a list of features that were found to help LEP minority and new immigrant students be successful in school (see Appendix B in this chapter). We used these criteria to make the final selection of schools for our site visits.

The Selection Process. After delineating selection criteria for choosing schools, we began considering schools to visit. We wanted to study three schools: one elementary school, one middle school, and one high school. We also wanted these schools to be in different parts of the country and to reflect recent shifts in student demographics. One purpose for studying schools with this variation was to discover and explore common features of the schools. These features could then be a basis for developing grounded theoretical premises (Glaser & Strauss, 1967; Strauss, 1987) about effective multicultural schools that transcend grade levels and geographical boundaries. The resulting premises can be used to examine other effective school contexts. We also wanted to explore one school that was more stable demographically but that was still making curricular changes to align with the demands of a technological and multicultural society.

As we considered parts of the country that reflect the demographics we sought, we selected regions that are particularly crucial for studying increasing cultural diversity in students and that are reflective of the demographic transitions sweeping the entire country. Examples of these areas are Southern California and various states in the Southwest. These two regions are experiencing significant increases in Hispanic and Latino populations (e.g., Texas). Locations in the eastern United States are also experiencing demographic shifts, especially Florida. We decided that southern California, Texas, and Florida would be well suited to our needs. Consequently, the experiences of these regions are the likely future experiences of other parts of the country.

We used the "snowball sampling technique" (Bogdan & Biklen, 1992, p. 70) to purposefully select the three schools we studied. Using this technique, we relied on informed colleagues and other educators to recommend schools for our site visits. These colleagues were familiar with effective multicultural schools and provided us with valuable suggestions. We also reviewed the literature, especially ethnographies, on such schools and their communities. After a sample of schools was identified in the targeted geographical regions, telephone interviews were conducted with school administrators to determine how the schools aligned with our initial criteria and whether the administrators wanted to be part of our study. From this process, which took approximately 2 months, three schools were selected.

Strategies for Conducting Case Studies

Prior to the site visits, we developed a protocol for exploring each school. Following the work of Lucas et al. (1990), we determined that 4- or 5-day site visits to each school would provide us with sufficient time to make brief, albeit intense, immersions into the school contexts. During these site visits, we sought to develop an understanding of the sociological dimensions of the schools' contexts. As noted above, we wanted to examine how the schools were negotiating curriculum and instruction with students relative to cultural diversity. This need caused us to examine the sociological dimensions of the school, to capture the personal perspectives of educators at each site, and to look at the personal meaning that educators at each school derived as they socially constructed their classroom curriculum with students.

To examine each school, we gathered information on

- the demography of schools and their communities
- the nature of the curriculum
- student assessment strategies
- multicultural staff development
- educators' perspectives about cultural diversity
- special programs and activities for students
- teachers' instructional strategies
- school-community relations

This information was gathered with qualitative research methods recommended for educational settings (LeCompte & Preissle, 1993). These methods are useful when studying the unique local, naturally occurring qualities of school contexts. First, we held formal interviews and informal conversations with principals, assistant principals, counselors, teachers, students, bilingual directors, and curriculum directors. Second, we reviewed school documents, including school curricula, classroom curricula, district policy statements, and program descriptions. Third, we observed classroom teaching and the overall school environment. Fourth, during our site visits, we explored the communities that surrounded the schools. Finally, we examined all transcripts developed from formal interviews conducted at the schools.

During the first 2 days of our visits, we worked together as a team to become familiar with each school environment. We interviewed school principals, counselors, and other administrative personnel. We toured the campus, met with auxiliary staff, ate in the school cafeteria, and visited teachers' workrooms and the school district office. We also reviewed school documents.

During the final 2 days of our site visits, one of us (Powell) made focused observations of one teacher at each school. These teachers, who were selected by administrators prior to our visit, were known to be particularly sensitive to the needs of all students. These teachers were also known for their ability to develop and implement culturally relevant instruction. The selected teachers were contacted by phone prior to our visit to answer questions about our upcoming observations. At the school sites, conversational interviews (Oakley, 1981) were conducted with each of these teachers. Each interview, which lasted approximately 1 hour, was taped and transcribed. The interview protocol that guided conversations with these teachers is in Appendix C of this chapter. All teachers were given the interview protocol prior to the site visit so that they could have time to reflect on their perspectives and personal theories about teaching culturally diverse students.

Strategies for Interpreting School Information

Because each school site was visited by at least two of us,* we were able to discuss and interpret the information as we gathered it. This process, called **peer debriefing** (Lincoln & Guba, 1985), was useful in analyzing school sites from multiple perspectives.

To be consistent with constant comparative methods of qualitative data analysis (Strauss, 1987), we organized school information, observation data, interview data, and our subjective insights about the schools into distinct thematic categories. We continuously compared newly gathered information with the categories we had developed earlier. This process helped us clarify and refine our categories, eliminate categories that lacked support from information we gathered, and develop new categories as they surfaced from the data. From this process, which was used throughout all site visits, a number of themes that were shared by all schools emerged. Because of space limitations, we are unable to report all of these themes in this book. Four themes that were particularly salient at each school are reported in Chapter 6. The themes that were salient for the teachers are reported in Chapter 7.

APPENDIX B *Criteria for Selecting Culturally Diverse Schools*

This checklist includes features that have been found to promote the achievement of all students, especially language-minority and traditionally marginalized students. The eight categories of features are

1. Students' languages and cultures
2. High academic expectations
3. School leadership
4. Staff development
5. Courses and programs (curriculum)
6. Counseling program
7. Parental involvement
8. School staff

(adapted from Lucas et al., 1990)

---

* Porter Troutman, Professor of Multicultural Education at the University of Nevada at Las Vegas, visited each school site with us. Dr. Troutman provided many important insights into each school and was helpful in making comparisons of the three schools. Hollibrook Elementary School was visited by Richard Powell, Jesus Garcia, and Porter Troutman. Brown Barge Middle School was visited by Richard Powell and Porter Troutman. Mark Keppel High School was visited by Richard Powell, Stanley Zehm, and Porter Troutman.

1. Value is placed on **students' languages and cultures** by
   1.1 Treating students as individuals, not as members of a group
   1.2 Learning about students' cultures
   1.3 Learning students' languages
   1.4 Hiring bilingual staff with similar cultural backgrounds to the students
   1.5 Encouraging students to develop their primary language skills
   1.6 Offering advanced as well as lower division content courses in the students' primary languages
   1.7 Instituting extracurricular activities that will attract minority students
   1.8 Acknowledging ethnic holidays and other appropriate celebrations
2. **High academic expectations** of all students, especially minority students, are made concrete by
   2.1 Hiring minority staff in leadership positions to act as role models
   2.2 Providing a special program to encourage and/or prepare minority high school students for college
   2.3 Offering advanced and honors bilingual/sheltered classes in content areas
   2.4 Making it possible for students to exit ESL programs quickly
   2.5 Challenging students in class and providing guidance to help them meet these challenges
   2.6 Providing counseling assistance (in the primary language if possible) to help students fill out college and scholarship forms (high schools)
   2.7 Recognizing students for doing well
   2.8 Working with minority parents to gain their support for helping their children do well (and for going to college)
3. **School leadership** makes the education of minority students a priority by
   3.1 Holding high expectations of minority students
   3.2 Demonstrating knowledge of instructional and curricular approaches to teaching minority students (especially language-minority students) and communicating this knowledge to staff
   3.3 Taking a strong leadership role in strengthening curriculum and instruction for all students
   3.4 Hiring teachers who are bilingual and/or trained in methods for teaching minority students
   3.5 Planning staff development activities that help teachers develop classroom strategies for meeting the social, cultural, and academic needs of all students
4. **Staff development** is explicitly designed to help teachers and other staff serve minority students more effectively. Schools and school districts
   4.1 Offer incentives and compensation so that school staff will take advantage of available staff development programs relative to cultural sensitivity
   4.2 Provide staff development for teachers and other school staff in
      4.2.1 Effective instructional approaches for teaching in culturally diverse classrooms (e.g., cooperative team learning, sheltered English, reading and writing in the content areas)
      4.2.2 Principles of second-language acquisition

4.2.3 Cultural backgrounds and experiences of students

4.2.4 Languages of students

4.2.5 Cross-cultural communication

4.2.6 Cross-cultural counseling

5. A variety of ***courses and programs*** for minority students is offered. These courses and programs

   5.1 Include courses in ESL and primary language instruction and bilingual and sheltered courses in content areas

   5.2 Ensure that course offerings for minority students do not limit their choices or trap them in low-level classes by offering advanced and basic courses taught through bilingual and sheltered English

   5.3 Keep class size small to maximize interaction with minority students

   5.4 Establish academic support programs that provide help to all students (especially to language minorities so that they can better make the transition from ESL and bilingual classes to mainstream classes)

   5.5 Include authors of books and/or activities that reflect the ethnic diversity of society

6. A ***counseling program*** gives special attention to language-minority students through counselors who

   6.1 Speak the students' languages and are of the same or similar cultural backgrounds

   6.2 Are informed about and encourage students to explore vocational education in various professions

   6.3 Believe in, emphasize, and monitor the academic success of minority students

7. ***Parental involvement*** of all students, especially minority students, is encouraged. Schools can provide and encourage

   7.1 Staff who can speak the parents' languages

   7.2 On-campus ESL classes for parents, where needed

   7.3 Regularly scheduled parents' activities/nights at school

   7.4 Parental involvement with counselors in planning students' schedules

   7.5 Telephone contacts with parents whose children are truant

   7.6 Flexible opportunities for parents to meet with teachers and administrators

8. ***School staff*** share a strong commitment to empower minority students through education. This commitment is made concrete through staff who

   8.1 Give extra time to work with minority students, especially language-minority students

   8.2 Demonstrate willingness to incorporate innovative and nontraditional teaching methods for meeting the needs of ethnically diverse students

   8.3 Seek out training for working with minority groups and language-minority students

   8.4 Show willingness to go beyond regular job requirements to help minority groups

   8.5 Participate in community events related to minority activities

8.6 Participate in school decision making about student activities and classroom curriculum

8.7 Share a common vision of the school to educate all students with equal access to school curriculum, special programs, and other school activities

---

APPENDIX C   *Protocol for Interviewing Teachers*
Culturally Sensitive Instruction

1. What sensitivity do you have for teaching students who are ethnically diverse? How did you develop this sensitivity?

2. How can teachers develop a readiness for teaching in ethnically diverse classrooms, especially beginning teachers who have had limited experience with ethnic social groups other than their own?

3. What advice would you give a teacher, just starting out in a multicultural school, who has only limited, or possibly no, multiethnic and multicultural experiences inside or outside school?

4. Generally speaking, how can schools improve instruction for culturally/ethnically diverse schools?

5. We often hear the phrase, "Good teachers believe that all students are capable of learning, regardless of stanine groups and tracking." What does this statement mean to you?

6. What instructional strategies do you use and what personal qualities do you have that enable you to help all students achieve without causing them to lose a sense of personal and cultural identity?
   a. How did you develop these strategies?
   b. How did you develop these personal qualities?
   c. What suggestions do you have for other teachers, especially beginning teachers, to develop strategies and personal qualities that are effective in meeting the needs of ethnically diverse students?

7. Why should schools (and teachers) whose students are mostly monoethnic (e.g., mostly Black, mostly White, mostly Hispanic) develop culturally sensitive instruction, especially if the local community where students live is also monoethnic?

8. What is the greatest challenge in your teaching right now?

9. Your principal said that you are very good at meeting the needs of a diverse student population. Why do you think he or she said that?

Culturally Sensitive Classroom Curriculum

10. What is the nature of your classroom curriculum?
    a. What part(s) of your curriculum resembles the curriculum prescribed by the district?
    b. What part(s) of it have you created?
    c. How does your classroom curriculum align with the needs of your students, given their ethnic and cultural diversity?

11. On what do you base your classroom curricular decisions; that is, what has the greatest influence on the decisions you make about what and how to teach?

12. How much freedom do you have in selecting the instructional materials you now use?

13. Describe your classroom learning environment. In other words, if I looked into your classroom for the first time, what kind of classroom environment would I see?

14. What metaphor would you use for yourself as a teacher of ethnically diverse students? Why is this metaphor appropriate for describing your instruction?

15. Tell me what you know about the cultural and/or ethnic patterns of your students. For example, how are Hispanic students different in their social and academic needs from Black students? from Asian students? from White students? etc.

Personal Biography

16. What experiences comprised your formative years as a student?
    a. Elementary and secondary schools attended? ethnic diversity of schools?
    b. Best teachers? ethnic diversity of teachers?
    c. Peer groups? ethnic diversity of groups?
    d. Other?

17. What else have you done for a living other than teach, if anything? Explain.

18. What experiences have you had with minority and majority social groups, if any, outside school? How has this influenced your ability to interact with students in school?

19. What factors influenced your decision to become a teacher?

20. What is the relationship between your autobiography and your classroom instruction?
    a. What part(s) of your curriculum is prescribed by the district?
    b. What part(s) of it have you created?
    c. How does your classroom curriculum align with the needs of your students, given their ethnic and cultural diversity?

REFERENCES

Banks, J. (1994). *An introduction to multicultural education.* New York: Longman.

Beane, J. (1993). Problems and possibilities for an integrative curriculum. *Middle School Journal, 25*(1), 18–23.

Bogdan, R., & Biklen, S. (1992). *Qualitative research for education: An introduction to theory and methods.* Boston: Allyn & Bacon.

Brown Barge Middle School. (1993). *Middle school curriculum restructuring: A curriculum project of Brown Barge Middle School.* Pensacola, FL: Author.

Byrnes, D., & Cortez, D. (1992). Language diversity in the classroom. In D. Byrnes & G. Kiger (Eds.), *Common bonds: Anti-bias teaching in a diverse society* (pp. 71–85). Wheaton, MD: Association for Childhood Education International.

Carter, T., & Chatfield, M. (1986). Effective bilingual schools: Implications for policy and practice. *American Journal of Education, 95,* 200–232.

Cummins, J. (1986). Empowering minority students: A framework for intervention. *Harvard Educational Review, 56*(1), 18–36.

Doll, W. (1993). *A post-modern perspective on curriculum.* New York: Teachers College Press.

Eckert, P. (1989). *Jocks and burnouts: Social categories and identity in the high school.* New York: Teachers College Press.

Erickson, F. (1984). School literacy, reasoning, and civility: An anthropologist's perspective. *Review of Educational Research, 54*(4), 525–546.

Ernst, G., Statzner, E., & Trueba, H. T. (Eds.). (1994). *Anthropology and Education Quarterly, 25*(3).

Fine, M. (1991). *Framing dropouts: Notes on the politics of an urban public high school.* New York: SUNY Press.

Gadamer, H. (1975). *Truth and method.* New York: Seabury Press.

Garcia, J. (1993). A commentary on increasing minority faculty representation in schools of education. *Educational Forum, 57,* 420–429.

Garcia, J., & Pugh, S. (1992). Multicultural education in teacher preparation programs: A political or an educational concept? *Phi Delta Kappan, 74,* 214–219.

Gergen, K. (1991). *The saturated self: Dilemmas of identity in contemporary life.* New York: Basic Books.

Gibson, M. (1988). *Accommodation without assimilation: Sikh immigrants in an American high school.* Ithaca, NY: Cornell University Press.

Glaser, B., & Strauss, A. (1967). *The discovery of grounded theory: Strategies for qualitative research.* Chicago: Aldine.

Greenbaum, W. (1974). America in search of a new ideal: An essay on the rise of pluralism. *Harvard Educational Review, 44*(3), 411–440.

Hannan, B. (1982). The multicultural school: Or schools in search of their culture. In G. Dow (Ed.), *Teacher learning* (pp. 79–110). Boston: Routledge & Kegan Paul.

Hollins, E. R., & Spencer, K. (1990). Restructuring schools for cultural inclusion: Changing the schooling process for African American youngsters. *Journal of Education, 17*(2), 89–100.

Hollins, R. (1990). Debunking the myth of a monolithic White American culture: Or, moving toward cultural inclusion. *American Behavioral Scientist, 34*(2), 201–209.

Horton, J. (1992). The politics of diversity in Monterey Park, California. In L. Lamphere (Ed.), *Structuring diversity: Ethnographic perspectives on the new immigration* (pp. 215–245). Chicago: University of Chicago Press.

Howard, G. (1993). Whites in multicultural education: Rethinking our role. *Phi Delta Kappan, 75,* 36–41.

Kalantzis, M., Cope, B., Noble, G., & Poynting, S. (1990). *Cultures of schooling: Pedagogies for cultural difference and social access.* London: Falmer Press.

Kleifgen, J-A. (1988). Learning from student teachers, cross-cultural communicative failures. *Anthropology and Education Quarterly, 19,* 218–234.

Kliebard, H. (1987). *The struggle for the American curriculum 1893–1958.* New York: Routledge & Kegan Paul.

LeCompte, M., & Preissle, J. (1993). *Ethnography and qualitative design in educational research* (2nd ed.). New York: Academic Press.

Levin, H. M. (1987). New schools for disadvantaged students. In Chief State School Officers (Eds.), *School success for students at risk* (pp. 209–225). Orlando, FL: Harcourt Brace Jovanovich.

Lincoln, Y., & Guba, E. (1985). *Naturalistic inquiry.* Newbury Park, CA: Sage.

Lucas, T., Henze, R., & Donato, R. (1990). Promoting the success of Latino language-minority students: An exploratory study of six high schools. *Harvard Educational Review, 60*(3), 315–340.

McCarthy, J., & Still, S. (1993). Hollibrook Accelerated Elementary School. In J. Murphy & P. Hollinger (Eds.), *Restructuring schools: Learning from ongoing efforts.* Newbury Park, CA: Corwin Press.

National Council for Social Studies. (1992). Curriculum guidelines for multicultural education. *Social Education, 56,* 274–294.

Oakley, A. (1981). Interviewing women: A contradiction in terms. In H. Roberts (Ed.), *Doing feminist research* (pp. 30–61). London: Routledge.

Pallas, A., Natriello, G., & McDill, E. (1989). The changing nature of the disadvantaged population: Current dimensions and future trends. *Educational Researcher, 18*(5), 16–22.

Paquette, J. (1991). *Social purpose and schooling: Alternatives, agendas, and issues.* London: Falmer Press.

Patthey-Chavez, G. (1993). High school as an arena for cultural conflict and acculturation for Latino Angelinos. *Anthropology and Education Quarterly, 24*(1), 33–60.

Stedman, L. (1987). It's time we changed the effective schools formula. *Phi Delta Kappan, 69,* 215–224.

Strauss, A. (1987). *Qualitative analysis for social scientists.* New York: Cambridge University Press.

Strommen, E., & Lincoln, B. (1992). Constructivism, technology, and the future of classroom learning. *Education and Urban Society, 24*(4), 466–476.

Suarez-Orozco, M. (1987). "Becoming somebody": Central American immigrants in U.S. inner-city schools. *Anthropology and Education Quarterly, 18,* 287–299.

Trueba, H. (1989). *Raising silent voices: Educating the linguistic minorities for the 21st century.* New York: Newbury House.

Trueba, H., Jacobs, L., & Kilton, E. (1990). *Cultural conflict and adaptation: The case of Hmong children in American society.* London: Falmer Press.

Villegas, A-M. (1988). School failure and cultural mismatch: Another view. *Urban Review, 20*(4), 253–265.

Vogt, L., Jordan, C., & Tharp, R. (1987). Explaining school failure, producing school success: Two cases. *Anthropology and Education Quarterly, 18,* 276–286.

Chapter 7[1]

Discovering the Strategies of Effective Teachers

One of the first things I tell my class when I introduce myself is, "I'm Ms. Castro, and I'm a history teacher, and I was born in Costa Rica." I tell them all this flat out. I'm proud of that. By telling the kids in my class all this, I give them the message that it's OK to be part of your culture. You don't have to lose yourself into this melting pot thing. (Gissella Castro, Mark Keppel High School, 1993)[2]

The popular notion that a teacher must be from the same culture as his or her students in order to successfully navigate within and appreciate that culture is, to put it baldly, wrong. (Wigginton, 1992, p. 62)

Gissella Castro (see quote above) is a history teacher at Mark Keppel High School (MKHS) in Alhambra, California (see Chapter 6). MKHS has a high percentage of Asian Students (61 %) and a moderately high percentage of Hispanic students (31 %). So, Gissella Castro, who is a bilingual Latin from Costa Rica, teaches primarily Asian and Hispanic students. Quite obviously, these students represent cultural backgrounds different from Gissella's, although Hispanic and Latino cultures share the same language. Yet, Gissella navigates successfully within all of her students' cultures. Ask Rudy Chavez, the principal of MKHS; or Linda Mariyott, the assistant principal for instruction at the school; or any other colleagues of Gissella, and they'll tell you, just as they told us, that she is an outstanding teacher who knows how to reach all of her students personally and academically.

This chapter is about Gissella Castro and three other teachers who move comfortably and capably among the many cultures of their students. The teachers described in this chapter use the cultural backgrounds of their students to enrich their daily teaching practice. The purposes for describing these teachers are to help you

- develop an appreciation for teacher effectiveness in culturally diverse classrooms
- develop a fuller understanding of the strategies selected teachers use to successfully reach culturally diverse classrooms
- consider specific qualities that help selected teachers be effective with diverse learners
- understand the relationship between the cultural backgrounds of your students and effective classroom teaching

DISCOVERING THE QUALITIES OF EFFECTIVE MULTICULTURAL EDUCATORS

Teacher Effectiveness

Every teacher likes to think she or he is effective in some special way. In fact, thinking about yourself as an effective teacher, as reaching students in important ways, is the fuel that keeps you going in the classroom day after day. Few topics in education, however, are more debatable than "effectiveness" as it relates to teaching diverse learners. For example, some educators equate teacher (and school) effectiveness with increased gains in test scores. Other educators equate teacher effectiveness with sustained meaningful relationships between teachers and students in the classroom. In reality, so many factors must be considered when defining effectiveness that most educators realize this concept cannot be reduced to only a set of test scores or to only personal relationships in the classroom.

What is teacher effectiveness? And how do you know when you are effectively reaching all of your students, especially when so many of them have different cultural backgrounds?[3] Answering these questions with simple, straightforward answers just isn't possible.[4] What is possible, however, is to learn about effectiveness by studying the actual skills, strategies, thoughts, perspectives, and behaviors of teachers who are deemed effective by their peers and supervisors. With each effective teacher you observe and with each effective teacher you talk with, you become more knowledgeable about how to successfully reach diverse learners. Studying these kinds of teachers, as we did for this chapter, helps you develop a practical understanding of how to best reach diverse learners. As you build this understanding, your expertise for reaching these students grows and your standards for teaching in culturally diverse classrooms grow.

Visions of the Possible

The four teachers described in this chapter are, by selected standards, successful in helping most of their students meet their personal and academic needs. Three of the teachers were teaching in schools discussed in Chapter 6. A fourth teacher, who was in a longitudinal study on teacher development that one of us (Powell) conducted, was selected because of her demonstrated ability to create culturally relevant instruction.

The teachers we studied are

Karen Donathen
Hollibrook Elementary School (HES)
Houston, Texas

Linda Fussell
Brown Barge Middle School (BBMS)
Pensacola, Florida

Gissella Castro
Mark Keppel High School (MKHS)
Alhambra, California

Joanie Phillips
Las Vegas High School (LVHS)[5]
Las Vegas, Nevada

Selecting the Teachers.   The approach we used to identify successful teachers was to rely on the expert opinions of school administrators.[6] We asked the principal in each school to identify a teacher in the school who was particularly effective at meeting the needs of all students.[7] We said we wanted to study a teacher who very clearly exhibited these five qualities:

1. Demonstrates keen sensitivity for the cultural backgrounds of students
2. Motivates students from all cultural groups
3. Uses culturally relevant instructional activities
4. Creates a culturally relevant classroom curriculum
5. Uses instructional strategies that engage all students in meaningful learning

We mentioned to the principals that although several teachers at their schools may have these qualities, we could study only one teacher who is clearly superior in all five qualities.[8] The teachers listed above were among the immediate first choices of the principals. A fourth teacher, Joanie Phillips, was also invited to be part of this project, as noted above.[9] During this study, Joanie demonstrated continuously the five qualities listed above.

Visiting the Teachers.   After teachers were identified, we contacted them to discuss our intentions and to seek their permission to study their teaching. All of the teachers gave us permission to visit their classrooms and to talk extensively with them about their teaching. Prior to visiting their classrooms, we developed questions that guided our case studies of the teachers:

1. What biographical factors of teachers contribute to their successful teaching of diverse learners?
2. What classroom strategies do teachers use to effectively reach diverse learners academically and personally?
3. What personal and professional qualities do teachers have that enable them to be culturally sensitive?
4. How do culturally sensitive teachers interact with students both inside and outside the classroom?

To find answers for these questions, we explored the teachers' beliefs and knowledge about teaching diverse learners and sought to understand their dispositions for interacting with students.[10] We also tried to understand how these dispositions were transformed into classroom instruction.

We spent 2 full days shadowing each teacher at school.[11] During this time, we observed their interactions with students in the classroom and reviewed their teaching materials. After school we conducted extensive interviews with each teacher. Each interview, which lasted 60 to 90 minutes, was taped and transcribed.[12] We also had numerous informal conversations with them throughout the 2-day site visits. And we observed the teachers during their after-school activities with students. To gain additional insights into the teachers' instruction, we talked with administrators, other teachers, and students.

Admittedly, the scope of these case studies is limited; in 2 days, only a glimpse of teachers' lives at school can be made. Yet, the multiple sources of information we gathered provided a somewhat comprehensive view of the unique qualities of their teaching. And the extensive interviews and conversations we had with each teacher helped us capture important parts of their classroom wisdom.

As we conducted each case study, common qualities among the teachers emerged. The particularly salient qualities for all teachers, which we call "instructional themes," are described below. Prior to this discussion, however, biographical sketches of the teachers are provided.

BIOGRAPHICAL SKETCHES

Because biography is such a powerful factor in the classroom lives of teachers,[13] we asked the teachers to tell us about their life experiences prior to becoming a teacher.

We were especially interested in learning about prior experiences they had both in-side and outside school with various cultural groups; we assumed that these expe-riences might help them be more sensitive to the cultural diversity in their class-rooms. Background information about the teachers' professional careers is shown in Table 7–1.

Karen Donathen

Karen Donathen, a music teacher who has taught school for 16 years, grew up with a family of educators. Her mother taught third grade for 33 years, and her aunt and grandmother were teachers. Karen feels a certain closeness with this educational heritage, which influ-enced her decision to enter teaching. Karen's formative years as a child were spent in a small Indiana town called North Liberty. Karen described her home town racially as "all White." She noted, "I had no contact with other cultures until I got to college. I went K–12 in all-White schools." At the private university she attended, she said, "There was a percentage of Black kids from Gary, Indiana, that I befriended. And that was the first experience with ethnic diver-sity I touched."

Karen began her teaching career in Indiana, but financial cutbacks in local schools soon after she began teaching caused her to look for teaching jobs in other parts of the country. Personnel recruiters from Houston schools offered Karen the chance to move there, and she accepted a position as a music teacher in the city. With only limited and brief multicultural ex-periences and with no formal multicultural education at the university or in her former school districts where she taught, Karen chose to enter the culturally diverse schools of Houston.

Although Karen has taught in upper, middle, and lower income bracket schools and has taught in schools that range from mostly all White to mostly all Hispanic, her very clear prefer-ence is to teach in schools like Hollibrook Elementary School (HES), where she now teaches, which has 86% Hispanic students. Karen noted, "I would never want to teach anywhere again except in this kind of situation."

Table 7–1 Features of selected teachers who are deemed successful in teaching diverse learners

Feature	Teacher			
	Karen Donathen	Linda Fussell	Gissella Castro	Joanie Phillips
Current Grades Taught	1–5	7–8	10–12	9–11
Past Grades Taught	6–12	9–12	7–8	6–8
Years Teaching	16	15	13	2
Teaching/Second Career	no	no	no	yes
Subjects Taught	music	history	history	English ESL
Settings Taught	suburban, urban	rural, suburban, urban	urban	urban
Positions Held	teacher	teacher, counselor	teacher	teacher

Linda Fussell

Linda Fussell teaches social studies at Brown Barge Middle School (BBMS) in Pensacola, Florida. Her thinking about student diversity, her beliefs about equitable learning, and her commitment to helping all students succeed are grounded partly in her childhood experiences growing up in Atlanta, Georgia. Her beliefs about teaching diverse learners have also developed during her 15 years in the classroom.

Linda's sensitivity for cultural and racial groups began at an early age. Her family moved to Atlanta when Linda was very young, and she completed her precollege schooling there. About her home in Atlanta, Linda noted,

> Where I lived in Atlanta in 1968 became a transitional neighborhood with Black and White persons. And my parents became involved in a dialogue group in the community with Black and White neighbors in an effort to find out about each other and to look for similarities. In these dialogue groups, I was able to see people of other races in the same position as my parents and my family. I learned that the goals of the families were similar: good education, comfortable lifestyle, career success. The Catholic high school I attended was totally integrated. I started high school in 1967, way before the court order to integrate the schools in Atlanta.

Linda's memories of that earlier part of her life also included watching Ku Klux Klan members in uniform handing out leaflets. And she recalls when Blacks in Atlanta were made to sit in the back of the city bus. Linda recalled, "I would sit down [on the bus] next to a Black person. But there were other kids, older kids, that would not sit down with Blacks. That never made sense to me."

Linda started teaching in a rural Southern community. In this first teaching job, Linda had to face the reality of student gender and racial discrimination at her school.

> One of the things I remember very explicitly from my early teaching . . . is the discrimination that the Black kids endured there. Such incredible discrimination! It was horrendous. And . . . the people in the Black community were so powerless. And the girls were powerless too.

Linda recalled that many of the young girls in that community went to work in the local factory immediately after graduating from high school and that they worked most of their lives there. Linda taught in this small community for 7 years.

For the next 3 years, Linda was a teacher and guidance counselor in Boone County, West Virginia. About this experience, Linda noted, "That was a real eye opener. I thought I had seen poverty before in Georgia, but I had never seen poverty like that. And it was White poverty."

Linda described her teaching as having a humanistic orientation, a likely function of being prepared to teach by the Center of Humanistic Education and Psychology of West Georgia College. She attended this college specifically so that she could be part of its humanistic center, which she described as nontraditional. According to Linda, not until her present teaching position at BBMS has she had the freedom to bring her well-developed humanistic skills for interacting with students to the classroom.

Gissella Castro

Gissella Castro has been teaching high school history at Mark Keppel High School (MKHS) in Alhambra, California, for 13 years. Her teaching career began at a junior high school in Los Angeles, where she taught social studies for 1 semester. She then accepted a teaching position at MKHS, where she is now teaching. Gissella described her teaching experiences this way:

> I taught in LA for a little over 1 semester at a junior high. Then the major cuts came with Proposition 13. And so I was the last in and the first out of that [junior high] school. I moved outside of the LA district, and I've been here [at MKHS] ever since.

Gissella arrived in the United States from Costa Rica with her parents when she was 9 years old. She learned English in the public schools of Los Angeles, and she now speaks both Spanish and English fluently. She noted, "When I was 9, I went through the travails of learning English and learning how to pronounce English words correctly."

Gissella described herself as "bicultural and biliterate," characteristics that she says "make me who I am." Gissella is proud of her Latino heritage, as suggested by the opening quote to this chapter and as suggested by the following comment:

> Some people say about themselves, "I'm color-blind. I'm seeing only the person." And that says to me that you are just negating who I am if you tell me that. If you tell me you don't see me as a Latina, then you aren't seeing who I am. Because a big part of what I am is being Latina.

Gissella can't recall ever being in monoethnic school or community environments. Her high school years were filled with cultural and ethnic diversity. She described her high school as being very culturally diverse.

> I had Black teachers, Asian teachers, Anglo teachers. All this diversity was a given part of school for me. I never thought of it as anything else. I never lived in a monoethnic environment. And the education I received was in the same vein. I guess I was at an impressionable young age when I was around this diversity. Now I'm very comfortable being around people whose culture and traditions are very different from mine. And now I acknowledge this cultural diversity in my classes [at MKHS].

Gissella doesn't think about multicultural education; indeed, she has had no formal training in it. Yet, she continuously infuses, smoothly and seemingly without effort, components of Latino, Anglo, Asian, and other cultures into her daily lessons.

Joanie Phillips

Joanie Phillips entered teaching as a second career later in life. Although Joanie was only in her second year as a teacher when this chapter was written, we discovered her views about classroom instruction, her wisdom for how to reach adolescents in the classroom, and her insight into cultural diversity to be extraordinary.

Prior to entering teaching, Joanie was a floral designer for 17 years in Alaska, Kansas, and Texas. Many years as a floral designer gave Joanie a disposition to be progressive in her teaching, to always try out new things, and most of all, to be creative with her lessons. She noted,

> As a floral designer, I always had to stay current on what was happening in the field. If you weren't constantly creating new floral designs, the competition next door would pass you by. As a florist, I was constantly moving forward with my work, always looking for new ways to be better. And that's the way I think teaching should be. It should be creative and inventive. That's how to engage kids in the content.

Joanie grew up in Anchorage, Alaska, where she attended a high school that she described as "mostly White." She recalls that her friends and peer groups at school were White and that she interacted with "only a few minorities." At home, however, Joanie became acquainted with other cultures. Her father was a church minister who had many visitors from other countries staying in their home. Joanie recalled,

> There were people in my home from other countries all the time. I remember one person who lived with us from Puerto Rico. I remember another person from Japan who lived with us for months. A whole group of Japanese students stayed with us for a week. And the Native Alaskans would come from the villages and visit our home all the time.

The ministry of Joanie's father also provided her with early opportunities to fill the role of teacher. She noted, "When I was 10 years old, I was taking care of children during church services. And by the time I was 12, I was teaching Bible clubs."

From an early age, then, Joanie has filled the role of teacher in church settings. These early experiences were just the beginning of what has become a life of service to her church. As part of these church activities, Joanie spends time with adolescents in detention centers. The hours she has spent with young persons in these centers has helped her develop strategies for understanding the special needs of adolescents and skills for communicating effectively with them.

SHARED THEMES OF TEACHERS' CLASSROOM INSTRUCTION

As we studied the teachers in their own schools, we compared and contrasted their cultural and biographical backgrounds, their beliefs about teaching, and ways they interacted with students. We looked for features of their teaching that put unique trademarks on their classrooms. We also wanted to identify features of their teaching that they shared, that somehow linked their classrooms together. These shared features, which we describe as themes below, provide insight into successful classroom strategies and beliefs for teaching diverse learners: reshaping traditional classroom curriculum, rethinking the role of teacher, and acquiring and using cultural sensitivity,

Reshaping Traditional School Curriculum

Traditional school curriculum, what Doll (1993) and Perkinson (1993) call a modern curriculum, assumes a specific form and uses a characteristic terminology. The elementary, middle, and high schools you attended most likely had a modern curriculum, especially if you heard teachers use phrases like "daily objectives," "cover the material," "we're behind and have to get caught up," and "we have to be on a specific chapter by the end of the grading period." An assumption that underlies comments like these is that students are in school to receive a specified body of knowledge that remains mostly constant over time. From this modern curriculum perspective, teachers are viewed as filling up students' "bucket-like minds by transmitting knowledge to them" (Perkinson, 1993, p. 3). The means to this end (filling up minds) is student mastery of content.[14] Students in effective schools, according to this model, demonstrate greater mastery of content than students in less effective schools.

Although the four teachers we observed were very concerned about engaging students in the content, their teaching strategies for doing this differed significantly from the idea of filling up students' minds with prescribed information. They reshaped the curriculum of their school districts to meet the needs of students more appropriately. In the classrooms of Linda Fussell and Karen Donathen, the classroom curriculum was re-created altogether. One of the processes that all teachers used to do this is what McNeil (1981) calls the social negotiation of classroom curriculum.[15]

This kind of negotiation occurs when teachers and students together determine what content will be taught and how it will be presented. Negotiations between teachers and students are not always explicit and verbal, but they most often occur when students and teachers develop a gradual accrued awareness of each other. Gissella Castro, for example, who teaches in a tracked high school, had different classroom curriculum activities for lower level and higher level students; the activities were based on her awareness of these students' needs and learning potential. Such a basis reflects an implicit negotiation of classroom curriculum and related activities.

For Linda Fussell at BBMS, social negotiations of content with students have led to a culturally responsive classroom curriculum in which students' personal, academic, and cultural needs are met. To develop this kind of classroom curriculum, Linda has moved away almost entirely from the modern form of curriculum described above. The nontraditional approach to teaching at BBMS allows her to do this. Linda admitted that BBMS can be a stressful school for teachers who prefer the traditional model of schooling, in which teachers view themselves as content specialists and content is determined irrespective of student needs (without curriculum negotiations). Linda reported,

> This school is a very stressful place for teachers who worry that they're not teaching content. Because they are most comfortable when they are within the structure of the content, I feel that people who won't work well at this school are just afraid to see themselves from another teacher perspective. They're afraid to give up their traditional roles. But those roles won't work anymore, especially here.

Joanie's description of her social negotiations with students about classroom curriculum was similar to Linda's. And Joanie, like Linda, was able to distinguish between the nature of some of her classroom curricula, which put students first, and the nature of her colleagues' classroom curricula, which put content first. Using the metaphor of farmer and musician, Joanie noted,

> I love my students like a farmer loves the field, like a musician loves the melody. I don't see the content I teach as the field. You know how a farmer loves the land, and the farmer says, "I've worked *with* nature to produce something valuable." I know teachers who feel that way about the subject matter. But I feel that way about the kids. And musicians don't love their instruments as much as the music, as the sound. But some teachers are in love with the instrument and not the music. The music is what happens with the kids. The music is why I teach.

For Karen Donathen, social negotiations over classroom curriculum occur not just with whole classrooms of students but also spontaneously with individual students throughout each day. Consequently, her curriculum is frequently molded to the needs of each student. She noted,

> A boy in one of my third-grade classes cannot read. He has a learning disability, and he doesn't read English or Spanish. He doesn't recognize numbers either, but he is very oral. I knew that if I could go through the musical rhythms with him, he would remember them. And he did every time.

As teachers reshaped their classroom curriculum, then, they demonstrated a willing disposition in several key areas:

- They reshaped traditional curricula to fit the personal, cultural, and academic needs of students.
- They negotiated classroom curriculum with students to put students first and content second.
- They changed classroom curriculum on the basis of implicit and explicit negotiations with students.
- They explored students' needs in order to make these needs central to their curriculum.

These willing dispositions, however, required teachers to rethink their role as a teacher, to view themselves as facilitators, guides, and risk takers.

Rethinking the Role of Teacher

The view that teachers had of themselves came partly from their life experiences and partly from their teaching experiences. None of the teachers saw themselves as filling traditional classroom roles, such as subject matter expert, sage, or authority. And none of them considered themselves to be "in charge" of students. Rather, they saw themselves as facilitating students in the learning process.

Gissella Castro viewed herself as a "mentor-friend" to her students. She grounded this view in her cultural heritage as a Latina. She reported,

I'm very academic in my classroom. I encourage my students academically, but I also see myself as a mentor-friend to them. And maybe I have this role because I teach in high school. But I never really accepted the American view of a rebellious [adolescent] that is between adulthood and childhood and that has to be held in with a tight rein. That's not the Latino view. We don't even have a concept of teenager. And so I'm a mentor-friend from that basis, that my students are more adult than anything else.

Linda Fussell, at BBMS, saw herself as a "facilitator" of student learning. She related this to being a humanistic educator. Linda also suggested that the curriculum structure of BBMS requires teachers to be facilitators of student learning, rather than authorities of content knowledge. She noted,

Education should be humanistically oriented. That means being teacher as facilitator and empowering kids. What is important, particularly at this school, is that teachers have to learn to be facilitators and share in the learning with kids. Teachers can't be afraid to come down from that authoritarian sphere. They sometimes feel as though they have to be authoritarian because they don't know how to maintain order and control through learning. We need to help guide students. For ourselves as teachers, we just have to quit thinking we're the most important thing around here. And that's what many teachers think.

Similar views of self as teacher were expressed by Joanie and Karen. To fill these alternative teacher roles in the classroom (e.g., mentor-friend, guide, facilitator, humanist), the teachers demonstrated a willingness to set themselves apart from other teachers, to become risk takers; this perspective was reflected in the words they used to describe their classroom instruction. Joanie saw herself as "a renegade" and expressed concern that she might become "like teachers who are more traditional." She asked herself these questions: Am I so arrogant that I think I'm right and they [traditional teachers] are wrong? Will I conform to their standards, fall into their mold, buy into their kind of instruction and their kind of thinking about students?

Similarly, Karen described herself in the classroom as "a risk taker." Karen also admitted that Roy Ford, the principal of Hollibrook Elementary School, gives her unlimited autonomy to create instruction and to be an instructional risk taker. She noted,

I have full reign of my classroom. I can do anything I want. The district does have a curriculum, but I've chosen not to use it. I don't stick with that curriculum in the least. But I try to use what I know the kids need.

For Linda Fussell, taking risks meant moving from traditional norms of classroom instruction to the leading edge, or to "the front," as expressed by Linda. She reported,

I like being out in front. I like being on the radical edge. While I've been afraid to take risks from time to time, I've always been glad I did. I think the benefits for students are so much greater when I take risks.

Being autonomous risk takers, these teachers were continuously trying out new instructional strategies and searching for relevant content; they avoided routine teaching, and they all believed that the prescribed curriculum was unable to meet the needs of their diverse student population. They were also continuously learning about students' cultural backgrounds and about culturally relevant ways to communicate with them. Karen and Joanie both had a high percentage of Hispanic and Latino students when we visited their classrooms, and they were learning Spanish to communicate more effectively with these students. Gissella Castro, who speaks Spanish and English fluently, had learned many Chinese phrases to communicate better with the Asian students she taught.

As these teachers reconsidered their relationships with diverse learners, they demonstrated a willingness to rethink the role of teacher. Through this process, the teachers

- gave up the traditional role of teacher as content specialists
- became facilitators and guides of student learning
- took instructional risks (reshaping the curriculum as they deemed necessary)
- became "cultural anthropologists," thus learning about the cultural realities of students

Acquiring and Using Cultural Sensitivity

Acquiring Cultural Sensitivity.   One reason that teachers saw themselves as different (e.g., facilitators) from their more traditional colleagues (e.g., content authorities), perhaps the same reason they were willing to take risks in their classrooms in order to meet the needs of all students, was the sensitivity they acquired for students' cultural backgrounds. For each teacher we studied, classroom decision making was based, at least in part, on students' cultural backgrounds. The instructional risks these teachers took affirmed their strong belief that traditional, content-centered curriculum (i.e., a prescribed set of knowledge and skills reflective of one cultural value system) was no longer effective for classrooms of diverse learners.

An obvious means for acquiring cultural sensitivity for students is knowing about their cultural backgrounds and knowing how these backgrounds influence classroom teaching. Another means is learning the first language(s) of students, for communicating with them in ways that build trust and respect. Karen, who had only limited experience with diverse cultures prior to teaching in Houston, began acquiring her sensitivity for the many Hispanic students she taught by learning the Spanish language. She explained,

> When I first came here, I didn't have any experiences with minority students. I was an outsider, and I felt like an outsider with the kids. When I got into this teaching job, I took Spanish classes immediately. I knew that speaking Spanish would help me communicate better and build trust with the kids. Once I began speaking Spanish with my students, they got an understanding that I was making an attempt to communicate better with them.

As Karen continued teaching at HES, where a high percentage of the students are Hispanic and/or Latino, she soon realized that culturally sensitive teaching meant more than only learning the Spanish language. She realized that it meant affirming the cultural values and norms of her students. She noted,

> To teach in this kind of setting, you have to be extremely open minded and open hearted. You don't take your values and give them to students. You accept the whole cultural picture of the community.

One way that Joanie Phillips acquired cultural sensitivity for her students, especially Hispanic and Latino students, was by having them write about many aspects of their lives outside school. She admitted that when she started teaching, her sensitivity for students' cultural backgrounds was lacking. She noted,

> Can you say that you have to be culturally sensitive and that you have to be culturally aware when you begin teaching? I don't think so. I wasn't.

Joanie demonstrated a strong disposition to meet students' needs, to always put students first. In her first teaching job, she taught ESL to limited-English-proficient Hispanic and Latino students. She saw these students as having many personal and academic needs. Consequently, she spent many hours thinking about and creating new kinds of instruction for these students. She searched for literature of Mexican or Latino authors to use in her lessons. She had students continuously write about their lives outside school so that she could gain insights into their cultures. And Joanie visited students' homes so that she could build a fuller and more complete understanding of their home and family cultures. The following comment summarizes Joanie's views about developing cultural sensitivity and reflects her perspective of a culturally sensitive work environment. Like Karen Donathen, Joanie linked cultural sensitivity to language.

> The thing that's beautiful about this school is you can hear all different kinds of languages in the hall. That should be affirmed and encouraged. It seems to me that if you're a professional and the place you work is very multicultural, then you better make it your business to find out what [your students] are saying, to learn enough of their language. Or if you don't learn the language, then get to know the kids well enough so you know what they are up to regardless of what they are saying. So if you're going to be in this school, it would help you to see a little bit of what Hispanic culture is all about. Go to Hispanic special events outside school, go to Hispanic homes. Learn how children are treated in these homes.

Like Joanie, Gissella Castro linked cultural sensitivity to knowing students' cultural backgrounds and knowing what needs reside in these backgrounds. Gissella's cultural sensitivity is also rooted in her Latin heritage. She reported,

> A big part of what I am as a teacher is being Latino. And I think that's what I try to get across to my kids and how I interact with them. Their culture, their family, their traditions, are just as legitimate, are just as important, as anything else.

Gissella's Latin background has given her insight into how best to communicate with Latino students:

For the Spanish-speaking kids, the kids that come from a Latino background, the affective level has to be established first. And that means establishing respect with the kids immediately. "I respect you, you respect me. You cannot deny the dignity I have as a human being." And from that you can play your teacher role. Teachers who don't do this and who don't become familiar with student backgrounds get into problems.

Linda Fussell's sensitivity for students' cultural backgrounds is grounded in her experiences with White and Black students. She noted,

I think that White teachers often think they know what it takes for a Black child to succeed. I think a lot of times they try to make them White, to impress upon them the importance of things they know will make them successful by White standards, like correct grammar and certain behavior qualities. Maybe what these teachers need to be looking at is students' cultural learning styles, then work up lessons around these learning styles.

Using Cultural Sensitivity.   One way in which the teachers demonstrated cultural sensitivity was their tendency to be involved in culturally related positions of leadership at their schools. For example, Karen Donathen began an after-school program for students of all ages. The program, called After School Activities Program (ASAP), is an alternative place for students to go after school. ASAP provides a refuge for Hispanic students from the many street gangs in the immediate area. By seeking donations from the church that she attends, Karen was able to purchase various games, baseball equipment, and Ping Pong tables for ASAP. Karen and a group of teacher volunteers stay very late after school 3 days a week to manage the program.[16]

As another example of school leadership relative to cultural issues, Linda Fussell is the instructional leader of the American Tapestries Stream at BBMS. The Tapestries Stream is a 12-week unit, taught by an interdisciplinary team of four teachers, that many students at the school complete. The purpose of the Tapestries Stream is to engage students in readings, activities, field trips, and writing projects all related to ethnicity and race.

Joanie Phillips is the school sponsor for the Hispanic Club. In this role, she helps students plan special Hispanic-sponsored events, including dances and field trips. And Gissella Castro, at MKHS, is one of two teachers who planned, developed, and now teaches a course titled Conflict Resolution. The purpose of the course is to help students understand how personal and cultural characteristics may be misunderstood. Another purpose is to help students develop conflict mediation skills for resolving conflict in nonviolent ways.

A second way in which the teachers demonstrated cultural sensitivity was their reluctance to implement a curriculum they thought was culturally insensitive and irrelevant. Knowing the cultural backgrounds of their students, all teachers thought their school districts' prescribed curricula were not culturally relevant to students' lives and so disengaged students from meaningful learning. The comments by Joanie Phillips perhaps summarize this sentiment most clearly. Joanie was concerned about the literature that her department expected her to teach. The literature was extremely traditional, and Joanie described it as "the great literature that everyone in school always has to read." Joanie thought the literature alienated many of her minority students. She noted,

> I'm not saying that great literature is irrelevant. It's relevant in that it helps you to see the world in a broader way. But it's not relevant if it alienates you. And many of my students just don't connect with this literature. For my students, I try to choose literature that is culturally inclusive. You know that a lot of my students are Hispanic, and right now I have my kids reading selected chapters from Rodriguez's autobiography, *Always Running*. It's about gangs in LA. It's literary enough to justify reading it. And now students who are reading it are paying attention and reading like I've never seen them read before. And I know that I might be criticized harshly for using this literature, but it's worth the risk because it engages my students, it causes them to want to read.

Joanie thought books such as *Always Running* and other culturally relevant literature should help students connect with other forms of literature, including literature that is more traditional.

All four teachers diversified their classroom curricula despite their districts' established curricula; this action could be viewed as a highly subversive activity by officials of other schools. Signing a teacher contract is usually a commitment to teach the established curriculum, even if this means teaching to a standardized test or to an adopted textbook. The teachers described in this chapter, however, were able to restructure their curricula to fit students' cultural and personal needs without risking their employment security. As a teacher, you might not have this freedom. How, then, can you take instructional risks and support student creativity in the face of school and district expectations to teach an established curriculum if you know the curriculum is culturally insensitive and is disengaging some of your students from learning the content in a personally meaningful way? As schools continue to become more culturally diverse, more teachers will have to find a suitable answer to this question.

The third way in which teachers demonstrated cultural sensitivity for students was by extending their classrooms to the home and family cultures of students. All of the teachers acknowledged their students' home lives in various ways. They also acknowledged the profound influence that social and cultural factors outside school have on life in school. By doing this, the teachers and their students were connected, not just by their standard roles at school but also by family culture and related values. Karen Donathen thought she finally began reaching students when she made the extra effort to spend time with parents in their homes. She noted,

> Making the extra effort to really spend time with parents in their homes, getting to know them as families, helped me understand the students at school.

Joanie Phillips, like Karen, acknowledged the importance of moving beyond the classroom walls to create effective and meaningful classroom curriculum. She expressed frustration with some of her colleagues who, according to Joanie, limit their understanding of students, and consequently their instruction, to only their classrooms. Joanie noted,

> I wish that somehow I could *force* some teachers to take another look at some of their students, to see beyond their four classroom walls and beyond the things that are convenient for them. You can't make assumptions about students until you move beyond the classroom, until you see them in their culture. Why do so many teachers choose not to do this?

The cultural sensitivity that Karen, Linda, Joanie, and Gissella acquired and used was central to their teaching. Because of this cultural sensitivity, these teachers

- continuously explored students' cultural backgrounds and family lives
- understood how students' cultural backgrounds influenced classroom instruction
- linked student needs with student culture
- assumed various leadership positions in school that were related to learner diversity
- created and implemented alternative classroom curricula
- viewed their classrooms as an extension of students' cultural and family backgrounds

---

SUMMARY

The innovative teaching strategies of the teachers described in this chapter helped them meet the personal and academic needs of their diverse learners. The teachers also met their students' needs by engaging them in the content in culturally relevant ways; that is, the teachers connected students with the curriculum and made students' cultural backgrounds a real part of the school environment. Because of their demonstrated success, the qualities shared by the teachers in this chapter must be considered carefully as viable means for reaching diverse learners effectively in other school settings.

Perhaps what is most interesting about these teachers is how they aligned so closely with recent suggestions for culturally relevant teaching. Yet, none of them had formal educational experiences in teaching diverse learners (e.g., multicultural education courses in their teacher preparation programs). Their intuition for meeting students' needs and their commitment to putting students ahead of curriculum in their classroom decision making helped them learn experientially about the value of bringing together students' cultural backgrounds with their classroom instruction.

As classroom populations become increasingly diverse and as differing cultures with differing values for education meet and mingle inside schools, new instructional demands have come to the forefront of classroom teaching. One of these demands, which is central to this book, is the pressing need to rethink teaching, school curriculum, and classroom instruction in terms of multiple student cultures. The teachers described in this chapter provide one set of qualities for how this can be done.

RESEARCH TOPIC

Exploring Teaching Strategies for Diverse Learners

Problem Posing

The purpose of this research project is to help you explore successful teaching strategies used in culturally diverse classrooms. To conduct this research project, you may use the methods we used to conduct our case studies of Karen Donathen, Linda Fussell, Joanie Phillips, and Gissella Castro. And you may compare the shared qualities of these teachers (see Table 7–2) to the teaching strategies you discover during your project.

Note that the shared qualities listed in Table 7–2 were not determined prior to this study, but rather emerged as we made observations and as we examined the information we gathered from each teacher during our case studies. Because the qualities are specific to the four teachers we observed, you should use caution when trying to generalize them to all teachers in all classrooms. The themes are intended to be used as a basis for comparing the traits of the teacher(s) you observe with the traits of those teachers described in this chapter. Because teachers vary in the many

Table 7–2   Qualities of selected successful teachers of diverse learners

Curriculum Qualities

- reshape prescribed curriculum
- negotiate classroom curriculum with students
- consider students first in curriculum decision making
- change classroom curriculum based on implicit and explicit negotiations with students
- explore students' academic, cultural, and social needs and then make these needs central to classroom curriculum

Teacher Qualities

- give up the traditional role of teacher as content specialist
- become facilitator and guide of student learning
- take instructional risks in planning and implementing lessons
- become teacher as cultural anthropologist
- hold leadership positions in school that are related to learner diversity
- understand how students' cultural backgrounds influence classroom instruction

Cultural Qualities

- learn about students' cultural backgrounds and family lives
- link students' classroom needs with students' cultural backgrounds
- create and implement alternative classroom curriculum that is relevant to students' cultural backgrounds
- view classrooms as extensions of students' cultural and family backgrounds

ways they interact with diverse learners and because school contexts vary, you likely will identify qualities that were not part of the teaching we observed. Therefore, the list in Table 7–2 should not be used as an evaluation checklist, but rather as a basis for comparing and discussing teaching strategies demonstrated by individual teachers.

An interesting aspect of features in Table 7–2 is their high degree of alignment with the qualities of successful teachers of diverse learners reported elsewhere. Comparing your observations with other reports can provide yet another basis for helping you understand the activities of successful teachers. For example, reports developed by Delgado-Gaitan (1991); Foster (1993); Hollins (1982, 1993); Ladson-Billings (1990); McDiarmid, Kleinfeld, and Parrett (1988); Moll (1988); Trueba (1989); Wigginton (1991); Zeichner (1993), among others, can provide multiple sources for assessing the classroom teaching you are observing.

As we noted earlier in this chapter, four questions initially guided our case studies. You can use these questions to begin the study of your selected teacher(s):

1. What biographical factors of teachers contribute to their successful teaching of diverse learners?
2. What classroom strategies do teachers use to effectively reach diverse learners academically and personally?
3. What personal and professional qualities do teachers have that enable them to be culturally sensitive?
4. How do culturally sensitive teachers interact with students both inside and outside the classroom?

Exploration and Discovery

With the assistance of school administrators, university faculty, practicing teachers, or other persons, identify one or more teachers who are deemed effective in meeting the needs of all students academically and culturally. The qualities we used to identify the teachers described in this chapter are as follows:

1. They demonstrate keen sensitivity for the cultural backgrounds of students.
2. They motivate students from all cultural groups.
3. They use culturally sensitive instructional activities.
4. They create a culturally sensitive classroom curriculum.
5. They use instructional strategies that engages all students in meaningful learning.

You can use these qualities when asking for teacher recommendations for your project. After identifying and gaining permission to study a selected teacher, make observations of classroom teaching. Try to observe the teacher with students inside and outside the classroom and, if possible, attend after-school and/or extracurricular activities with the teacher. To explore the background of the teacher and how this background might be related to teaching diverse learners effectively, use the interview protocol in Appendix C in Chapter 6.

The questions in Table 7–3 can serve as another means to explore the teacher's classroom instruction for cultural relevancy. These questions were derived from the features shown in Table 7–2. They help you compare and contrast your observations with our observations of the successful teachers we studied.

Reflection and Modification

After you have gathered and examined various sources of information about the teacher you studied (e.g., observations, formal interviews, informal conversations, teaching materials), respond to the following questions. What did you discover about culturally relevant teaching? How is the teacher you studied similar to and different from the teachers we described in this chapter? What features of successful teaching, in addition to those in Table 7–2, did you discover about your teacher? List these features below.

1. _____

2. _____

3. _____

Table 7–3　Considerations for exploring successful teaching of diverse learners

Curriculum Considerations

In what ways, if any, has the teacher reshaped the prescribed curriculum to be culturally relevant to students?

How does the teacher negotiate classroom curriculum with students?

What changes has the teacher made in classroom curriculum on the basis of negotiations with students?

How does the teacher infuse students' needs into the classroom curriculum?

Teaching Considerations

In what ways does the teacher reflect the roles of teacher as facilitator and teacher as guide of student learning?

What kinds of risks does the teacher take, if any, to ensure that culturally relevant lessons are taught to students?

What understanding does the teacher have for how students' cultural backgrounds influence classroom instruction?

What instructional and/or extracurricular leadership positions does the teacher hold at school relative to student diversity?

Cultural Considerations

What strategies does the teacher use to learn about the cultural backgrounds of students?

What does the teacher know about students' cultural backgrounds and family lives?

How does the teacher ensure that students' cultural backgrounds will be part of the content taught to students?

In what way, if at all, does the teacher view her or his classroom as an extension of students' cultural and family backgrounds?

From studying the teachers in this chapter and from conducting your case study, what modifications have you made in your beliefs about successful teachers of diverse learners? Think about your own qualities as a teacher of diverse learners. What qualities do you have that are similar to those of the teachers described in this chapter and to those of the teacher you observed? What qualities do you have that are different from these teachers'?

To complete your case study, develop a report on the teacher you studied. Suggested sections for the report are (a) biographical sketch, (b) classroom curricular qualities, (c) teaching qualities, and (d) culturally sensitive qualities. In this report, speculate on the relationship between your teacher's biography and her or his classroom teaching. In a separate section of your report, compare your teacher with those we describe in this chapter. For a final section, describe how your views about culturally relevant teaching changed, if at all, during your study.

Description and Modification

Now that you have explored strategies for teaching diverse learners, what additional studies might you conduct that will help you develop a broader and more complete understanding of teacher effectiveness in culturally diverse classrooms? List and describe these studies below.

1. _____

2. _____

3. _____

NOTES

1. A version of this chapter was presented at the Annual Meeting of the American Educational Research Association, San Francisco, 1995.

2. Interview conducted with Gissella Castro at MKHS in December 1993.

3. Many reports discuss various dimensions of teacher effectiveness relative to teaching diverse learners. These reports are culture specific; that is, they are about effective teaching strategies for Black students or for Hispanic students. Consequently, deriving a generalizable definition for teacher effectiveness in culturally diverse classrooms is problematic. See Avery and Walker (1993); Foster (1993); Fuller and Ahler (1987); Hollins (1982, 1993); Kleifgen (1988); Ladson-Billings (1990); McDiarmid, Kleinfeld, and Parrett (1988); Moll (1988); Reed and Simmons (1991); Short (1992); Tippeconnic (1983); Trueba (1989); and Zeichner (1993).

4. Zeichner claims that the teacher education community knows very little about how prospective teachers develop cognitions, beliefs, and skills relative to teaching diverse learners. See Zeichner, K. (1993, April). *Educating teachers for cultural diversity.* Paper presented at the Annual Meeting of the American Educational Research Association, Atlanta.

5. During the school year that we studied the teachers, Las Vegas High School had 2,511 students. The composition of these students was 45.7% White, 31.9% Hispanic, 12.2% Black, 9.3% Asian, and 1% American Indian.

6. Because of the limited time we had at each school site (4 days), we were unable to observe a number of teachers and then purposively select one or two of them for our study. Therefore, we relied on the expert opinions of the school principals and assistant principals for the selection of teachers.

7. Because of limited time and resources, we were able to study closely only one teacher at each school.

8. See Hollins, E. (1982). The Marva Collins story revisited: Implications for regular classroom instruction. *Journal of Teacher Education, 33*(1), 37–40. We also mentioned to the principals that a higher level of student achievement, though very important, was not a primary factor in the selection of teachers. Ladson-Billings reported that achievement indicators such as test scores, when viewed alone, fail to reveal successful teachers of diverse learners. See Ladson-Billings, G. (1990). Like lightning in a bottle: Attempting to capture the pedagogical excellence of successful teachers of Black students. *Qualitative Studies in Education, 3*(4), 335–344.

9. We did not rely on the expert opinion of Joanie's administrator. In a brief conversation with the principal, however, we learned that one reason Joanie was invited to join the faculty at the school was her demonstrated sensitivity to student needs during her beginning year of teaching at a middle school in the same district.

10. See also McDiarmid, G., Kleinfeld, J., & Parrett, W. (1988). *The inventive mind: Portraits of rural Alaska teachers*. Fairbanks, AK: Center for Cross-Cultural Studies.

11. Limited resources prevented us from spending more than 2 days with the teachers. Because Joanie Phillips was part of a longer study in progress during the writing of this chapter, additional time was spent with her. In a phone conversation prior to our visits, we emphasized to the teachers that we wanted to observe them teach "typical" lessons. Realizing that teachers might feel obligated to enhance their teaching for the short period we planned to visit, we asked them to show us, as much as they possibly could, regular teaching days.

12. See Appendix C in Chapter 6 for the protocol we used to interview the teachers.

13. The influence of biography on classroom instruction has been clearly documented by, for example, Bullough, Knowles, and Crow (1991); Goodson and Walker (1991); Knowles (1992); and Powell (1992).

14. Ladson-Billings (1990) criticizes the modern form of curriculum as assimilationist; that is, by remaining constant over time as learner diversity increases, the curriculum becomes culturally irrelevant to many students. Consequently, all students, regardless of cultural background and learning styles, learn the same prescribed curriculum—usually the White mainstream curriculum.

15. See also Boomer, G., Lester, N., Onore, C., & Cook, J. (1992). *Negotiating the curriculum: Educating for the 21st century*. London: Falmer Press.

16. Four months after visiting Karen, we received this correspondence from her: "ASAP has nearly grown beyond our resources. More and more middle and high schoolers have joined us. Fortunately, we've been doing quite a few speaking engagements to various organizations, which have resulted in many adult volunteers to the program. The program's five baseball teams are now in full swing and will begin league play at the end of the month. ASAP will run five days a week (four hours each day) during the summer. The official 1993 crime statistics reveal a fifteen percent drop in gang activity in the Hollibrook neighborhood. We can't take all of the credit, but I think we can take a pretty big chunk of the credit anyway."

REFERENCES

Avery, P., & Walker, C. (1993). Prospective teachers' perceptions of ethnic and gender differences in academic achievement. *Journal of Teacher Education, 44*(1), 27–37.

Boomer, G., Lester, N., Onore, C., & Cook, J. (1992). *Negotiating the curriculum: Educating for the 21st century.* London: Falmer Press.

Bullough, R., Knowles, G., & Crow, N. (1991). *Emerging as a teacher.* London: Routledge.

Delgado-Gaitan, C. (1991). Involving parents in the schools: A process of empowerment. *American Journal of Education, 100*(1), 20–46.

Doll, W. (1993). *A post-modern perspective on curriculum.* New York: Teachers College Press.

Foster, M. (1993). Educating for competence in community and culture: Exploring the views of exemplary African-American teachers. *Urban Education, 27*(4), 370–394.

Fuller, M-L., & Ahler, J. (1987). Multicultural education and the monocultural student: A case study. *Action in Teacher Education, 9*(3), 33–40.

Goodson, I. F., & Walker, R. (1991). *Biography, identity, and schooling: Episodes in educational research.* New York: Falmer Press.

Hollins, E. R. (1982). The Marva Collins story revisited: Implications for regular classroom instruction. *Journal of Teacher Education, 33*(1), 37–40.

Hollins, E. R. (1993). Assessing teacher competence for diverse populations. *Theory Into Practice, 32*(2), 93–99.

Kleifgen, J-A. (1988). Learning from student teachers' cross-cultural communicative failures. *Anthropology and Education Quarterly, 19,* 218–234.

Knowles, J. G. (1992). Models for understanding preservice and beginning teachers' biographies: Illustrations from case studies. In I. Goodson (Ed.), *Studying teachers' lives* (pp. 99–152). New York: Teachers College Press.

Ladson-Billings, G. (1990). Like lightning in a bottle: Attempting to capture the pedagogical excellence of successful teachers of Black students. *Qualitative Studies in Education, 3*(4), 335–344.

McDiarmid, G. W., Kleinfeld, J., & Parrett, W. (1988). *The inventive mind: Portraits of rural Alaska teachers.* Fairbanks, AK: Center for Cross-Cultural Studies.

McNeil, L. (1981). Negotiating classroom knowledge: Beyond achievement and socialization. *Journal of Curriculum Studies, 13*(4), 313–328.

Moll, L. C. (1998). Some key issues in teaching Latino students. *Language Arts, 65*(5), 465–472.

Perkinson, H. (1993). *Teachers without goals, students without purposes.* New York: McGraw-Hill.

Powell, R. (1992). The influence of prior experiences on pedagogical constructs of traditional and nontraditional preservice teachers. *Teaching and Teacher Education, 8*(3), 225–238.

Reed, D., & Simon, D. (1991). Preparing teachers for urban schools: Suggestions from historically Black institutions. *Action in Teacher Education, 13*(2), 30–35.

Short, G. (1992). Responding to racism in prospective teachers. *Journal of Education for Teaching, 18*(2), 173–183.

Tippeconnic, J. W. (1983). Training teachers of American Indian students. *Peabody Journal of Education, 61*(1), 6–15.

Trueba, H. T. (1989). *Raising silent voices: Educating linguistic minorities for the 21st century.* New York: Newbury House.

Wigginton, E. (1991–1992). Culture begins at home. *Educational Leadership, 49,* 60–64.

Zeichner, K. (1993, April). *Educating teachers for cultural diversity.* Paper presented at the Annual Meeting of the American Educational Research Association, Atlanta.

Chapter 8

Discovering Beliefs About Cultural Diversity in Your Community, District, and School

How can . . . teachers understand their part in the cultural conflict affecting the instructional process?   (Trueba, Jacobs, & Kirton, 1990, p. 124)

There are balances and harmonies always shifting, always necessary to maintain.   (Silko, 1977, p. 130)

INTRODUCTION

One way you can understand your part in the cultural dynamics that affect the instructional processes in your classroom, the very same way you can understand the cultural dynamics that affect your school, is to look closely at the beliefs that your community, district, and school have about cultural diversity. Not only must you look at these beliefs, but, more important, you must also look carefully and critically at whose beliefs are transformed into curriculum and instruction. You must also consider how these beliefs are balanced and harmonized among various cultural groups attending school and examine how changing student demographics locally and nationally are requiring shifts in these beliefs in order to attain educational equity and excellence (Gay, 1990, 1993).

Earlier in this book, you explored your own beliefs about cultural diversity and pluralism as core values for education. This task helped you gain a perspective on the role you play in the cultural dynamics of your classroom learning environment. You also considered which of your beliefs about teaching, if any, might need restructuring, or shifting to follow Silko's (1977) reasoning above, if you are to maintain cultural harmony in your classroom and, consequently, an equitable learning environment. Now that you have considered your own beliefs in this chapter, you will consider the beliefs of educational leaders, including teachers. You will also examine the beliefs of a selected school and school district. You then will determine the extent to which these beliefs support cultural diversity as a core value and consider shifts in beliefs that may be needed before cultural diversity can become a core value for your school district and school.

Traditional patterns of behavior, particularly of belief and world outlook, change only under considerable social pressure (Spindler, 1963). Today, at a time when the world is experiencing ethnic cleansing atrocities, lifestyle conflicts, culture wars, sexual harassment, and discrimination of the aged, only one source of pressure can marshall the power to change the culture of communities and their schools into new patterns of belief wherein racism is not tolerated and cultural diversity is affirmed. This power is not necessarily found in antidiscrimination laws, which have been on the books for years without consistent enforcement. The only place you will find the power for changing people's beliefs about the core value of cultural diversity is in the hearts and minds of school and community leaders.

LEADERSHIP FOR CULTURAL DIVERSITY

Effective leaders possess the power to assist others in the creation of new norms, new standards, and new ways of behaving and believing in the communities and schools. In such places, courageous leaders have taken a stand to end all forms of discrimination in school. They have implemented community and school programs aimed at making cultural diversity a core value. Their leadership is paving the way for a new community understanding of what it means to be part of a pluralistic society.

ACTIVITY 8.1   Discovering Leadership for Cultural Diversity

Identify a school known to value cultural diversity. Talk with persons familiar with the school, including students, parents, teachers, administrators, community members, and business persons. Ask them to help you identify community and/or school leaders, the "movers and shakers" who consistently affirm their belief in cultural diversity as a core value of the community and its schools.[1] Write the names and roles of these persons below. You will use this list in Activity 8.2.

Leaders Who Support Cultural Diversity

Name   Role

_____   _____

_____   _____

_____   _____

ACTIONS OF COMMUNITY AND SCHOOL LEADERS

In school and community programs in which cultural diversity is a core value, you will likely find key individuals actively involved in planning for and implementing bold strategies for change. Such strategies may reflect the initiatives listed below for schools that build successful programs around the cultural and linguistic diversity of their students (Lucas, Henze, & Donato, 1990).

- Value is placed on the home languages and cultures students bring with them to school.
- Educators work with parents to maintain high expectations of culturally diverse students.
- School leaders make the education of language-minority students a priority.
- Ongoing staff development is provided to help teachers provide culturally sensitive instruction.
- A variety of support programs are provided to enable minority students to find academic success.
- Specialized counseling is provided for culturally diverse students to help them meet their academic and vocational needs.
- Parents are encouraged to become involved with community-school programs that support their children's education.
- School and community leaders are committed to empower minority students to become successfully involved in school-community activities.

In many ways, you as a teacher are a leader for students; indeed, you are a role model for learning, for establishing mutual respect, and for establishing the inherent goodness of every student. With this leadership responsibility comes a moral obligation to provide your students with equal access to learning regardless of their ethnicity, social class, home background, or other cultural features. Nieto (1992) suggests that when you provide students with such equal access, you strengthen your relationship with students while building their self-esteem and academic success. And when you provide all students with equal access to learning, you very likely will demonstrate many of the initiatives listed above.

As you read the following story, notice how the classroom teacher, whom we view as an instructional leader, uses many of the strategies listed above (Lucas et al., 1990). By using these strategies, the teacher reflects a strong belief in cultural diversity in the classroom.

A STORY OF CLASSROOM LEADERSHIP FOR CULTURAL DIVERSITY

Miguel Martinez, a prospective teacher, began his preservice field experience with a mixed sense of excitement and fright. He wasn't even sure whether he wanted to be a secondary teacher. He was frightened when he contemplated such formidable issues as "classroom discipline," "at-risk students," and "teacher burnout." Conscious of his fear, he was eager to get into the real life of classroom teaching.

Miguel's first field experience assignment was in a suburban middle school in a community known for its commitment to education. Most parents in the community had achieved their upward social mobility as a result of their successes in higher education. They wanted the same educational advantages for their children.

This initial field experience was designed by Miguel's teacher education program to assist him and other teacher education students to observe the critical elements of teaching, learning, and living in the middle school environment. During his first few observational periods, the principal shared with Miguel the "big picture" of their middle school. He emphasized the philosophy of their restructured middle school, which was, he was careful to point out, "grounded on experienced-based learning activities aimed at providing social, emotional, and academic success for all students."

Although Miguel was impressed with the middle school philosophy and its focus on success for all students, he sensed a gap in the school's philosophy. In the big picture described by the principal, he could find little to indicate that a respect for cultural diversity was a core value in the school's philosophy. The community in which the school was located was, he knew, a largely middle-class, White suburb. But he also knew that significant numbers of Black and Hispanic students were bused to the middle school each day.

Miguel was culturally sensitive and particularly proud of his Mexican heritage. The lack of a genuine emphasis on the core value of cultural diversity bothered him. He wanted to know, up front, whether his ability to operate as a bilingual, bicultural teacher would be perceived as making him more potentially effective with all students who would one day be assigned to him. He queried the principal.

"I really am impressed with your restructured middle school," Miguel addressed the principal, "but I am surprised that I have not seen where the different cultural backgrounds of your students fit into the big picture of your school as a core value."

The principal paused, collected his thoughts, and responded calmly, "We do things differently at this school, Mr. Martinez. We are color-blind. We treat all students alike, regardless of their ethnicity, gender, or religion. You'll be a more effective teacher if you act the same way." With that terse explanation, the principal gave Miguel his observation assignment and abruptly ended the "big picture" orientation.

During the next few days, Miguel became increasingly concerned about the principal's comment. In fact, he thought about withdrawing from the field experience altogether. He consulted his field experience coordinator from his teacher education program, and she also expressed concern about the principal's perspective. When Miguel asked the coordinator whether he could move to a school that supported a more realistic view of cultural diversity, she thought for a moment and then said, "You know, Miguel, you may be able to learn more about teaching and learning in this environment than you expect. This field experience is meant to give you the time and direction to observe the critical features of classroom life. You can learn some positive lessons even from situations that seem to be really negative. We would like all of our school leaders to be real supporters of cultural diversity and multicultural education. And we would like them to understand that having a culturally sensitive school environment means more than claiming that you and your faculty are color-blind. But, it has been my experience that, for some issues such as cultural diversity to get addressed in the school, the most effective kind of leadership is classroom leadership. Go to your classroom observation; you may be surprised to find that the teacher you observe is more culturally sensitive than the principal."

Fortunately for Miguel, this prediction is exactly what happened. As he observed Mrs. Walker's classroom teaching from his seat in the back of the room, Miguel realized that much more was involved in culturally sensitive instruction than colorful bulletin boards and banners. In Mrs. Walker's instruction, he witnessed a classroom teacher who was demonstrating what he interpreted to be culturally sensitive instruction, and she was doing this spontaneously and intuitively. Mrs. Walker was reading a children's book to her class, two thirds of whom were White and the remaining third equally divided among African American and Hispanic American students.

Miguel was surprised to find these sophisticated seventh graders entranced by the language, humor, and illustrations of a children's picture book. The book, *The Dragon Takes a Wife* (Myers, 1972), was not one known to Miguel, but as he listened to it, he, too, became caught up by the charm of the book. He wondered how Mrs. Walker would use it to teach important lessons about cultural diversity to all of her students.

The story revolved around how a Black fairy used her magical powers to help a dragon defeat the knight in battle, find his true love, and live happily ever after. The fairy used street language to give advice to the dragon. Miguel observed the Black students to see whether they might be uncomfortable with the nonstandard English as he had been made to feel as a limited-English-proficient junior high school student. He made a note to talk with Mrs. Walker about this practice.

Before she finished this engaging modern fairy tale, Mrs. Walker closed the book, broke the class quickly into six learning teams, and assigned a leader to each team. Mrs. Walker then said, "I want each group to come up with what you think the dragon's number one problem is. Second, I want your group to come up with the advice you would give the dragon to help him solve his problem if you were the fairy. Please select a recorder to write down your responses to these tasks and pick a reporter to present your ideas to the class. I'll give you about 10 minutes to do this."

Miguel was surprised by the seriousness with which these seventh graders undertook their tasks. Their group work was punctuated occasionally by outbursts of laughter, but Miguel soon realized this behavior was not the result of fooling around, but rather was humor that resulted from students brainstorming a real-life problem they found meaningful. As he observed the groups, he was struck by the fact that the African American and Hispanic American students were not sitting on the fringes of the group, excluded as he felt many times when he was in junior high school. Almost every one of the students in the class was actively involved in the exercises. He wondered how this could be happening. He made another note to discuss this with the teacher after class.

The final surprise came a few minutes later, when he listened to the students share the results of their teams' brainstorming. "We think the dragon's problem is that he is his own biggest enemy," Laronda reported to the class. "We think he should forget about the magic stuff and start believing in himself. We say, 'Harry, don't be afraid to be a dragon. You've got all the firepower and storming power you need to permanently slam the knight and take care of yourself. Go for it, Harry!'"

Miguel noticed that the class applauded the findings from this final report, without any cue from the teacher, just as they had expressed their genuine approval of all the team reports. The bell rang, and the students assembled their gear to head for their next class. "Mrs. Walker, you never finished the story," one of her students proclaimed, with obvious distress. "I will tomorrow," she quickly replied, "I will tomorrow, I promise!"

During the next few weeks, Miguel recorded his observations of Mrs. Walker's class. He also carefully transcribed the substance of their discussions. As you read the following three excerpts from Miguel's diary, notice how he not only learned the value of multicultural education from Mrs. Walker but also recognized its value in becoming an effective classroom leader.

EXCERPTS FROM MIGUEL'S OBSERVATION JOURNAL

Journal Entry: Wednesday, October 13th

Today was my first observation in a middle school classroom. Right now, I'm not really sure what I saw. I know I observed a super teacher, but I'm not sure about all the things that make her effective. She obviously cares about every one of her students. She does not appear to buy into the "color-blind" philosophy of her principal. Her classroom is decorated in a way I never remember seeing when I was in junior high. There are quotes, poems, and the like displayed on her classroom walls that represent the contributions of many different cultural groups.

I'm sorry Mrs. Walker didn't have time to talk with me after class this morning, but she promised to make time for me tomorrow. I'm anxious to ask her some questions about what she did in the class I observed today; I'm also interested in hearing the end of the story about Harry the dragon, and Mabel Mae the Black fairy.

Journal Entry: Wednesday, October 14th

Wow! What a terrific class I observed this morning! I guess I expected to see a teacher say, "Put away your work sheets, it's time for multicultural education." Not this teacher. Mrs. Walker weaves multicultural concepts, ideas, and values into almost everything she teaches. For example, after she finished the story, she led a class discussion on the "standards of English" usage. This blew my mind. I remember when I first entered American schools as a young Mexican adolescent being regularly put down by classmates and a few teachers because I did not speak "Standard English." I felt so ashamed that I coped by keeping my mouth shut most of the time. Needless to say, this strategy preserved me from further embarrassment, but it did not help me learn English.

Mrs. Walker pointed out that Mabel Mae used an informal standard of English that many African Americans speak at home. Her students also learned that all users of English use a variety of standards of English, from the very formal standards in the public forum, to the very informal in more private situations. I knew Mrs. Walker was my kind of teacher when she said, "Many people have been put down for the language they bring from their home cultures . . . African Americans for the Black dialects they invented at home . . . Hispanics for Spanish language they speak at home."

I was disappointed when Mrs. Walker approached me after class and apologized for not being able to see me again after class as she had promised. "I've got an important battle to fight this afternoon, and I want to be ready," she said without elaboration. She promised to make time for me after my next observation.

Journal Entry: Tuesday, October 20th

Mrs. Walker gives her class the opportunity to explore their own beliefs and values about who they are, about their cultural identities. She has one class rule that is emblazoned on a banner, NO SLAMS! She has the same high expectations for the personal, social, and academic behavior of all her students.

What I was especially surprised to observe was a genuine attitude of respect the students demonstrated for each other. I could especially see this in their cooperative learning groups, where they had to give and take to come up with a group consensus, as in the activity with Harry the dragon and Mabel Mae the Black fairy. Sometimes, when the team members don't agree, Mrs. Walker permits the disagreeing team member(s) to give a "minority report."

After class, Mrs. Walker invited me into the teachers' lounge for our promised get-together. We sat by ourselves in a quiet corner. Before I could ask her my set of questions, she began . . . "I'm sorry I had to postpone our last meeting, but I had to get ready for a big battle that's been brewing as we move from a teacher-centered junior high school to a student-centered middle school."

Mrs. Walker shared with me the list of major issues the faculty were battling over. The issue I was most interested in was making multicultural education not just a timeout for an occasional Cinco de Mayo or a Martin Luther King Day, but a regular, daily part of all of the middle school exploratory activities.

"But how can you hope to accomplish that at a school where a principal maintains a color-blind policy?" I asked her.

Mrs. Walker smiled a knowing kind of smile and hesitated before she responded. I could sense she was looking for words to talk about this situation. She said, "Well, some people still believe that effective education in culturally diverse settings is related to the color-blind idea, which means to see all students the same regardless of their ethnicity. But that perspective is changing. We know that every person is not the same. Every student represents some kind of culture. This might be ethnicity, religion, or even family background."

She then told me about what she had learned in a graduate leadership class she took last summer. "One powerful lesson I learned was that to make the revisions necessary to become an authentic middle school, we had to get political. Now, those of us who genuinely believe in cultural diversity as a core value in our school are beginning to use positive, healthy confrontation as a political tool to find the energy and resources to make multicultural education an everyday reality in our learning experiences for all students. I'm confident that we are winning."

"But why are *you* doing this, and not the principal?" I asked her. She paused, looked me right in the eye, and said, "Because I believe it is the right and just thing to do; because it is my moral duty to help each of my students find his or her unique identity as an individual and a descendant with a rich cultural heritage."

The bell rang, and Mrs. Walker jumped up and exclaimed, "See you tomorrow, Miguel. Gotta beat the kids into my room!"

ACTIVITY 8.2   Interview Educational Leaders

In the story above, Miguel learned how Mrs. Walker used one of the four leadership frames—the political frame, developed by Bolman and Deal (1990, 1993)—to discover the energy and resources she and her fellow teachers could use to establish and implement a vision for valuing cultural diversity in her classroom and school. Using this political frame, educational leaders, most especially teacher leaders, can guide communities and schools in the establishment of new ways of believing and acting about the value of cultural diversity to our nation.

Return now to the list of names you compiled in Activity 8.1. Ask two persons on your list for an interview about their views on cultural diversity. You may use the four questions below, which are structured around Bolman and Deal's four frames, as one basis for your interview.

1. What political strategies do local community and school leaders use to encourage needed social/educational change?
2. What issues are likely to be the most volatile and political that a community and school leader must address?
3. What strategies can community and school leaders use to involve constituents in healthy and positive political confrontation?
4. What is your best example of something beneficial that has resulted in this community from political action?

EXAMINING DISTRICT CULTURAL DIVERSITY POLICIES

Effective leaders, those who support cultural diversity as a core value, often develop official policies that give legal teeth to their convictions. Two sources of official policies you can use to help you examine your school district for the degree to which cultural diversity is a core value and an integral part of the educational endeavor are a school district's official mission statement and a school district's vision statement. In this section, we ask you to examine the official mission statement of the Spring Branch Independent School District in Texas, the district in which the Hollibrook Elementary School, discussed in Chapter 6, is located.

The purpose of looking at these documents is to find language that demonstrates whether or not cultural diversity is a genuine core value recognized and supported by the official policy makers of a school district. In the next section, you examine the degree to which this official district mission is translated into the vision statement of the Hollibrook staff and community.

The official mission statement and policies of local school districts, approved by an elected board of trustees, the official representatives of the local community members, provide schools with mandates on what must be included in the curriculum, textbooks, and instructional programs. If the elected members of the school board and the school administrators of a school district feel pressure from their constituents to make cultural diversity a core value, you will likely find evidence of this pressure in the official policies of the district.

ACTIVITY 8.3   Examining a School District Mission Statement

Carefully review the official mission statement of the Spring Branch (Texas) Independent School District (ISD) below.

Spring Branch ISD Mission Statement

Spring Branch Independent School District is dedicated to providing a quality education to meet the needs of a diverse student population in an environment of acceptance. All learners will be successfully prepared for their roles as responsible citizens in a global society.

Use the following questions to examine the Spring Branch mission statement.

1. Can you identify specific language in the mission statement that focuses on cultural diversity?
2. How effective is this mission statement in recognizing the belief in cultural diversity as a core value of the district/school?
3. How effective is this mission statement in identifying cultural diversity as a valuable resource for global understanding and commerce?
4. To what extent does this mission statement demonstrate acceptance of ethnic and linguistic diversity?
5. To what extent does this mission statement show a recognition of the importance of students' prior knowledge and background as key to academic and social success?

6. How effective is this mission statement in demonstrating an understanding of the importance of pride in cultural background to a healthy self-esteem?
7. To what degree does this mission statement emphasize the importance of knowing the historical contributions of ethnically diverse citizens?
8. Does this mission statement recognize and celebrate cultural diversity as an end in itself, as a significant part of our American immigrant heritage?
9. To what degree does this district policy recognize the need to enhance beliefs in cultural diversity?

Now that you have completed your analysis of the mission statement from the Spring Branch Independent School District, locate the official policies and mission statement that govern your school district's educational practices related to multicultural education, cultural pluralism, and excellence and equity in education. After you have collected these materials, use the nine questions above to evaluate the effectiveness of your district's mission and policy statements in affirming the belief in and support for multicultural education.

EXAMINING YOUR SCHOOL'S COMMITMENT TO CULTURAL DIVERSITY

You may encounter another set of political realities as you examine the commitment to cultural diversity of the school in which you are conducting your field experience. You may find no obvious commitment to cultural diversity at the district level but a firm belief in multicultural learning among the principal, teachers, and parents on the school level.

Now that you recognize the realities of school and district policies, you are ready to examine the commitment to the core value of cultural diversity of your own school. Many schools today have prepared policy statements, which might be called vision or mission statements, that identify what the staffs and parents of the schools consider essential. Locate this statement and any other available written material within your school that translates the intentions of the district mission and policies you identified above into evidence of ongoing school practice. For example, you may find that your school has developed a mission or vision statement that identifies its beliefs about the importance and place of cultural diversity in the school's curriculum.

ACTIVITY 8.4   Comparing Vision and Mission Statements

In this activity, you compare and contrast the focus on cultural diversity in the vision statement of Hollibrook Elementary School with the mission statement of its home district, the Spring Branch Independent School District (see above). The Hollibrook Elementary School vision statement demonstrates how this school elaborated on the district mission to include elements its staff and parents considered essential to effective learning in their school. As you read the vision statement, recognize how diligently the Hollibrook teachers, administrators, and parents worked to craft a statement that reflects their commitment to helping all students construct a solid understanding of and appreciation for ethnic, linguistic, and cultural diversity.

Hollibrook Elementary School Vision Statement

Hollibrook (Elementary) will strive to create an equal, equitable, and excellent people-centered institution where all cultures and languages are respected. We respect and fully expect to achieve biliteracy, creativity, independent thinking, giftedness, cooperative risk-taking, developmental learning, and heterogeneous grouping. We respect our teachers, colleagues, administration, and staff and fully expect to be the preferred employer in education, providing for a professional environment that recognizes the value of intellectual, physical, and spiritual balance. All children can learn when teachers are proactive researchers and continuous learners in an environment that supports change and enhances self-esteem. Realizing that parents are the first teachers, entrusting us with their best, we recognize that we must all be responsible for educating children in a cooperative effort.

As you compare the vision statement of Hollibrook Elementary School with the mission statement of its home district, check the statements for similarities and differences. Describe how and why they are different. Discuss with your peers the effectiveness of these statements as they regard cultural diversity. You will probably notice that differences between the statements are not in substance, but rather in level in specificity.

BEYOND THE RHETORIC: EXAMINING SCHOOL PRACTICES

As you completed the activities in this chapter, we hope that you found official policies and mission statements in your district and school that support the offering of multicultural learning experiences for all students. We also hope that, in your analyses of these policies, you found a genuine depth of commitment to the cultural diversity of students from all cultural groups.

The rhetoric of the official district and school policies may be just empty words if there is no corresponding evidence in the daily curricular experiences that students are presented with in their classrooms. Although the policies describing a district's or school's beliefs about cultural diversity are very important, how these policies are transformed into classroom practice for fostering student learning is more important. The ultimate test of school policies is found in the effectiveness of the learning experiences that a school intentionally selects to help all students build essential multicultural attitudes, knowledge, and skills. The ultimate test of school leadership is found in the willingness that leaders demonstrate for recognizing shifts in student demographics and then adjusting curriculum and instruction to maintain educational balance and harmony for all students.

NOTE

1. This process is how we identified the successful teachers in Chapter 7. Moreover, Ladson-Billings (1990) identified successful teachers by using a similar strategy.

REFERENCES

Bolman, L., & Deal, T. (1990). *Reframing organizations.* San Francisco: Jossey-Bass.

Bolman, L., & Deal, T. (1993). *The path to school leadership.* Newbury Park, CA: Corwin Press.

Gay, G. (1990). Achieving educational equality through curriculum desegregation. *Phi Delta Kappan, 72,* 62–62.

Gay, G. (1993). Ethnic minorities and educational equality. In J. Banks & C. M. Banks (Eds.), *Multicultural education: Issues and perspectives* (2nd ed., pp. 171–194). Needham Heights, MA: Allyn & Bacon.

Ladson-Billings, G. (1990). Like lightning in a bottle: Attempting to capture the pedagogical excellence of successful teachers of Black students. *Qualitative Studies in Education, 3*(4), 335–344.

Lucas, T., Henze, R., & Donato, R. (1990). Promoting the success of Latino language-minority students: An exploratory study of six high schools. *Harvard Educational Review, 60*(3), 315–340.

Myers, W. (1972). *The dragon takes a wife.* Indianapolis, IN: Bobbs-Merrill.

Nieto, S. (1992). *Affirming diversity: The sociopolitical context of multicultural education.* New York: Longman.

Silko, M. (1977). *Ceremony.* New York: Penguin Books.

Spindler, G. (1963). *Education and culture.* New York: Holt, Rinehart & Winston.

Trueba, H., Jacobs, L., & Kirton, E. (1990). *Cultural conflict and adaptation: The case of Hmong children in American society.* New York: Falmer Press.

Chapter 9

Assessing Learning in Culturally Diverse Learning Environments

Since all forms of assessment are inevitably culture bound, one can only attempt to ensure that those that are used are as culture fair as possible to all pupils. (Figueroa, 1992)

Schools need new measures of processes and outcomes in addition to achievement tests in order to monitor how their programs, teaching, and administrative practices affect the opportunities, experiences, achievements, attitudes, and social development of different groups of students. And, they need to use the information they collect to continue to improve their programs for effective students. (Epstein, 1988)

INTRODUCTION

One of the biggest challenges that many teachers face is the day-to-day assessment of their students' learning. One of the biggest challenges that most school administrators face is the overall assessment of whole student populations. These tasks might be easier if schools contained students who were essentially homogeneous —that is, if all students had the same potential for learning, the same interests, and similar family backgrounds. As we suggest in this book, however, the homogeneous classroom is a myth. Schools are filled with students who differ in their ethnicity, language competence, background knowledge, interest, religious beliefs, family support, and personal motivation for learning. These differences are further influenced by economic and gender differences that make assessment of their learning even more challenging.

Whether you are just beginning your teaching career or you already have several years of teaching experience, there is much you can learn in the areas of traditional and alternative assessment (Stiggins, 1991). In this chapter, however, we do not try to teach you everything you need to know about assessing student learning. Nor do we provide you with an exhaustive discussion of alternative assessment, which has now become an important part of schoolwide assessment of student learning. Rather, the purpose of this chapter is to help you consider various dimensions of the assessment controversy that surround contemporary, culturally diverse classrooms. To do this, we introduce you to concerns raised over traditional assessment strategies, particularly standardized testing. Borrowing from the work of Howard Gardner (1983), we discuss an alternative framework for assessing student learning. We provide an overview of alternative assessment strategies, including portfolios. As you read this chapter, keep in mind that alternative assessment is for every student, not just for those who historically have been labeled minority.

PURPOSES FOR ASSESSING LEARNING AND TEACHING

Traditional Assessment

Traditionally, educational assessment has had three overarching purposes. First, educational assessment has long been used to sort and sift students for placement in academic tracks or ability-level groups, reading groups, and college prep programs (Brooks & Brooks, 1993; Darder, 1993; Kozol, 1990; Mercado & Romero, 1993). Second, educational assessment has been used to provide accountability to political authorities and policy makers regarding the effectiveness of educational programs (Linn, 1990). Third, educational assessment has been used to provide parents, teachers, students, administrators, and school policy makers with information about the academic growth of students and to compare this growth with that of other students. The importance given to each of these purposes can differ from one community to another.

In recent years, these three traditional purposes have been vigorously challenged. These challenges have focused primarily on the negative effects that traditional standardized tests have had in turning student learning into the memorization of fragmented bits of facts that can be bubbled into multiple-choice tests.

Alternative Assessment and Learning Style Theory

In place of traditional assessment, new strategies (those called alternative assessment) are being increasingly implemented (Garcia & Pearson, 1994). Traditional assessment generally involves the use of paper-and-pencil tests and related methods, such as multiple-choice tests. In place of these more traditional assessment strategies, which are viewed by some educators as being educationally insensitive to some student groups who have traditionally been marginalized in schools, alternative assessment strategies are coming to the forefront of classroom teaching. Alternative assessment strategies are viewed as having the potential to acknowledge students' individuality and personal predispositions for learning (Au, 1993; Dunn, 1993; Dunn, Dunn, & Price, 1989; Gilbert & Gay, 1985; Hale-Benson, 1982; Nine-Curt, 1977; Shade, 1982; Worthen, 1993).

Much work remains to be done before we have a better understanding of how to appropriately and effectively assess student learning. A body of work has accrued, however, that supports learning style theory as a framework for both teaching and assessment of learning. Tailoring instruction to specific styles of learning, or so proponents of learning style theory claim, helps you develop instruction that is culturally sensitive. We agree with Zeichner (1993) that an overreliance on learning style theory, which tends to cause typification of whole groups of students, increases the chances for stereotyping students; thus, you generalize learning dispositions to whole cultural or ethnic student groups (e.g., the way a typical Latino student learns, the way a typical Black student learns) instead of acknowledge unique learning dispositions of individual students. Rather than rely too heavily on academic constructs such as learning style theory, Zeichner suggests that

> teachers need to be capable of . . . gaining information from their own students and the local community and learning how to transform it for pedagogical use. . . . The disposition and skill to conduct research on their own students and their students' families and communities is a necessary addition to the more general knowledge about human development and general cultural knowledge because, in the final analysis, it is each student's everyday life experiences, influenced in unique ways by factors such a social class, ethnicity, language, culture, and gender, that affect the academic and social development of students. (p. 23)

The central premises for this book align with Zeichner's comment that one must learn about each student's unique needs and dispositions, rather than risk an overreliance on "scientific" learning style theory that focuses mostly on student ethnicity, that purports to be generalizable to groups of students, and that increases the possibility of unnecessarily stereotyping students.[1] For an alternative discussion of learning style theory, see Grant and Sleeter (1989), who suggest that a teacher's common sense and intuition can be equally important as scientific learning style theory when assessing the learning of culturally diverse students. We suggest that you reference Grant and Sleeter's suggestions for exploring learning styles of students in a manner that avoids the stereotyping and categorizing inherent in generalizable learning style theories.

MULTIPLE INTELLIGENCE (MI) THEORY

A promising approach for assessing a fuller range of student abilities is Gardner's theory of multiple intelligences (Gardner, 1983, 1991).[2] Although Gardner does not address cultural differences directly in his theory of multiple intelligences, Nieto (1992) believes that Gardner's theory has important implications for making learning experiences more culturally compatible:

> According to [multiple intelligences] theory each human being is capable of several relatively independent forms of information processing and each of these is a specific "intelligence": logical-mathematical, linguistic (the two most emphasized in school success), musical, spatial, bodily kinesthetic, interpersonal, and intrapersonal. Intelligence is defined here as the ability to solve problems or develop products that are valued in a particular cultural setting. The salience of what may be cultural differences in intelligence becomes apparent. Gardner's research has demonstrated that individuals differ in the specific profile of intelligences that they exhibit. These differences may in effect be due to what is valued in their culture. The importance of this research lies in the fact that because a broader range of abilities is considered, the talents and abilities of individuals previously considered inferior or unexceptional may be brought to the surface. (p. 113)

In terms of MI theory, part of your success as a teacher depends on your ability to help students discover their individual intelligences and unique strengths. Gardner (1983) describes these intelligences, as Nieto notes above, as linguistic, musical, logical-mathematical, spatial, bodily-kinesthetic, and personal. Assessing these kinds of intelligences requires more than traditional paper-and-pencil tests; alternative strategies are needed that give you more effective tools for the ongoing assessment of student learning in your culturally diverse classrooms.*

An example of how Gardner's MI theory has been translated into curriculum and instruction is found at the Key School, a magnet elementary school in the Indianapolis, Indiana, school district.[3] Following the visionary leadership of Patricia Balanos, the school, which is based exclusively on Gardner's work, has an MI curriculum.[4] About the Key School, Gardner (1993) writes,

> One of the [Key school's] founding principles is the conviction that each child should have his or her multiple intelligences ("MI") stimulated each day. Thus, every student at the Key School participates on a regular basis in the activities of computing, music, and "bodily-kinesthetics," in addition to theme-centered curricula that embody the standard literacies. (p. 113)

---

* Further reading on Gardner's MI theory is found at the end of this chapter.

A salient feature of the MI curriculum at the Key School is student projects. These projects aren't like those you might think are routinely assigned as part of a regular curriculum, perhaps done with one or two visits to the school library and stiffly presented to a class of peers. These projects are theme based and engage students in concentrated effort on one topic for a 10-week period. These projects engage students in more than just logico-mathematical and linguistic intelligences; the projects are intended to allow students to demonstrate unique intelligences and abilities in the other areas of intelligence that Gardner describes.

Using primarily traditional strategies (e.g., paper-and-pencil tests, traditional book reports) for assessing student learning at the Key School is clearly inappropriate; that is, the MI curriculum at the school is designed to build on multiple intelligences. Assessment strategies aimed exclusively at measuring how much subject matter content a student has mastered will not determine growth and development in the intelligences of, for example, kinesthetics or music. The Key School staff make videotape portfolios of students and their individual projects. The staff also use a pupil progress report form based on the seven intelligences that Gardner describes. Research is being conducted at the Key School on appropriate ways to assess students' projects and related learning. One assessment matrix that Gardner reports (1993, pp. 114-116) includes five dimensions: (a) individual profile; (b) mastery of facts, skills, and concepts; (c) quality of work; (d) communication; and (e) reflection. Appendix A at the end of this chapter contains additional reading on the Key School in Indianapolis and on how the MI theory has been applied to this school.

Alternative assessment strategies like those being considered at the Key School help you gain a fuller view of unique student strengths, other than those traditionally assessed by standardized tests that focus mostly on students' mathematical and linguistic abilities. Another important feature of some alternative assessment strategies, such as videotape portfolios at the Key School, is that they avoid comparisons among students within and between schools. Rather, genuine alternative assessment strategies theoretically chart growth of each student's abilities over time, particularly related to unique strengths. As Nieto (1992) argues, these strengths are often culture-specific and provide students whose cultural backgrounds differ the opportunities to be successful in school in ways other than with strategies that have predominated school learning environments for most of this century. Notice, however, that your increased proficiency in alternative assessment of student learning in culturally diverse classrooms is not intended to make you more *tolerant* of minority students (Garcia & Pugh, 1992); rather, alternative assessment gives you the tools to provide your culturally diverse students the access to present and future learning in an intentional manner. Providing access to learning for all of your students is the primary purpose of your classroom assessments.

ACTIVITY 9.1   Classroom Assessment of Student Learning

As you interact with teachers and students at school and as you observe the classroom instruction of other teachers, notice the different ways assessment is used to determine the qualities of student learning. Try to determine how all students are assessed. Talk with a selected teacher about how he or she assesses student learning. Ask about the kinds of "intelligences" the teacher is assessing and compare this with Gardner's theory of multiple intelligences. Ask whether alternative assessment strategies are used or whether traditional assessment (e.g., paper-and-pencil tests, chapter tests) is the primary means for assessing learning. Compare and contrast what you find about assessment from your observations and teacher interview with how your own learning was assessed when you were a student in elementary, middle, and high school.

STANDARDIZED TESTING AND CULTURAL DIVERSITY

Many factors interfere with accurate assessment of learning in culturally diverse classrooms. Some of these factors are obvious, such as the culturally biased items on standardized tests. Significant national efforts are being made to reduce these forms of culture-biased assessment. In this section of the chapter, you consider the effects of standardized testing on culturally diverse students. To help you do this, we describe four aspects of standardized testing: (a) historical roots of standardized testing, (b) culture-bound nature of standardized assessments, (c) uses and misuses of standardized tests, and (d) strategies to minimize the negative effects of standardized testing on students.

Historical Roots of Standardized Testing

During World War I, Louis Terman, president of the American Psychological Association and professor of psychology at Stanford University, was asked by the government to prepare a written test to be administered to thousands of men who were being recruited for military service. The purpose of this test was to sort and sift the new recruits roughly into two categories: (a) those possessing the intelligence to be officers and (b) those with lower levels of intelligence to be the "dough boys," the ordinary foot soldiers. Terman had already been working on revising the intelligence test of Alfred Binet, whose test had been commissioned by the French government in 1904 to identify "mentally subnormal" students for placement in separate schools (Mercer, 1989). Following World War I, Terman and associates redoubled their efforts to refine and market the Stanford-Binet Intelligence Test and later the Stanford Achievement Test for use in the public schools.

The connection of these tests to Binet is important because Binet was most insistent that his test did not measure intelligence as a fixed entity, a claim that is antithetical to the very use of these tests today. To Louis Terman, H. H. Goddard, and the other American developers of standardized tests, however, the test was assumed to measure intelligence quantitatively, without any regard to the subject's experience, culture, age, or gender (Hakuta, 1986).

The second root of the American standardized test, the Alpha Test, also was developed by Terman for the government during World War I. Terman and associates are responsible for making the assessment of students' intelligence supposedly more "scientific" and "efficient." Because Terman initially developed the test for use by the

U.S. Army, the military culture can still be found in contemporary standardized tests. Recall your own experiences with standardized tests. You may have had a warm, supportive, caring fourth-grade teacher like Miss Fithian. On test day, however, her caring behavior was radically transformed when she administered the Test of Basic Skills or some other standardized test. She became stern-looking (like an officer). She barked commands (e.g., "Don't open the test book until I tell you to" [like a sergeant]). Like a company commander, she crisply and coldly read the directions, laced with more imperatives ("Don't . . .," "Open the test booklet now," "Begin," "STOP!"). Remnants of the Army Alpha Test continue to be found in many contemporary standardized tests. These remnants clearly inhibit the performance of limited-English-proficient students, immigrant students, and many students whose cultures provide them little experience in understanding and coping with this vestige of military culture.

The Culture-Bound Nature of Standardized Tests

In the opening quote of this chapter, Peter Figueroa (1992) asserted that all assessments are culture bound. Relative to standardized testing, this means test items that are intended to assess students' knowledge and skills reflect the standards of language and points of view of the test writers. "Content bias" is the technical descriptor for this culture-bound dimension of standardized tests. When students take a standardized test that reflects the vocabulary, topics, and life experiences typical of, for example, the White mainstream culture, the content bias of the test, which results from the implicit predominance of mainstream values and language in test items, interferes with accurate assessment of what students from other cultures know and are able to do relative to their own cultures.

Figure 9.1 contains an example of a culture-biased test item. A matching item similar to this appeared in a national standardized test. Students who moved to the United States from Cuba and Haiti may be unfairly penalized by this item because it does not accurately reflect their personal knowledge and home experience. Apples are not grown in the Caribbean, where children see their mothers cooking oranges and bananas in pots.

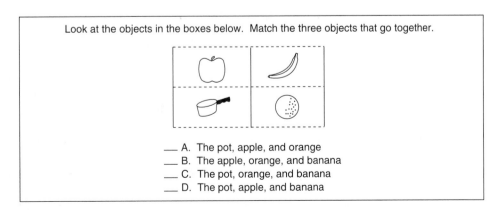

<figure>
Look at the objects in the boxes below. Match the three objects that go together.

___ A. The pot, apple, and orange
___ B. The apple, orange, and banana
___ C. The pot, orange, and banana
___ D. The pot, apple, and banana
</figure>

Figure 9–1 Culturally biased test item

The results of content-biased tests and, consequently, items like those in Figure 9–1 will not likely provide you with any information you can use to improve the learning of students. The results will not give useful diagnostic information about their respective levels of reading comprehension (Langer, 1987) or provide you with information you can use to assess your students' mathematical thinking and problem-solving abilities (Ginsburg & Allardice, 1984). Several attempts have been made to develop "culture free" standardized tests, with test items devoid of content bias. These laudable attempts have been roundly criticized as impossible to attain. Other test designers have attempted to build "culture fair" tests for which they claimed to have test items within the experience of students from all cultures. Culture-fair tests also failed to live up to their promise of providing a reliable assessment of the learning of students from all cultures. In the final analysis, we have come to realize that all tests are, indeed, culture bound.[5]

The use of standardized tests with students for whom English is not their first language gives unreliable and invalid results of student learning. The tests given to these students to determine their dominant language may meet the legal requirements for student eligibility and placement in bilingual and English as a Second Language (ESL) programs. However, these tests provide teachers with very little information regarding the linguistic and instructional needs of these students. According to Mercado and Romero (1993), "the major problem with assessment as it has evolved in bilingual education, is that it has responded to legal concerns and political pressures rather than to the real needs of students. . . . Traditional testing of both language proficiency and academic achievement has yielded very little information about bilingual students as learners" (p. 153).

The Uses and Misuses of Standardized Testing

Standardized testing traditionally serves two basic functions in the public schools: administrative functions and instructional functions. Administratively, tests are used regularly to determine whether a student is eligible for special services offered by the school through an entitlement program. For example, before students from migrant Mexican families can become eligible for bilingual services at school, they must complete a language dominance test to identify her or his primary language. Tests are also used to place students, however questionable this practice might be, in ability tracking, remedial programs, gifted programs, advance placement programs, and the like. Finally, the results of standardized tests are used to evaluate the overall effectiveness of educational programs and to compare student achievement in one school with student achievement in other schools.

Although standardized achievement is being challenged on social, cultural, and political grounds, it remains the predominant means of assessing student learning. A 1993 report from the U.S. General Accounting Office indicated that more than 80% of tests that school districts use are formal achievement tests (Garcia & Pearson, 1993). This finding means that the predominant form of student assessment used to measure the knowledge and skills that students acquire is some form of standardized testing.

Research on standardized testing clearly demonstrates the limitations of this type of assessment in evaluating the learning of culturally diverse students. Historically, the poor performance of Hispanic and African American students on the tests provides a quantifiable, though highly questionable, rationale for segregated schools. The continued use of these tests to identify a disproportionate number of minority students from regular classrooms for ability tracking is a de facto form of segregation. Schools continue to use test scores to justify the placement of large numbers of minority students in classrooms where they are often provided with a custodial form of instruction (keeping them in their seats, doing busy work that requires lower levels of thinking). In these kinds of learning environments, expectations for student academic achievement are drastically lowered. Students of color, low-income students, and students for whom English is a second language follow the textbooks rigidly and routinely in these low-track and remedial classrooms. They are constantly grilled and drilled with batteries of paper-and-pencil tests that keep the instructional focus on the lowest conceptual level. According to Garcia and Pearson, (1993), "since most of the tests used in these programs focus on discrete skills, low-income students tend to receive a fragmented, skills-based curriculum" (p. 354).

Indeed, the politics of testing remains intense. Most teachers are required to administer some form of standardized testing to their students, and these tests have very high stakes for both students and teachers. School districts continue to describe their success in terms of higher test scores, and those scores are often the result of much pressure on teachers to raise scores. So much importance has been placed on the results of student performance on standardized tests that high stakes have been attached to their local, state, and national use (Linn, 1990). When politicians make promises to reform education—for example, promising to make the performance of U.S. students in mathematics number one in the world by year 2000—the stakes attached to standardized testing in mathematics are inevitably raised. When school funding, for another example, is tied to student performance on a national standardized test, principals and teachers almost feel compelled to employ a curriculum tightly coupled to the test. This coupling is what is meant by "teaching to the test." Finally, when larger numbers of culturally diverse students, including students from low-income families, are in a particular school locale, you will more likely find a high percentage of teachers teaching to the test (Rothman, 1992).

To avoid the high-stakes consequences of test results of low-performing students, many school districts place more students into special education, the majority of whom are low-income students, students of color, and students for whom English is a second language. This practice allows schools to exclude these students from taking the standardized tests (see Garcia & Pearson, 1993, p. 355, for more information regarding this claim). The exclusion of large numbers of students from high-stakes assessment may be one explanation for the Lake Woebegone effect: All of the children are quantitatively above average. Although standardized tests are constructed to create a bell curve in which 50% of the students score above the national percentile ranking and 50% below, all 50 states report state average scores above the 50th percentile ranking. Interesting, to say the least!

Minimizing the Negative Effects of Standardized Testing

What can you as a teacher do to minimize the negative effects of standardized testing on your students? It is obvious that you will not be able on your own to eliminate standardized testing or to rid these tests of their inherent biases. However, you can begin a number of actions now to minimize the negative effects of standardized testing on culturally diverse students.

First, through reading and personal inquiry, you can learn more about assessing the learning of all of your students, especially students of color, low-income students, and students for whom English is a second language. Richard Stiggins (1991) has carried on a one-person campaign to help teachers learn more about assessment of learning. He adamantly believes that teachers must have more complete understanding of assessment if they are to make informed decisions regarding the learning needs of students, communicate achievement expectations to students, and organize classroom learning environments more effectively (see Stiggins, 1991, p. 8). Until you and your colleagues learn about the political dimensions of standardized assessment and until you become aware of their discriminatory effects on some student groups, you can expect that students will benefit little from the many tests to which they are subjected.

Second, you can help students take more responsibility for assessing their own learning. You can do this by helping them understand how they learn new concepts and recognize the obstacles that hinder their learning. Many students suffer test anxiety, which interferes with their readiness to do their best on a test. You can help them learn how to take tests. Many "testwiseness" packages are on the market; you can adapt your own lessons on effective test-taking strategies. Let's face it, we live in a testing society. Your students will not be able to go to college, serve in any branch of the Armed Forces, or get a job in the United States Postal Service unless they can pass a test. Test taking is a survival skill. Because there is nothing unethical or illegal about teaching test-taking skills, we encourage you to add relevant instruction in test-taking skills to your instructional repertoire.

Third, you can help parents become better informed about assessment issues. Many parents still have high levels of anxiety about testing, which they pass on to their children. Not being aware of alternative strategies for assessment, most parents maintain a strong belief in the validity of standardized tests as measures of their children's intelligence and academic achievements (Ohlhausen, Powell, & Reitz, 1994). In the section that follows, we describe selected alternative assessment strategies you can use to assess learning on levels that standardized testing is unable to do. Many of these strategies are based on teacher judgments of student performance. We cannot expect the parents of minority students to believe in the efficacy of these new assessments based on teacher judgments unless we communicate with parents and demonstrate to them how these assessments are more culturally fair, especially compared with standardized tests.

ALTERNATIVE ASSESSMENT STRATEGIES

Earlier in this chapter, we mentioned nontraditional forms of assessment that educators are finding useful for providing information about student learning. Various assessments that fall under this category are being called "alternative assessments"—that is, alternatives to formal standardized tests and to other paper-and-pencil tests that you may regularly be using (Worthen, 1993).

Characteristics of Alternative Assessments

Although alternative assessments come in many forms, they share many of the following characteristics:

- Encourage students to demonstrate authentic knowledge and skills they find personally valuable and worth knowing
- Provide rich cultural contexts that stimulate oral and written responses of students
- Focus on the big ideas related to real life, rather than bits and pieces of fragmented information
- Build on measuring the quality of what students can do; quality products and performances
- Actively involve students in assessing their own performances and those of their peers
- Use performance standards and criteria known by the student prior to the assessment
- Depend on the mature, culturally sensitive judgments of teachers and peer evaluators; require these judgments be translated into a scoring system
- Produce results that can be reported to and understood by students, parents, and taxpayers
- Affirm multiple ways that students learn
- Acknowledge learning as problem framing and problem finding
- Give control of student assessment to teachers and their expertise about student learning

Potential Benefits of Alternative Assessments

The characteristics of alternative assessment above give it the potential to provide you and your students with more useful, up-to-date, and culturally sensitive assessment information. Just as we have observed that all students learn in unique ways, the major advantage of alternative assessment is that it gives teachers a variety of assessment options to match more effectively with the variety of ways in which students learn. For example, when you use techniques for assessing students' oral fluency, you will find another way to build on the verbal strengths of many students who may not be ready to express themselves to the same degree in writing.

Another benefit of alternative assessment lies in the integrity this approach brings to teaching, learning, and assessment. The many forms of standardized testing require that instruction stop completely when testing begins. Alternative assessment, however, is inseparable from instruction. Instruction continues as you assess your students' learning. Because of this close connection of assessment with teaching and learning, Mercado and Romero (1993) recommend the use of alternative assessment with bilingual students. They contend that assessment must be viewed as an ongoing, dynamic, collaborative, and reciprocal process which is inseparable from teaching and learning. . . . Rather than being a "race to cover content," to "catch up," and to "perform" in English, as is often the case, teaching becomes a form of research—a journey into discovering how and what students are learning and the type of support they may need at any given time. (p. 158)

Garcia and Pearson (1993) identify another benefit of alternative assessments in encouraging teachers to build on and honor the cultural resources of their students (pp. 360–361). They describe the results of two studies involving Hawaiian and Native American children. Both studies demonstrate the benefits that students can derive when teachers adapt curriculum and instruction to reflect students' cultural resources and values and when teachers assess student learning with alternative assessment strategies.

Classroom Challenges to Alternative Assessment

Although alternative assessment can provide a more culture-fair assessment of student learning, we must draw your attention to three challenges they pose for your classroom. We share these with you, not to discourage you from using forms of alternative assessment in your classroom, but so that you will be prepared for these challenges whenever you implement alternative assessment practices in your classroom.

First, no critical mass of field research indicates the effectiveness of alternative assessment in providing for a more culture-fair evaluation of student learning. Garcia and Pearson (1993) remind us that "few, if any, researchers have specifically investigated the cultural bias of authentic classroom assessment of performance assessment" (p. 356). Moreover, critics of alternative assessment claim that this kind of assessment, in whatever form it takes, is fraught with subjectivity (Ohlhausen et al., 1994). The subjective judgments from culturally insensitive teachers have the potential for resulting in harsher impediments to the learning of culturally diverse students than those experienced from the cultural bias of standardized tests. Conversely, teachers who are unreasonably sensitive may inappropriately ease up on instruction and assessment measures, thus ensuring lower quality instruction.

A second limitation of the alternative assessment process can be foreseen in the complexity this process could bring to your classroom. To start and maintain an alternative assessment system requires considerable time. If you are to implement a sound system of alternative assessments, you must commit yourself to learning about alternative assessment tools and then select those that are most appropriate for your students.

After you begin to implement an alternative assessment system, you must examine its effectiveness. You will need to determine the cultural fairness of your strategies and make changes as needed. Notice also that your alternative assessment system will result in confusion if you try to make an alternative form of assessment fit a traditional, teacher-centered approach to instruction. Unless you are convinced that your classroom is a place where students of all cultural backgrounds can use their interests and strengths to become actively involved in exploring their world, in seeking solutions to real problems, and in the processes of discovering and using their authentic voices, you will experience a severe mismatch between your instructional and assessment practices.

Alternative Strategies for Monitoring Student Learning

For decades teachers have been using many alternative strategies for monitoring student learning. The following are brief descriptions of a few alternative assessment strategies we consider especially useful for assessing student learning in all classrooms. In the field activity that follows these descriptions, you search for classroom applications of these and other useful alternative assessment strategies.

Student Observation. Teachers have long used observation as a means of assessing student learning. Student observation, or "kid watching" as it has been called by Goodman (1985), is one key to effective, culture-fair assessments of student learning. Elementary teachers who work with one class for an entire academic year have an opportunity to refine their observational skills to collect information regarding student learning. Secondary teachers might be more challenged to use observations as a means to collect information about student learning. Instead of working closely with one class of 25 to 30 students all year in an elementary classroom, secondary teachers often have 100 to 150 students rotating through their classrooms during the 5 or 6 periods of a school day. Nevertheless, secondary teachers can use observation of their students as a very function of their job to learn about how their assessment strategies are working. Simple things like anecdotal records in the margins of your grade book are helpful when you must later make judgments about student learning.

You can use the information you get from observing students to assist all of them in meeting the same high standards of performance. Moreover, careful, systematic observations of the cultural variation among your students can help you identify cultural characteristics that can become a source of pride and mutual esteem and then motivate the individual learning of your students.

Conferences. Many elementary schools use parent conferences as means for teachers and parents to share their ongoing observations and assessments of student learning. Educators are finding parent conferences to be an effective means for parents to share their home values and worldviews with teachers (Delgado-Gaitan, 1991). This sharing, in turn, helps you better understand the cultural dynamics that influence the social, emotional, and intellectual growth of students at home.

Another way to collect information for assessing student learning is student conferencing. We have observed both elementary and secondary teachers regularly having conferences with their students. Conferences offer culturally diverse students, especially those with limited-English-speaking skills, a safer setting to demonstrate their oral skills and relational styles.

Portfolios.[6] Just as the artist uses a portfolio to display his or her artistic abilities and products, so teachers in elementary, secondary, and postsecondary schools are finding portfolios to be effective alternative assessment tools. A student portfolio is a collection of student-developed products and processes that teachers can use as tools for monitoring student growth. This use of the portfolio can be especially effective in culturally diverse classrooms (Au, 1993). We have found them most effective when teachers include the following guidelines in their portfolio protocols:

- Provide clear information to students and their parents about how portfolios will be used in assessing student learning and in assigning grades to students' academic performance.
- Provide a balance of processes and products of student learning in the portfolios.
- Establish clear criteria and a usable system for judging the effectiveness of student products/performances. Use this system and criteria to make sure the portfolios "count."
- Give students major responsibility for choosing what to include in their portfolios and for providing the rationale to explain their choices.
- Provide students with opportunities to use their portfolios to make self-assessments of the processes and products of their own learning.

Projects/Demonstrations/Exhibitions.   Student projects, demonstrations, and exhibitions are additional sources you can use to assess student learning (Gardner, 1993). These provide you with a means for determining how students embed their acquired knowledge, skills, and culture into various kinds of performances. Additionally, students can use these performances to demonstrate responsibility, initiative, and creativity.

ACTIVITY 9.2   Appraising the Use of Alternative Assessment in Culturally Diverse Classrooms

In this activity, you look more closely at the kinds of alternative assessment practices you discovered in Activity 9.1. Use Figure 9–2 to compile information on the nature of student assessment used by a teacher you have selected for study.

1. Observe the kinds of alternative assessments, if any, that teachers use to measure student learning in culturally diverse classrooms. For each kind of assessment strategy, determine the following and record in Figure 9–2.
   a. Method of documentation
   b. Frequency of use
   c. Application to final "grade" of student progress
   d. Rationale for use
   e. Rationale for non-use of other strategies
2. Record your observations of the alternative assessment strategies you discover. Elaborate on the kinds of assessment you observe (e.g., frequency of use, how the assessments are recorded, how the assessment information is shared with students, how culturally sensitive the assessments are).

Teacher:
Grade Level:
Subject(s) Taught:

Use	Assessment Strategy	Documentation[1]	Frequency[2]	Rationale[3]	Percentage[4]
yes no	observation record				
yes no	individual student projects				
yes no	group student projects				
yes no	student self-assessment				
yes no	portfolios				
yes no	parent conference sheets				
yes no	student conference sheets				
yes no	paper-and-pencil tests				
yes no	anecdotal records				
yes no	reading logs				
yes no	other				

Figure 9–2   Assessment Strategy Observation Record

[1] Method for gathering information on student learning

[2] Number of times the strategy is used in a designated grade period (e.g., 6 weeks, 9 weeks)

[3] Reason for use

[4] Weight the strategy has in overall assessment of student learning for a designated assessment period of time

3. Compare and contrast your observations with those of peers and/or colleagues. Consider the degree to which alternative assessment is used and the degree to which it is sensitive to the various backgrounds of all students.

4. Assessment that is culturally sensitive will foster individual growth for students without excess comparisons to other students. Assessment that is more traditional and standardized will compare the progress of one student with the progress of other students. To what degree, therefore, are the assessment strategies you observed culturally sensitive? How might you make them more sensitive if you deem them to be insensitive?

SUMMARY

Traditional forms of assessing student learning in contemporary classrooms have become increasingly invalid as contemporary society and its schools have become more globalized and, consequently, as student populations in many locations have become increasingly diverse. Given that instruction in many classrooms is driven by local assessment strategies and thus tends to foster instruction that is commonly called "teaching to the test," the immediate and pressing need is for all educators to explore strategies that appropriately, effectively, and validly assess the learning of all students. This is no simple challenge, especially given the widespread use of institutionalized standardized testing and the general belief, though a misconception, that this form of testing validly indicates the "intelligence" of students. New ways of conceptualizing student learning—for example, Gardner's theory of multiple intelligences—are providing alternative frameworks for assessment, as clearly demonstrated at the Key School in Indianapolis. As part of your life-long professional development as a teacher, you must not accept traditional forms of assessment as always valid and "correct" for all students; rather, you must continuously search for ways to more appropriately assess student learning, both for your own classroom learning and for schoolwide assessment.

RESEARCH TOPIC

Examining School and Classroom Assessment Practices

Problem Posing

Assessment is the driving force that shapes curriculum and instruction in many schools. The notion of teaching to the test, though unwantingly admitted by educators, is a piece of school reality that all teachers and administrators deal with each school year. The purpose of this research project is to examine the nature of assessment in a selected school context and to determine how assessment practices influence curriculum and instruction in that school. After completing this project, you will have considered the impact of standardized achievement tests on the overall school climate and on individual classroom instruction. You will also have considered the nature of classroom assessment that teachers use throughout the year to determine the growth of their students in specific subject areas.

Given the central purpose of this research project, the following questions can serve as an initial framework for gathering information. The first set of questions focuses on standardized testing in the school you observe. The second set of questions focuses on assessment in teachers' classrooms.

Standardized Testing.   Questions that can provide an initial framework for your observations are:

What kinds of standardized tests does the school administer each year?

What is the purpose for the tests?

Who requires that the tests be administered?

How does the school prepare students for taking and teachers for giving these tests?

What is the impact of the tests on teachers' classroom curriculum and instruction?

How do the standardized tests affect the progress of students in school?

What information do teachers learn about improving student learning from these tests?

How are the results of the tests used by teachers? by administrators? by students? by parents?

Is the test administered in more than one language?

What testing accommodations does the school make for students whose first language is not English?

In what ways is the test culturally sensitive? culturally insensitive?

Which students in the school are exempt from taking the test, if any?

What is the ethnic composition of students who are exempt from the test, compared with the ethnic composition of the entire school population?

Classroom Assessment.   Classroom assessment varies within and among schools. Although each teacher may have a personal trademark for her or his grading policy, the school may overshadow this with schoolwide assessment policies. Moreover, assessment in elementary classrooms may be very different from assessment in secondary classrooms. And in secondary classrooms, assessment strategies for the art and music teachers may vary considerably from those of the English, history, and mathematics teachers. Although the following questions are intended to cut across grade levels and subject matter boundaries, you might need to add questions that are more germane to the classroom and grade level you observe and investigate.

What kind of assessment is being used by the teacher?

Are traditional assessment strategies used (e.g., mostly paper-and-pencil), or are alternative assessment strategies used in place of or in addition to traditional strategies?

Are letter grades the main indication of student learning?

From the work of Gardner (1983), what kinds of intelligences are assessed by the teacher?

Does the teacher vary assessment strategies because of cultural diversity, or is the same assessment strategy used for all students?

Exploration and Discovery

To find answers for the two sets of questions above, arrange for interviews with selected students, teachers, and administrators. Interviewing students from various cultural and ethnic groups enables you to compare and contrast student views of assessment strategies used by the school administration and by various teachers.

To obtain information on standardized testing used in the school, try to obtain sample copies of the tests that are administered. As you seek answers to each question posed above and as you find answers for other questions you might have, remain mindful of the sensitivity that usually surrounds these tests. Many standardized tests have high stakes for the school; that is, the results of the test might result in additional state funds for the school, among other benefits.

Keep an accurate record of the information you find out about standardized testing for the school. As you talk with administrators, determine the stakes involved with the tests that are administered. Find out whether the tests are sensitive to culturally diverse student populations. As you talk with teachers, listen for how standardized tests influence classroom curriculum and instruction. Ask teachers about any professional pressure they feel because of the tests. When you talk with students, explore their feelings and thoughts about the tests. Which students benefit most from the tests, and which students think the tests are discriminatory? What pressure do students feel from taking the tests? Determine what stakes are involved with various students who take the tests.

As an added dimension to your study of standardized tests, reflect on your own experiences with these tests when you were a student in elementary and secondary school. How do your reflections, thoughts, and insights about the tests compare with those you hear from administrators, teachers, and students?

After compiling school information on standardized testing, explore how a selected teacher carries out the day-to-day assessment of his or her students. To gain further insight into this kind of assessment, compare and contrast the assessment strategies of several teachers. If you are doing this research project in a secondary school, compare strategies used by teachers of different subject areas—for example, art and science. In what ways are the assessment strategies in different subject areas similar and different?

Of importance to this book is the notion of culturally sensitive assessment strategies. To explore this idea, determine the ways, if any, the teacher you are observing uses alternative assessment strategies that enable students from various socioeconomic, cultural, and ethnic groups to demonstrate their level of learning. Determine the kinds of intelligences mentioned by Gardner (1983) that are assessed. Using multiple intelligence theory as a framework, determine whether assessment of one kind of intelligence in the teacher's classroom predominates other kinds of intelligences.

As you gather information on classroom assessment, compare the information you gather from students, teachers, and administrators. Find areas of agreement and disagreement among these groups. Then compare and contrast the information gathered with that gathered by your peers and colleagues working in the same school and with others working in different schools. From this comparison, determine whether school context and student diversity influence the nature of assessment used at various schools by different teachers.

Reflection and Modification

As you reflect on the results of your research on student assessment, consider areas in which the assessment strategies you observed were culturally sensitive and others in which they were culturally insensitive. If Gardner's theory of multiple intelligences is culturally sensitive, as Nieto (1992) claims, then how are the standardized assessment and classroom-based assessment you observed culturally sensitive? Was the assessment you observed primarily aimed at determining one kind of intelligence? If so, what kind? If not, what other forms of intelligence were being assessed by the school and by the teachers you observed?

As you ponder the nature of culturally sensitive assessment, you soon will discover that this is a complicated phenomenon for schools, given the political pressures they are under. Many schools are constantly under pressure to raise their standardized test scores to more favorably compare with other schools locally, nationally, and globally. What suggestions can you make for alternative, culturally sensitive assessment of student learning in schools that are under pressure to do well on standardized tests? The tendency to teach to the test in these schools is strong, and the school curriculum is often designed to help students do well on these tests, thus minimizing the potential that teachers have for being creative and spontaneous in their teaching.

Discovery and Speculation

After gathering information on assessment of student learning, you have probably discovered some things you did not previously know, especially political implications of standardized testing. By considering multiple intelligences theory, you also became aware of intelligences for which students can be assessed other than logical-mathematical intelligence, which usually predominates standardized tests. From what you discovered about student assessment, what additional studies might you conduct that would further inform your perspective of student assessment? List these studies below.

1. _____

2. _____

3. _____

4. _____

NOTES

1. Bennett's (1990) discussion of learning style theory provides an overview of generalizable learning style theory.
2. A recent discussion of multiple intelligence theory can be found in *Teachers College Record, 95*(4), 1994, pp. 555–592. Contributing to this discussion are Eisner, Sternberg, Levin, and Gardner.
3. For additional reading on the Key School, see Balanos, P. (1990). Restructuring the curriculum. *Principal, 69*(3), 13–14; Balanos, P. (1994). The Key Renaissance Middle School: Extending the notion of multiple intelligences. In J. Jenkins, K. Louis, H. Walberg, & J. Keefe (Eds.), *World class schools: An evolving concept* (pp. 18–25). Reston, VA: National Association of Secondary School Principals; Gardner, H. (1993). *Multiple intelligences: The theory in practice.* New York: Basic Books; Interview with Howard Gardner. (1993, April). *Think: The Magazine on Critical & Creative Thinking,* pp. 2–5; Interview with Pat Balanos. (1993, October). *Think: The Magazine on Critical & Creative Thinking,* pp. 3–10; Key Elementary School. (1991). *NEA Today, 10*(1), 10–11; Steinberger, E. (1994, January). Howard Gardner on learning for understanding. *School Administrator,* pp. 26–31.
4. For an overview of how the school was conceptualized and developed, see the video *The Making of a School,* available from Phi Delta Kappa, P.O. Box 789, Bloomington, IN 47402-0789.
5. See Garcia and Pearson (1993, pp. 345–346) for a more complete discussion of these attempts to build culture-free and culture-fair tests.
6. For additional information on portfolios, see, for example, Black, Daiker, Sommers, and Stygall (1994) and Graves and Sunstein (1992).

FURTHER READING ON MULTIPLE INTELLIGENCE THEORY

Gardner, H. (1983). *Frames of mind.* New York: Basic Books.

Gardner, H. (1985). *The mind's new science: A history of the cognitive revolution.* New York: Basic Books.

Gardner, H. (1989). *To open minds: Chinese clues to the dilemma of contemporary education.* New York: Basic Books.

Gardner, H. (1991). *The unschooled mind: How children think and how schools should teach.* New York: Basic Books.

Gardner, H. (1993). *Creating minds: An anatomy of creativity seen through the lives of Freud, Einstein, Picasso, Stravinsky, Eliot, Graham, and Gandhi.* New York: Basic Books.

Gardner, H. (1993). *Multiple intelligences: The theory in practice.* New York: Basic Books.

REFERENCES

Au, K. H. (1993). Portfolio assessment: Experiences at the Kamehameha Elementary Education Program. In E. Hiebert, P. Afflerbach, & S. Valencia (Eds.), *Authentic reading assessment: Practices and possibilities.* Newark, DE: International Reading Association.

Balanos, P. (1990). Restructuring the curriculum. *Principal, 69*(3), 13–14.

Balanos, P. (1994). The Key Renaissance Middle School: Extending the notion of multiple intelligences. In J. Jenkins, K. Louis, H. Walberg, & J. Keefe (Eds.), *World class schools: An evolving concept* (pp. 18–25). Reston, VA: National Association of Secondary School Principals.

Banks, J., & Banks, C. M. (Eds.). (1993). *Multicultural education: Issues and perspectives* (2nd ed.). Boston: Allyn & Bacon.

Bennett, C. (1990). *Comprehensive multicultural education: Theory and practice* (2nd ed.). Boston: Allyn & Bacon.

Black, L., Daiker, D. A., Sommers, J., & Stygall, G. (Eds.). (1994). *New directions in portfolio assessment: Reflective practice, critical theory, and large-scale scoring.* Portsmouth, NH: Boynton/Cook.

Brooks, J., & Brooks, M. (1993). *The case for constructivist classrooms.* Alexandria, VA: Association for Supervision and Curriculum Development.

Darder, A. (1991). *Culture and power in the classroom.* New York: Bergin & Garvey.

Delgado-Gaitan, C. (1991). Involving parents in the schools: A process of empowerment. *American Journal of Education, 100*(1), 20–46.

Dunn, R. (1993). Learning styles of the multiculturally diverse. *Emergency Librarian, 20*(4), 24–32.

Dunn, R., Dunn, K., & Price, G. (1989). *Learning Style Inventory.* Lawrence, KS: Price Systems.

Epstein, J. L. (1988). Effective schools or effective students: Dealing with diversity. In R. Haskins & D. MacRae (Eds.), *Policies for American public schools.* Norwood, NJ: Ablex.

Figueroa, P. (1992). Assessment and achievement of ethnic minority pupils. In J. Lynch, C. Modgil, & S. Modgil (Eds.), *Cultural diversity and the schools.* Washington, DC: Falmer Press.

Garcia, E. A., & Pearson, P. D. (1994). Assessment and diversity. In L. Darling-Hammond (Ed.), *Review of research in education* (pp. 337–392). Washington, DC: American Educational Research Association.

Garcia, J., & Pugh, S. (1992, November). Multicultural education in teacher preparation programs. *Phi Delta Kappan, 74*(3), 214–219.

Gardner, H. (1983). *Frames of mind.* New York: Basic Books.

Gardner, H. (1991). *The unschooled mind: How children think and how schools should teach.* New York: Basic Books.

Gardner, H. (1993). *Multiple intelligences: The theory in practice.* New York: Basic Books.

Gilbert, S., & Gay, G. (1985). Improving the success in school of poor Black children. *Phi Delta Kappan, 67,* 133–137.

Ginsburg, H., & Allardice, B. (1984). Children's difficulties with school mathematics. In B. Rogoff & J. Lave (Eds.), *Everyday cognition: Its development in social context* (pp. 194–219). Cambridge, MA: Harvard University Press.

Goodman, Y. (1985). Kid watching. In A. Jaggar & M. T. Smith-Burke (Eds.), *Observing the language of learning.* Newark, DE: International Reading Association.

Grant, C., & Sleeter, C. (1989). *Turning on learning.* Columbus, OH: Merrill.

Graves, D. H., & Sunstein, B. S. (1992). *Portfolio portraits.* Portsmouth, NH: Heinemann.

Hakuta, K. (1986). *Mirror of language.* New York: Basic Books.

Hale-Benson, J. (1982). *Black children: Their roots, culture, and learning styles.* Baltimore: Johns Hopkins University Press.

Key Elementary School. (1991). *NEA Today, 10*(1), 10–11.

Interview with Howard Gardner. (1993, April). *Think: The Magazine on Critical & Creative Thinking,* pp. 2–5.

Interview with Pat Balanos. (1993, October). *Think: The Magazine on Critical & Creative Thinking,* pp. 3–10.

Kozol, J. (1990). The new untouchables [Special issue]. *Newsweek,* pp. 48–53.

Langer, J. (1987). The construction of meaning and the assessment of comprehension: An analysis of reader performance on standardized test items. In R. Freedle & R. Duran (Eds.), *Cognitive and linguistic analyses of test performance* (pp. 225–244). Norwood, NJ: Ablex.

Linn, R. (1990, Spring). Essentials of student assessment: From accountability to instruction aid. *Teachers College Record, 91*(3), 422–436.

Mercado, C., & Romero, M. (1993). Assessment of students in bilingual education. In M. B. Arias & U. Casanova (Eds.), *Bilingual education: Politics, practice, and research: Ninety-Second Yearbook of the National Society for the Study of Education. Part II.* Chicago: University of Chicago Press.

Mercer, J. (1989). Alternative paradigms for assessment in a pluralistic society. In J. Banks & C. Banks (Eds.), *Multicultural education: Issues and perspectives* (pp. 289–304). Boston: Allyn & Bacon.

Nieto, S. (1992). *Affirming diversity: The sociopolitical context of multicultural education.* New York: Longman.

Nine-Curt, C. (1977). *Non-verbal communication in Puerto Rico.* Cambridge, MA: Evaluation, Dissemination, and Assessment Center.

Ohlhausen, M. M., Powell, R., & Reitz, B. S. (1994). Parents' views of traditional and alternative report cards. *School Community Journal, 4*(1), 81–98.

Rothman, R. (1992, October 21), Study confirms "fears" regarding commercial tests. *Education Week,* pp. 1, 13.

Shade, B. (1982). Afro-American cognitive style: A variable in school success? *Review of Educational Research, 52*(2), 219–244.

Steinberger, E. (1994). Howard Gardner on learning for understanding. *School Administrator, 51*(1), 26–29.

Stiggins, R. (1991, Spring). Relevant classroom assessment training for teachers. *Educational Measurement: Issues and Practice,* pp. 7–12.

Worthen, B. (1993). Critical issues that will determine the future of alternative assessment. *Phi Delta Kappan, 74*(6), 444–457.

Zeichner, K. (1993, April). *Educating teachers for cultural diversity.* Paper presented at the Annual Meeting of the American Educational Research Association, Atlanta.

Chapter 10

Rethinking Management in Culturally Diverse Classrooms: Alternative Strategies

Negotiation is the basis for establishing "power with" students, rather than simply "power over" them. . . . It is built on a desire to determine shared interests, an ability to confer about decisions to be made and curricular ideas to be plumbed, and a willingness to face up to conflict and then share a compromise. There are important questions to be asked about whose interests are shared in classrooms and about how issues of gender, culture, and social class arise in these discussions.   (McLaughlin, 1994, p. 80)

As teachers gain a greater understanding of students' lives outside of school, they are more able to create opportunities for classroom dialogue, which assists bicultural students to affirm, challenge, and transform the many conflicts and contradictions they face as members of an oppressed group.   (Darder, 1992, p. 115)

INTRODUCTION

In the preceding chapter, we helped you explore assessment of student learning in culturally diverse classrooms, an ongoing challenge you face every day as you interact with students who represent various ethnic, religious, and economic groups. In this chapter, we focus on another challenge, perhaps equally as demanding: managing student learning and maintaining a classroom learning environment that fosters learning for all of your students. Much has been written on the topic of classroom management, yet little of this literature focuses on creating and managing learning environments in which students represent four or five nationalities and in which they might speak three or four first languages. Given the changing nature of student demographics in today's classrooms, you must openly ask, Does one style of classroom management fit all students in all classrooms, as suggested by traditional management strategies?

Reports during the past few years have shed light on the need to consider alternative management strategies for culturally diverse students and for differing school contexts. For example, the case studies of successful classroom teachers in rural Alaska (McDiarmid, Kleinfeld, & Parrett, 1988) indicate that management strategies for students in that location may be very different from strategies needed for new immigrant Latino students in inner-city Los Angeles (Patthey-Chavez, 1993).

Because of the culture-specific nature of classroom management in contemporary classrooms, we do not propose a set of rules, algorithms, or procedures that will automatically and "scientifically" ensure a productive learning environment for all of your students. Rather, one purpose of this chapter is to help you reflect closely on traditional management practices, to think critically about their efficacy in contemporary classrooms. Another purpose is to encourage you to consider alternative management practices that may very well enhance your ability to manage and organize more productive learning environments for all students.

THE CONTINUUM OF CLASSROOM MANAGEMENT

Classroom management is a broad concept that encompasses many aspects of classroom life. Some preservice and beginning teachers, however, think that management amounts to little more than correcting student misbehavior and upholding a fixed discipline policy. One of the greatest concerns of most persons entering teaching is unquestionably how to maintain a productive classroom learning environment by disciplining students effectively and efficiently. Although student discipline is certainly an important part of classroom management, it is not the only part, as most experienced teachers realize.

What, then, is classroom management, and how can you manage contemporary classrooms effectively? One way to consider classroom management is to think about it as a continuum from complete teacher-centered decision making on one end to complete student-centered decision making on the other end. Both ends reflect a certain perspective regarding the purposes of education. The "control" end of the continuum—that which is teacher centered—tends to represent a content-centered, traditional approach to management, what we call a "factory model of management" in this chapter. The "negotiation" end of the continuum—that which is student centered—tends to reflect a collaborative approach to management. The ends of the continuum and the many variations in between provide specific perspectives for how you ultimately create and implement management strategies, including time management, learning environment management, curriculum management, student behavior management, instructional materials management, bureaucratic management, and so on.

Viewed in broader terms, classroom management is everything you and your students do. How you ultimately manage your classroom depends, of course, on many factors. District and school policy have a strong bearing on your management strategies. Another factor influencing your classroom management is the primacy of your former schooling, including the industrial, factorylike model of management that was most likely part of your former school learning environments.

In their discussion of the factory model of management, Bullough (1994) and McLaughlin (1994) argue that this form of management may be ineffective in contemporary school classrooms. Bullough in particular argues that the management metaphor—that which is embedded in the factory model and discussed more fully below—has a powerful hold on how both new and experienced teachers view their roles as teachers. Although the factory model has various strengths, it also has obvious limitations (Boomer, Lester, Onore, & Cook, 1992; Bullough, 1994; Gergen, 1991; McLaughlin, 1994). Because of these limitations, Bullough contends, educators must begin rethinking the management metaphor for today's classrooms.

RETHINKING THE CLASSROOM MANAGEMENT METAPHOR

Educators in most school settings have been using the traditional model of management since the turn of the century. The traditional model is also known as the factory model (Bullough, 1994) because its basic structure is grounded in the industrial model of management. As its name suggests, the metaphor of a factory implies that the school is operated in an efficient and productive manner. The initial intention of transferring the factory model to schools was to establish an orderly and safe environment where the education of large numbers of students could be "managed" with the least amount of unnecessary disturbance and the greatest amount of learning. As with any model that is generalized to large numbers of similar institutions, the factory model of management has both strengths and limitations for school classrooms. If you fail to understand the implications of the factory metaphor for your own teaching, you will very likely use it in a wholesale fashion, without being aware of its limiting effects on student learning.

The Factory Metaphor for Schooling

To understand the factory model as a metaphor for school classrooms, consider its use in the play *Cheaper by the Dozen,* which was later made into a movie. The play, which remains a favorite for performances by high school theater departments, tells the story of a family of 12 children that was "managed" efficiently and economically by a father who ran his home like a factory. As in a factory, this family was ruled by the clock, with all family events beginning and ending on time. In the morning, 20 minutes after the wake-up alarm sounded, the father, clutching a silver stopwatch, would stand at the bottom of the stairway on the first floor of their home and blow a loud whistle. Immediately, the 12 children began to scurry down the stairs and line up from the oldest to the youngest. When the last of the children was in place, the father would stop the watch and give them an efficiency rating on their performance. This is how the father, an efficiency expert employed by a factory, managed his 12 children.

Cheaper by the Dozen has remained popular because of the humor the audience recognizes in the misapplication of the factory metaphor for managing children in a family setting. Although you might appreciate the obvious humor of applying the factory metaphor to family activities, you might not readily recognize the factory as a prevailing metaphorical foundation on which your school and classroom management practices are built (see Bullough, 1994, p. 7).

One of us (Zehm) attended a lecture by Professor David Tyack at Stanford University several years ago in which this eminent education historian told an educational version of the *Cheaper by the Dozen* story. It involved the application of factory management practices by the superintendent of schools in Portland, Oregon, in the 1880s. "I can look at my watch at any time during the school day," Tyack read from his notes about the superintendent from Portland, "and tell you exactly which page in the textbook any teacher is on anywhere in the Portland schools!" Although this incident may be laughable and remote from contemporary practice, it remains a part of the unbroken line of educational practice built on the factory metaphor. More contemporary examples of the factory metaphor, with its emphasis on controlling student behavior and managing overall learning of students, can be seen in reading and mathematics management systems, management by objectives, assertive discipline techniques, tracking, letter grading, national standards, national curriculum, and other dimensions of schooling. The implications of the factory model for school practice are depicted in Table 10–1. There remains little question that the factory model has strongly influenced school practice, including your own thinking about teaching.

Table 10–1   Comparison of factory practice and school practice

Factory Practice	School Practice
1. Truck in raw materials	1. Bus in diverse students
2. Sort/sift raw materials	2. Testing/ability grouping
3. Process raw materials	3. Prepackaged curriculum
4. Assembly line startup	4. Grade level assignments
5. Quality control measures	5. Standardized testing
6. Eliminate defective products	6. Expel deviant students
7. Packaging of products	7. Minimum exit standards
8. Labeling of products	8. College prep, vocational
9. Product shipping/sales	9. Jobs/college/service

Many preservice, in-service, and experienced teachers are indoctrinated to the factory model of classroom management, which tends to be content centered and teacher centered. Without critical reflection on how your beliefs and practices about classroom management have been shaped by the factory metaphor, you may not be able to implement egalitarian measures that make your classroom a democratic learning community. However, moving from a traditional, factorylike model of management to one that is more equitable is not a simple and straightforward process. Most schools, especially those with very large student populations, openly prefer traditional models of management. Proponents of these models contend that such management ensures safe and orderly interactions among students and provides clear boundaries for student learning and for student behavior.

If you are a beginning teacher, you will be particularly challenged when rethinking traditional forms of management. Bullough (1994) explains the tension that beginning teachers feel when they want to implement innovative classroom techniques such as alternative management:

> When tension exists between a personal metaphor and institutionally preferred teacher-student relationships, as it often does, the beginning teacher is placed in an extremely difficult position that calls forth a variety of public and private coping strategies. Quite commonly the beginning teacher seeks in the privacy of her room to negotiate a teaching role that is personally satisfying and, at the minimally acceptable level, institutionally fitting. Facing students used to being managed and disciplined, and resistant to teacher attempts to develop different quality relationships, beginning teachers often accommodate. (p. 6)

If you are an experienced teacher and have been teaching within the factory framework of schooling, you will be equally challenged by the same limitations as beginning teachers. Unless your teacher preparation program and related school-based field experiences helped you look critically at traditional models of management, and unless you are encouraged by school administration to consider alternative management strategies, you might not even have considered the limitations of the factory model of management for culturally diverse student populations. We urge caution, therefore, if you plan to implement, in a wholesale fashion, the alternative forms of management we discuss later in this chapter. Nor do we want you to believe that these models can be easily put into place in schools that have a long-standing tradition in the factory model of management. We do encourage you, however, to reflect critically on traditional forms of management and to explore possibilities of implementing alternative strategies. Our purpose here is not to provide you with a lock-step procedure to implement alternative strategies. Indeed, most alternative strategies, such as the negotiation model suggested by Boomer et al. (1992), negate the very existence of lock-step procedures and managerial algorithms. Nor is our purpose to provide you with an academic discussion of implementation strategies. Rather, our purpose is to encourage you to think conceptually about classroom management, to consider the very roots of your personal beliefs about how classrooms should be managed, and to think critically about the efficacy of the factory model for contemporary culturally diverse classrooms.

ACTIVITY 10.1   The Factory Model of Schooling

One way to explore the factory model of management is to study an existing school and/or classroom learning environment for how students are permitted to participate in school decision making. As noted above, the factory model of management tends to be more content centered and teacher centered; students usually don't play an active part in these schools in negotiating, for example, school rules, nature of classroom curriculum, types of evaluation, and content to be learned. Some models of management, such as the negotiation model described by Boomer et al. (1992), give students a strong voice in making decisions about organizing and maintaining the school environment.

Become familiar with a school and/or classroom learning environment. To do this, you need to make observations of the environment over time, talking with teachers and students and, in general, "hanging around" school and specific classrooms to get a sense of the local school and classroom management strategies. Arrange for interviews with selected students, teachers, and administrators to get their impressions of the items listed in Table 10–2. For each item, rate the level of student involvement. Items that you rate as low or none will tend to reflect the factory model of schooling. Items that you rate high or middle will tend to reflect an alternative model of schooling that is more negotiatory with students.

The following questions, which can be answered from the information you gathered for Table 10–2, will help you further consider the factory model of school management. Discuss your reactions to these questions with colleagues and peers.

1. How much shared decision making did you discover overall for students in the school you observed? Would you appraise the school as being more factorylike or more negotiatory?

Table 10–2   Assessment of shared decision making by students in school and classroom learning environments

Item	Level of Student Decision Making											
	Student Perspectives				Teacher Perspectives				Administrator Perspectives			
	none	low	middle	high	none	low	middle	high	none	low	middle	high
School Policies												
School Practices												
School Traditions												
Daily Routines												
School Climate												
Official Documents												
Architecture												
Organizational Structure												
Curriculum												
Assessment Practices												
Instructional Materials												
Extracurricular Activities												

2. What differences did you discover in the perspectives of students, teachers, and administrators relative to shared decision making in the school?
3. If the school is more factorylike, what advantages and disadvantages are there for students? What changes would you need to make to involve students more in school decision making? What might be the consequences of such an involvement of students?
4. If you discover that students have more of a voice in school and/or classroom decision making, what advantages and disadvantages result from this?
5. What new skills, if any, would teachers and students need in order to move from a factory management model to more of a shared management model?
6. What challenges might beginning teachers face, in addition to those mentioned above by Bullough (1994), in trying to implement an alternative model of management in a school with a factory orientation? What challenges would you face with students? colleagues? administrators? parents? your own beliefs about management?

TOWARD AN ALTERNATIVE MODEL OF MANAGEMENT

Various dichotomies can be drawn between the traditional factory model and alternative models of management. For example, the factory model, on the one hand, tends to align with direct transmission of information from teacher to student; hence, it is more content centered and teacher centered. Alternative models of management, on the other hand, put teachers in the role of facilitator of student learning, thus making teachers co-learners with their students. The factory model tends to require conformity and obedience, not only in behavior but also in thinking. Alternative models, however, foster critical and open questioning. As another example, the factory management model tends to acknowledge single ways of knowing, usually ways that are consistent with the mainstream culture. Alternative models usually acknowledge multiple ways of knowing and hence are culturally sensitive. This last quality of the factory model—that it is reflective of the mainstream culture's ways of knowing and thinking—is viewed by critics as limiting learning opportunities for students who are not part of the mainstream culture because of their ethnicity, religious beliefs, home cultures, or other personal qualities.

The dichotomies drawn above are not intended to suggest that the factory management model is fully inappropriate. The model has many strengths and, in some schools, does provide an important structure for students. The factory management model emphasizes efficiency and productivity, two traits deeply embedded in industrial and corporate ideologies. Given the increase in cultural diversity in most classrooms, however, and the growing concern that the factory model of management discriminates against nonmajority students, a question surfaces: Is the traditional management model, which tends to build on a single way of knowing, appropriate in a society that has become increasingly diverse and in classrooms where multiple ways of knowing predominate classroom learning environments?

Although we do not believe that you should cast aside entirely the central elements of the factory model of schooling, we do believe that you must consider ways of managing classroom environments that affirm multiple cultures, rather than a single culture, and that engage all students in meaningful learning. Trying out alternative models of management, as we describe below, can be a challenge even for those who are the most determined to transform traditional school structure into more contemporary practices.

TRYING OUT ALTERNATIVE MODELS

Once you recognize the factory metaphor and its features as a powerful and over-riding management model for most school learning environments, you will better understand how to apply other management metaphors to your classroom. Finding workable alternative metaphors, however, is challenging for two reasons. First, the largely unexamined and uncontested use of the management model, as embedded within the factory metaphor, during the past century has resulted in firmly entrenched patterns of working with students in school classrooms. Dealing with and changing such firmly entrenched patterns is tough work. Second, replacing the factory metaphor requires the reeducation of teachers and parents in the why's and how's of an alternative paradigm for guiding relationships between students and teachers. Don't think, however, that this reeducation will come easily. However you approach it, moving from one paradigm of management (e.g., factory model of management) to another (e.g., negotiation and shared decision making) will assuredly shake up the schooling beliefs of many people. When you challenge others' beliefs with progressive ideas, you might be viewed as a useful change agent by some, but as an educational radical by others. Certainly, there is nothing wrong with being viewed as a radical, as the teachers in Chapter 4 viewed themselves, if this is what is needed to improve learning conditions for all students.

CONTRACTUAL MODEL OF CLASSROOM MANAGEMENT

Although the task of replacing the factory metaphor, with its implications for managing and controlling students, is challenging, it already has been done in individual schools (see Chapter 6) and in individual classrooms (see Chapter 7) by educators whom we discovered to be culturally sensitive. Teachers who have consciously rejected the management metaphor have developed their own strategies for establishing relationships with students, strategies built on alternatives to the factory metaphor. We describe below an alternative to the prevailing factory management paradigm; this alternative can help you meet the learning needs of all students. We give the name *contractual model* to this alternative way of thinking about classrooms.

In simple terms, the contractual model relates to the ethical and moral contracts you implicitly assume with students when you become a teacher. We agree with Sergiovanni (1993) that teachers must consider their contracts as a solemn, moral obligation to provide for the learning needs of all students. The contractual model also relates to the explicit interactions you have with students, the interactions that overtly reflect the degree to which you permit students to have a voice in what goes on in your classroom. Below are central features of the contractual model of school management.

Features of the Contractual Model

Empowerment.   The first feature of the contractual paradigm focuses on teacher empowerment and on the source of your classroom authority. Factorylike schools tend to disempower teachers. This is not necessarily a function of unreasonable administrators. In fact, you might work with some of the finest administrators anywhere. The factory model, however, centralizes school authority in administrative offices—for example, the principal's office, the assistant superintendent for curriculum's office, and the assistant superintendent for instruction's office. Factory schools continuously strive for increased efficiency, shuffling large numbers of students here and there with the least amount of disruption, often putting them into ability groups (e.g., tracking) to enhance instructional efficiency. If you teach in such a school, the curriculum you use is very likely predetermined. Moreover, standardized tests that your school uses to measure degree of student learning are beyond your jurisdiction to regulate and construct; school rules are preestablished; and evaluations of your teaching, on whatever basis they are carried out, are based on how efficiently you run your classroom, including objective-based instruction, lesson transition, starting and stopping lessons in a smooth and timely manner, and related factors. Things like relevancy of your lesson to the needs of society, sensitivity of your instruction to cultural diversity of students, and moral implications of the content you teach are rarely, if ever, included in evaluations of your classroom teaching. Yet, these latter factors have potential to connect your students more personally to the content you teach.

You might now be asking, Are teachers and students empowered by any part of the school system? Although the school system as a function of the factory model might be disempowering, parents of learners in your classroom empower you to care for the academic and social well-being of their children. This kind of empowerment is very important; with this empowerment comes a moral and ethical responsibility not only to teach students but to care for them. When you care for students, when you help them find their voice and their place within the complex arena of school, you empower them to become autonomous, authentic learners (Oldfather & McLaughlin, 1993; Powell, in press).

Mutual Respect.   The second feature of the contractual paradigm is mutual respect. We believe that teachers earn the respect of their students when they consciously work on being relationship specialists. When you understand that your role as a teacher obligates you to provide for the diverse learning needs of all students, you will appreciate the importance of becoming a relationship specialist. Think of the best relationships you have established with others. No matter the kinds of relationships, be they personal or professional, the best relationships are those in which the other person feels that his or her needs are being met (Zehm & Kottler, 1993).

One obligation you have as a teacher is to respect the inherent dignity of each of your students and the cultural beliefs they bring with them into your classroom. An obligation that your students have is to respect you and each other as learning occurs. Without the mutual respect that comes from understanding and appreciating other cultures and other ways of existing, culturally diverse classrooms will be chaotic places demanding you to act as an enforcer of rules and regulations, rather than as a facilitator of student learning. You will then be forced into using the factory model of classroom management, demanding obedience and compliance with externally imposed rules.

Solidarity.   If you are successful as a relationship specialist in establishing an environment where there is mutual respect for all, you will be on your way to establishing solidarity. Solidarity, the third feature of the contractual paradigm, occurs when there is a pervasive spirit of caring among teachers and students (McLaughlin, 1991; Noddings, 1986). In a classroom with solidarity, students understand that they are responsible for their own learning. They also understand their social responsibility to support the learning of classmates, peers, and fellow citizens.

Solidarity is built on a genuine mutual esteem for each student, especially for differences in language, ethnicity, gender, religion, and academic abilities. The classroom cohesiveness that results from solidarity will have the most positive effects in support of the teaching and learning enterprise. First, solidarity strengthens the other features of the contractual paradigm. It legitimates your authority in the eyes of students and possibly eliminates some major student disruptions of learning. Most students will not want to sabotage a teacher who genuinely respects them, who empowers them to be responsible for their own learning, and who communicates with them in a relationship of genuine caring.

A second and powerful effect of classroom solidarity is the increased access to learning for all students. Two decades ago, Rist (1974) observed the staggering influence that negative teacher and student expectations have on reducing the access to learning for students from low-income families. Cohen (1974, 1986) and Rosenholtz (1985) focused their research on the academic status disorders that arose when students viewed as having high academic status (e.g., those labeled as gifted, bright, academically talented) effectively blocked avenues to learning for students viewed as having lower academic status. Classroom solidarity has the potential to reduce, if not ultimately eliminate, these academic status disorders. Finally, classroom solidarity encourages students to take risks and to learn from their mistakes, two prerequisites to the nurturing of students' higher order thinking skills.

Negotiation.   The fourth primary component that is central to the contractual model of management is negotiation. Without a genuine commitment by you to negotiate with your students in areas of their vital interests—such as the content of curricular units, individual and group learning experiences, classroom roles and responsibilities, and disruptive conflicts between teacher and students and among students—the contractual paradigm is rendered meaningless.

We view negotiation as a particularly effective instructional strategy with students who have traditionally been marginalized in school. Many of these students have been shuttled from one pull-out program to another. They have learned to keep quiet in their regular classrooms, where they are provided with a custodial form of instruction recognizable by low-level, skills-based activities and an inordinate amount of individual, sit-in-your-seat, keep quiet, and fill-in-the-ditto-sheet learning activities. These students have also had their classroom voices silenced by a threatening program of tests: pretests, placement tests, skills tests, chapter tests, unit tests, criterion-referenced tests, norm-referenced tests, and posttests.

The very process of negotiation empowers students; it makes them part of the decision-making and planning process. When you empower students to assume responsibility for their own learning, and when you support them with a helping relationship based on individual and mutual respect, you likely will eliminate many negative student behaviors. In classrooms where all students are empowered to negotiate with their authentic voices, many negative student behaviors, such as temper tantrums, sullenness, hostility, and open disobedience, will be minimized. Students will have negotiated options to acting out these negative behaviors as a means of meeting their needs. They individually and collectively can negotiate with you to change the rules, modify the curriculum, or select alternative learning experiences.

We think negotiation has metaphorical implications that better fit contemporary classrooms than the factory metaphor. What is "negotiable," like coin of the realm, is something to which we assign a high value. The implication is that students will place more value on curricular experiences and classroom rules in which they have used their authentic voices in genuine negotiation (see Boomer et al., 1992; McNeil, 1981).

There will always be nonnegotiables, the givens that you may have no power to negotiate. You will not be able to negotiate a shorter school day, commandeer school buses for daily field trips, establish an additional recess period, or add activities that would create unsafe conditions (see McLaughlin, 1994, pp. 82–83, for more discussion on the limits of classroom negotiations). Nevertheless, in a classroom marked by solidarity, caring, and mutual respect, teachers can explore potential areas to access students' needs for redefining boundaries and to determine the possibility of negotiation.

Contractual Management Model at BBMS

A school that reflects the central elements of the contractual model is Brown Barge Middle School (BBMS) in Pensacola, Florida.* Students at BBMS have a shared voice in decision making about what is taught and how it is taught. In fact, the content taught at BBMS, divided into 12-week content units called streams, is derived from surveys completed by students and their parents. BBMS has an integrated curriculum that puts students together by streams to be studied, not by tracking or ability grouping. As students work closely together with their stream peers and with their stream teachers, over time they build solidarity.

Because students at BBMS have a strong voice in what they learn and in how they learn it, they are empowered by the school as they become proactive learners and critical thinkers about timely and relevant topics. They also assume responsibility to help peers learn because all students in the school work together collaboratively

---

* BBMS is discussed more fully in Chapter 6. We suggest that you review this section of the book to understand how the school reflects the contractual model.

in small groups. Moreover, because students have responsibility for their own learning and for that of their peers, they learn the real value of mutual respect.

ACTIVITY 10.2   The Contractual Model in Action: The Case of Katherine

Read Katherine's story, which follows. Katherine is a veteran elementary teacher whose story is relevant to all grade levels. Her story was reported by one of us (Zehm) in another book (Zehm & Kottler, 1993, pp. 111–115); we have abridged the story here to fit the confines of this chapter. Katherine knows the joys and trials of contemporary public school teaching, and she demonstrates on a daily basis the central elements of the contractual mode.

Katherine's Story

I have been an elementary teacher for the past twenty-three years. Twenty-three years is a long time, but I've enjoyed every minute of it. Well . . . most of them.

My principal tells people that I was born with the ability to motivate students. He embarrasses me when he calls me a "classroom wizard" who casts the spell of lifelong learning on students. This makes some of my colleagues joke that I use some enchanting incantation or magic wand to motivate students to become eager about learning.

I don't have any magic. Furthermore, I really don't believe that I can motivate my students to learn. I do believe now, after thinking about it for many years, that motivation must come from inside my students. If I have a secret, it is that I talk frequently with each of my students. I get to know all about them, their hopes, fears, what they dream about, the kinds of pain they have known. I try to find the gifts in all my students; I try to build on their strengths. Knowing as much as I can about them helps me find ways to tap into their inner motivation.

I consciously try to avoid naming and listing their limitations. When I discover their strengths, I help them choose significant learning experiences to build on these strengths. I try to structure my classroom space to encourage their active involvement in authentic learning. Most of the time, my students find success in these experiences, success which builds up their self-esteem.

I also try to establish a context for learning in which my students are encouraged to mutually esteem one another. I give them regular opportunities to share their lives and interests with one another. I try to make real-world alterations for routinized classroom activities. For example, rather than the traditional, boring "show and tell," I substitute a variation such as "show and tell smorgasbord." To do this, I ask five students to bring in an unusual object to share. In five groups with three to four students as an audience, the students show and tell about their objects to small groups. The student audience learns how to listen, observe, ask questions, and respect their peers. Every four minutes, the show-and-tellers switch to the next group to make their presentations again.

What keeps me coming back to my classroom year after year are the many new things I learn every day. I believe my enthusiasm for learning gives me a lot of material for teaching. I know it gives me real credibility with my students. They know I'm a lifelong learner because they see I am eager to learn outside of class and inside of class as well. Also, let me say this because it is true, I have learned so much from my students that has really enriched my life.

Please don't think that I have not had any challenges that have made me grow in my professional life. Just this year five Hispanic students were assigned to my class. They spoke no English; I spoke no Spanish. I really felt badly at first because we couldn't communicate with each other. I felt helpless; I was tempted to try and get them assigned to a Spanish-speaking teacher.

Then I began to see that these little "lost" ones were not so lost after all. I found that these children of migrant farm workers also possessed admirable strengths. They knew more math than my regular first grade students; they could make change, they could tell time, they knew weights and measures. They knew the geography of the United States better than I did because they had worked alongside their parents in many states. They also began to pick up fluency in English at an astonishing rate, mainly from interacting with their classmates.

Now we are learning from them. Every day, they are teaching us to speak Spanish. They are also teaching us about their culture, not about tacos and enchiladas, but about more important things such as the respect they have for their parents, the unselfish love they show their families, and the value they place on working hard to help each other. I am the lucky one to have them in my class.

Reflecting on Katherine

1. In what ways has Katherine intuitively applied the principal features of the contractual paradigm? How closely does she align with each feature?
2. How do your predispositions for using the contractual model of management compare and contrast with Katherine's?
3. Reexamine the autobiography that you developed in Chapter 3. From your own story, try to decide how you consciously or unconsciously might use the contractual model. For what reasons might you automatically, almost without thought, use the factory-driven model of classroom management?
4. Would Katherine's style of management, which we equate with the contractual model, work in every school and in every classroom? In which schools and classrooms might her style be more useful? In which schools and classrooms might her style be less useful?

ACTIVITY 10.3   Transition to a Contractual Model

Imagine that a school district has decided to move from a factory orientation to a contractual orientation. The school district, in only a few years, has experienced a rapid growth in student diversity, moving from a K–12 student population that was mostly homogeneous to one that is mostly heterogeneous relative to ethnicity, religious beliefs, and other cultural factors. School officials, in learning about negotiation models of management, thought that this upcoming change in teaching orientation would help all students be part of the learning environment at school. Traditionally, the school has been firmly entrenched in the factory model of management, and many teachers in the district believe this model to be effective.

1. How might school officials and administrators approach the teachers to encourage them to try out a negotiation model of management?

2. What in-service workshops should the district conduct for teachers to help them learn about the contractual model of management that it wants to implement? How many workshops should be planned? What should be done at these workshops? What support should teachers receive throughout the year to implement the contractual model?

3. What new skills would students need to learn to be successful participants in the contractual model, especially if they have been indoctrinated to the factory model of management?

4. If you were the personnel director of this school district, what questions would you ask candidates for teaching positions to ensure that they would support the contractual model of management?

ADDITIONAL MODELS OF MANAGEMENT

A number of existing models of teaching and learning for culturally diverse classrooms, like the contractual model, have their roots in democratic, human-centered principles, not in the behavior-centered principles of the factory paradigm. The models below, although briefly described, give an overview of the main features of each model and help you construct a broader understanding of the contractual paradigm.

Classroom Community Model

A growing number of elementary and secondary educators are restructuring their schools, departments, and classrooms by using the community metaphor to replace the factory metaphor implicit in the classroom management paradigm. Essential to the community metaphor is the pervasive caring recommended by Etzioni (1983, 1993), Peck (1986), and Noddings (1986). Genuine caring reduces the need for the mandated conformity that overshadows traditional classroom management models. The notion of classroom community, which respects ethnicity, gender, and home language of all members, is also recommended by the Holmes Group (1990) and the Association for Supervision and Curriculum Development (1990) as a restructuring model effective in culturally diverse classrooms.

The classroom as community model incorporates cooperative learning strategies to promote mutual respect and understanding among culturally diverse students. The model developed by Cohen (1986), for example, is especially effective in building a sense of community in school classrooms. Cohen's model of cooperative learning provides clear roles and responsibilities for all students so that they have regular opportunities to develop their academic and leadership skills.

Restructuring efforts that seek to replace the factory model with a community model are not without risk. For example, Bullough (1994) describes the restructuring efforts of a group of high school faculty who, with his assistance, built a curriculum on the learning community metaphor, only to have it terminated 2 years later. Teachers organized ninth-grade learning communities; developed integrated units of study in science, English, and social studies; and committed themselves to following their students from freshman to senior year. According to Bullough, "the Learning Community metaphor altered our ways of thinking about teaching, learning, and teacher-student relationship" (p. 7). Among the changed expectations of the participating teachers were a pervasive caring for all members of the community, an increased sense of student ownership of their own work, and a rejection of routine teacher-imposed disciplinary measures.

Yet, the community model did not last at this school. Bullough's (1994) explanation of why the program failed underscores the difficulty you might experience when you try out an alternative model of management, something other than the factory model, in traditional school settings. Bullough writes:

> While the teachers and students struggled to establish new roles and relationships associated with building a Learning Community, the rest of the school marched along as before, a fragmented factory but a factory nonetheless. Tensions built and eventually the nonparticipating teachers revolted. One issue was that some teachers, those included in the Learning Community, had an additional planning period. According to other teachers, this was unfair. In a factory, fairness is a matter of treating everyone the same way: teachers have the same student loads, do the same work, and get the same rewards. Any variation from the norm is unacceptable. Without an additional planning period, the [Learning Community] teams could not operate. Union regulations requiring that all teachers have exactly the same schedules and loads were invoked. The school board refused to back the program and fight the battles necessary to preserve it. And so, after two difficult but rewarding years, the program collapsed, or more accurately, was crushed. (p. 7)

Human Rights Model

The human rights model developed by Garcia (1991) extends the classroom community model by emphasizing the cultural and human rights of all members of the classroom community. Although Garcia links his model to the traditional management model, we believe it is more appropriately rooted in the contractual model we propose, because Garcia emphasizes the contractual obligations of both teachers and students as the foundation for the human rights strategies he advocates for use in culturally diverse classrooms. "Each student," Garcia explains, "as an individual member of the community, makes a social contract with the community: 'I will enter the community to pursue my self interest of learning; the community will insure my basic right to learn; I must respect the right of everyone else to learn'" (p. 194).

The human rights model also emphasizes another important dimension of the contractual paradigm, the moral obligation you have to provide for the learning needs of all students. Garcia (1991) describes this dimension as "ethical transcendence," which he defines as "a means by which teachers can transcend, in a morally appropriate manner, the many human differences that are manifest among students in classrooms" (p. 194).

Cultural Democracy Model

The cultural democracy model of teaching and learning rejects the factory metaphor and substitutes the metaphors of country, nation, apprenticeship, and citizenship.

First articulated by Dewey (1916), the model of cultural democracy has been more recently emphasized by a number of educators committed to building more culturally sensitive learning that empowers bicultural students (Darder, 1992; Freire, 1972; Giroux, 1988; Ramirez & Castaneda, 1974).

For Dewey the public school was an apprenticeship in democratic living where students were encouraged to recognize and respect cultural differences, to understand the moral imperatives of genuine democratic living, and to participate in dialogue and negotiation to resolve their conflicts and to expand their worldviews. Recent attention has been focused on democratic metaphors of schooling. Freire (1972) shares Dewey's conviction that the image of apprenticeship in democratic living is a more fitting metaphor for learning in culturally diverse classrooms. Freire envisions classroom teaching rooted in the democratic process of active participation, personal responsibility, social solidarity, and constant dialogue and debate. Giroux (1988) encourages learning experiences crafted from the personal histories of students and the community values, traditions, and ways of knowing that are frequently ignored by the dominant culture of the school. Darder (1992) provides a comprehensive analysis of the principles generated by cultural democracy. The principles Darder describes in the opening quote of this chapter and in the quote below are rooted in those features of the contractual paradigm we have described above. Darder writes,

> Central to any theory that speaks to the notion of democracy in the classroom is the necessary requirement that it address seriously the themes of student participation, solidarity, common interest, and the development of voice. . . . If bicultural students are to become competent in the democratic process, they must be given the opportunities to experience it actively as it gradually becomes a part of their personal history. (Darder, 1992, p. 67)

SUMMARY

Why schools today have such fidelity to the factory model of management in a society that is very different from the one that existed when the factory model was actually implemented is very perplexing, certainly very troubling, and—for many students in today's classrooms—very disengaging. Teaching traditions and habits embedded in factorylike school management, when combined with conservative mainstream values, collectively comprise a powerful hold on classroom teaching, on the minds of school administrators, and on teacher education. If you are helped to understand the inherent value in alternative management models in the face of this tradition and habit, and if you are helped to learn strategies for implementing alternative management models, you will very likely be frustrated when you are to comply with existing norms of traditional management. Studies suggest that this kind of frustration causes you to criticize your teacher preparation program, saying that it failed to prepare you to "fit into" the existing school system and that your teacher preparation was irrelevant because it taught you strategies that could not immediately be implemented. However, if you are not helped to question traditional models of management by teacher education programs and by colleges of education, then the road is paved for an unquestioning, wholesale use of factory management, a model being questioned for its efficacy in culturally diverse classrooms.

What, then, should we do as an educational community, especially when rapid and unprecedented changes in student demographics suggest the need for changes in existing school management practices? There is no simple answer to this question. Yet we can, as Bullough (1994) and Greene (1994) suggest, begin imagining school classrooms and our relationship with students, not as they now exist in traditional form, but as they might be in a new form. This awakening of imagination can indeed bring about significant changes in our perspectives and in our actions, as Kearney (1988) so eloquently explains, if we only would give ourselves the freedom to awaken our own imaginations for managing schools and classrooms in ways that engage all students in meaningful, relevant, and divergent learning.

RESEARCH TOPIC

Exploring Alternative Models of Management

Problem Posing

In this chapter, you compared and contrasted the traditional model of management, commonly called the factory model, with an alternative model of management, called the contractual model. You considered strengths and limitations of these models, and you considered obstacles you might face as you implement the contractual model of management. The overall purpose of this research project is to help you explore your alignment with traditional and alternative models in actual classroom practice. Another purpose is to help you consider various parts of your own teaching that might be more negotiable with students.

This project can be undertaken by preservice, beginning, and experienced teachers. Regardless of which developmental phase you are in, you face certain challenges when you try out an alternative model of management. If you are a preservice teacher, you very likely completed your K–12 schooling in a factorylike school. The primacy of these schooling experiences has a powerful influence on your assumptions about management. If you are a student teacher and you want to try out parts of the contractual model, you might be constrained if you are teaching with a cooperating teacher who endorses the factory management model. And if you are an experienced teacher, you might have been teaching with the factory model for many years and so have become habituated to the assumptions and actions of this model; thus, you will be required to rethink your relations with students, the content you teach, and your classroom decision making.

In this project, you explore how moving to a contractual model of management will effect changes in your classroom practice. And you explore obstacles to overcome, if possible, to make this move. The following questions can serve as a framework for your research, along with additional questions you might develop.

1. Depending on your developmental stage of teaching (preservice teacher, student teacher, beginning teacher, experienced teacher), what are the main obstacles you have to confront when trying out the contractual model? What are the consequences of overcoming these obstacles?
2. Which dimensions of the contractual model might you already be using in the classroom? If you are observing another teacher for this research project instead of studying your own teaching, what dimensions of the contractual model does the teacher demonstrate, if any?
3. What changes will occur in your classroom learning environment if you implement a management model more reflective of the contractual model?

Exploration and Discovery

To answer the questions above, you can study your own teaching or that of another teacher. You can answer the first question by filling in Table 10–3; to do so, first reflect in a realistic manner on your teaching situation or on the one you are observing and then make a list of obstacles to implementing the contractual model and the consequences of overcoming these obstacles.

Answering the second question above can be done by making observations of classroom teaching. You can view your own teaching with videotapes of your lessons. Be sure to compare your own teaching or the teaching of a peer or colleague to the dimensions of the contractual model described in this chapter. Take an inventory of your present skills. In Table 10–4, rate the degree of alignment you have with each dimension and give an example of how you exemplify the dimensions.

The third question in the problem-posing section above requires you to perform action research on your own instruction. You may do this with another teacher, however, if you locate one willing to try out the contractual model of management. To determine the consequences of the contractual model on actual classroom teaching,

Table 10–3   Answers for Question Set 1

Obstacles to Implementing the Contractual Model	Consequences of Overcoming the Obstacles
1.	
2.	
3.	
4.	

Table 10–4   Answers for Question Set 2

Dimension	Degree of Alignment	Example of Action
Empowerment		
Roles/Responsibility		
Mutual Respect		
Solidarity		
Negotiation		

select one dimension (e.g., negotiation). Develop an action plan and a timeline for implementing this dimension. As you carry out your implementation plan, record in a personal journal your successes, challenges, obstacles, and feelings about the implementation. Determine how the implementation affected your classroom learning environment and affected learning for students. Continue with this action research until you have tried out each dimension of the contractual paradigm. Determine which dimensions were most useful in engaging all of your students in your lessons and in enhancing your relationships with them.

Reflection and Modification

From what you learned about the contractual model, appraise the feasibility of continuing its use in your teaching. Think about changes you made in your teaching as you implemented various dimensions of the model. Which of these changes, if any, will you make a permanent part of your classroom, and which obstacles could you not overcome during implementation?

Discovery and Speculation

Given what you discovered in this research project, what further studies would help you deepen your understanding of classroom management? Describe these studies below.

1. _____
2. _____
3. _____
4. _____

REFERENCES

Association for Supervision and Curriculum Development. (1990). Restructuring: What is it? *Educational Leadership, 47*(7), 4–90.

Boomer, G., Lester, N., Onore, C., & Cook, J. (1992). *Negotiating the curriculum: Educating for the 21st century.* Washington, DC: Falmer Press.

Bullough, R. V. (1994). Digging at the roots: Discipline, management, and metaphor. *Action in Teacher Education, 16*(1), 1–10.

Cohen, E. (1974). Interracial interaction disability. *Human Relations, 25,* 9–24.

Cohen, E. (1986). *Designing groupwork: Strategies for the heterogeneous classroom.* New York: Teachers College Press.

Darder, A. (1992). *Culture and power in the classroom.* New York: Bergin & Garvey.

Dewey, J. (1916). *Democracy and education.* New York: Free Press.

Etzioni, A. (1983). *An immodest agenda: Rebuilding America before the 21st century.* New York: McGraw-Hill.

Etzioni, A. (1993). *The spirit of community.* New York: Crown.

Freire, P. (1972). *Pedagogy of the oppressed.* Auckland, New Zealand: Penguin Books.

Garcia, R. L. (1991). *Teaching in a pluralistic society: Concepts, models, and strategies.* New York: HarperCollins.

Gergen, K. (1991). *The saturated self: Dilemmas of identity in contemporary life.* New York: Basic Books.

Giroux, H. (1988). *Teachers as intellectuals.* New York: Bergin & Garvey.

Greene, M. (1994, April). *Beginnings, identities, and possibilities: The uses of social imagination.* Paper presented at the Annual Meeting of the American Educational Research Association, New Orleans.

Holmes Group. (1990). *Tomorrow's schools: Principles for the design of professional development schools.* East Lansing, MI: Author.

Kearney, R. (1988). *The wake of imagination: Toward a postmodern culture.* Minneapolis: University of Minnesota Press.

McDiarmid, G. W., Kleinfeld, J., & Parrett, W. (1988). *The inventive mind: Portraits of rural Alaska teachers.* Fairbanks, AK: Center for Cross Cultural Studies.

McLaughlin, H. J. (1991). Reconciling care and control: Authority in classroom relationships. *Journal of Teacher Education, 42*(3), 182–195.

McLaughlin, H. J. (1994). From negation to negotiation: Moving away from the management metaphor. *Action in Teacher Education, 16*(4), 75–84.

McNeil, L. (1981). Negotiating classroom knowledge: Beyond achievement and socialization. *Journal of Curriculum Studies, 13*(4), 313–328.

Noddings, N. (1986). Fidelity in teaching, teacher education, and research for teaching. *Harvard Educational Review, 56*(4), 496–510.

Oldfather, P., & McLaughlin, J. (1993). Gaining and losing voice: A longitudinal study of students' continuing impulse to learn across elementary and middle level contexts. *Research in Middle Level Education, 17*(1), 1–25.

Patthey-Chavez, G. G. (1993). High school as an arena for cultural conflict and acculturation for Latino Angelinos. *Anthropology and Education Quarterly, 24*(1), 33–60.

Peck, M. (1986). *The different drum: Community making and peace.* New York: Simon & Schuster.

Powell, R. R. (in press). Teams and the affirmation of middle level students' voices: The case of Jimmie and related thoughts of a concerned educator. In T. Dickinson & T. Erb (Eds.), *Interdisciplinary teaming at the middle level.* Columbus, OH: National Middle School Association.

Ramirez, M., & Castaneda, A. (1974). *Cultural democracy: Bicognitive development and education.* New York: Academic Press.

Rist, R. (1974). Student, social class, and teacher expectations: The self-fulfilling prophecy in ghetto education. *Harvard Educational Review, 40*, 411–451.

Rosenholtz, S. (1984). Treating problems of academic status. In J. Berger & M. Zeiditch, Jr. (Eds.), *Status, rewards, and influence.* San Francisco: Jossey-Bass.

Sergiovanni, T. (1993). *Moral leadership.* San Francisco: Jossey-Bass.

Zehm, S., & Kottler, J., Jr. (1993). *On being a teacher: The human dimension.* Newbury Park, CA: Corwin Press.

Chapter 11

Implementing Culturally Relevant Curriculum

I'm not saying that great literature is irrelevant. It's relevant in that it helps you see the world in a broader way. But it's not relevant if it alienates you.   (Joanie Phillips, September 1993)

Do we teach women's and African American's history in eleventh grade social studies? Do we read Toni Morrison and Alice Walker in twelfth grade literature? These are sociopolitical questions—that is, they involve power.   (Kincheloe, 1993, pp. 26–27)

Contingencies of the wider sociocultural system within which the pedagogical encounter is embedded provide patterns of constraint that shape the definitions, social objects, and the opportunities for choice that are present in the immediate scene of everyday [school] life as a "curriculum."   (Erickson, 1982, p. 167)

RECOGNIZING SOCIOCULTURAL DIMENSIONS OF CURRICULUM

Have you ever been in a classroom in which you felt alienated from the content you were expected to learn or read—you just couldn't connect with it? If there was a time when you couldn't connect, have you considered why this happened? Would some content, such as books by Alice Walker or Toni Morrison, have helped you feel more connected? Have you considered that the information you learned in school was influenced by many political factors and, consequently, was enmeshed in power struggles by various social groups outside school? The political factors that shaped the content you learned in school caused "patterns of constraint" that shaped which content was selected for you to learn, how it was taught, and why you were expected to learn it. These same patterns of constraint might have been one reason you couldn't connect with some of the content you were expected to learn.

The above discussion is related to your classroom curriculum, which we view in this chapter as essentially everything that happens in your classroom. Your curriculum is not just the specific content you teach, as some preservice and beginning teachers think. Your curriculum is the whole learning environment you create as you interact socially with your students. This means your curriculum is not only the set of textbooks you use but also the information you share with students, the strategies you use to bring students to this information, the materials you select to foster learning, and the social interactions you have with students. Whether you realize it or not, even the materials you (or your school) choose *not* to use in your classroom become part of your curriculum.[1]

An important part of your classroom curriculum is the social relationships you develop with students as you interact with them throughout the school year. Because these social relationships are developed in the midst of the content you teach, your classroom curriculum is socially constructed. At the risk of oversimplification, we explain briefly what we mean when we say your classroom curriculum is socially constructed.[2] At any moment of the school day, your classroom curriculum is comprised of many things, including the personal qualities and needs that you and your students bring to the classroom. As your personal needs and those of your students meet and mingle in the presence of some kind of content, and in the presence of overall school expectations, you socially construct a classroom curriculum together. Because you, as a function of being a classroom teacher, have both political and institutional power over your students, your personal beliefs about how students should learn, along with expectations of the school administrators, set the tone for your classroom climate and give shape to your classroom curriculum.

Your personal beliefs about how students learn determine the kinds of negotiations you have with students about your classroom curriculum.[3] During these negotiations, which occur every teaching moment of every school day, your personal sociocultural system (prior schooling, race, gender, class, religion, worldview, family, culture, beliefs about teaching and learning) and the sociocultural systems of your students (race, gender, class, religion, culture, family) interact to shape your classroom curriculum.[4]

When you are aware of your own sociocultural system, which you began to explore in Chapter 3, and when you become aware of the sociocultural systems of your students, you are better prepared to recognize which factors (personal, social, cultural, gender, class, religion) unnecessarily constrain or necessarily foster opportunities for student learning. Being sensitive to sociocultural systems also means thinking critically about your classroom curriculum and asking sociopolitical questions like, Whose knowledge am I teaching? Why am I teaching in this particular way? How can I effectively teach the histories and cultures of the majority of working people, of women, and of people of color to my students?[5] Asking these questions, regardless of your school context or school location, helps you understand the relevancy of teaching, for example, women's and African American history in 11th grade and reading Toni Morrison and Alice Walker in 12th grade. Having this understanding is an important step toward transforming your classroom curriculum into one that is culturally relevant.

UNDERSTANDING CULTURALLY RELEVANT CURRICULA

If curriculum is everything that goes on in the classroom, as we suggested above, how can you make your curriculum culturally relevant so that it can be personally meaningful to your students? There is much to consider here—for example, textbooks, other written teaching materials, evaluation and assessment strategies, seating arrangements, wall and bulletin board decorations, your interactions with students, students' interactions with other students, conflict resolution, classroom management, overall school expectations, communication styles, learning styles, students' home lives, and the list goes on. Talking about developing a culturally relevant curriculum, then, means giving full consideration to all of these items, not just the books, handouts, and other written materials you use in your instruction.

Making your classroom curriculum culturally relevant means weaving together students' cultures with all that goes on in your classroom on an ongoing basis. Such weaving makes your classroom curriculum culturally responsive, especially when you make students' cultures a naturally flowing part of your classroom learning environment. Weaving together students' cultures and classroom instruction may not be effective, however, unless you understand how to appropriately interact with students whose cultural patterns of communication and learning vary from yours. Frederick Erickson, an anthropologist of school classrooms, clarifies this in the following comment:

> If a child comes from a speech network (culture) in which direct questions are avoided because they are regarded as intrusive, when a teacher routinely asks that child a direct question in the classroom the child may be puzzled by the teacher's strange behavior, and assume that teacher is angry. (Erickson, 1987, p. 337)

An important point to be made from Erickson's observation is that having curriculum materials (e.g., books, handouts, bulletin boards) that you consider to be culturally relevant for students are by themselves only one part of a culturally relevant curriculum. Curriculum materials (e.g., textbooks) are tools available to teachers.[6] How you actually use these tools when you interact with students, how you communicate with students in class, and how you respond to their linguistic patterns of communication are just as important in developing a culturally relevant classroom curriculum as the actual teaching tools you use.[7]

ACTIVITY 11.1   Focusing on Sociocultural Phenomena That Influence Classroom Curriculum

In this activity, you explore some of the phrases we introduced in the introductory sections of this chapter. One way to explore is to make observations in a school classroom. Recall that we described classroom curricula as being socially constructed—as being influenced by many sociocultural factors. And we suggested that a classroom curriculum is all that goes on inside a school classroom. Seeing "all that goes on" in a classroom is, of course, limited by your personal perspectives of teaching and your prior experiences inside and outside school; that is, you can only perceive classroom events as much as your experiential background will allow you to perceive and comprehend (Neisser, 1976). Because each person has limited potential in what he or she can perceive, your understanding of what goes on in a selected classroom can be broadened and deepened when you listen to what your peers and colleagues are perceiving and comprehending.

Select a classroom to observe over a period of several weeks. Use the questions below to help you explore what goes on within the lived experience of this classroom.

1. What is happening in the classroom?
2. What has been (or is being) negotiated by teachers and students?
3. What sociocultural factors of the teacher are influencing the classroom curriculum?
4. What sociocultural factors of the students are influencing the classroom curriculum?
5. What sociocultural factors of the school are influencing the classroom curriculum?
6. How is the classroom curriculum being socially constructed? What appears to be having the most influence on how the curriculum is constructed?

After responding to these questions, describe how students' sociocultural systems are being woven into the classroom curriculum, if at all. If you find scant evidence, what changes would you make to the classroom curriculum to ensure that the weaving occurs?

TEXTBOOKS AND RELATED INSTRUCTIONAL MATERIALS

Now that you understand how a classroom curriculum is influenced by multiple dimensions, look more closely at one particular dimension—namely, the teaching tools you use, such as textbooks and related materials. The textbook remains the predominant medium for communicating content to students in most classrooms. As a teacher, you are a facilitator of student learning. Consequently, you have the important responsibility of choosing instructional materials, such as a textbook, or creating ones that are culturally sensitive, that engage students in culturally meaningful ways. This is not always a simple, straightforward process, especially when the materials and textbooks you use are prescribed by the school district where you work.

You might not have the freedom to choose the kinds of materials you would like to use for a specific group of students when your school district prescribes the content you teach. This problem can be disconcerting when you discover, like Bigelow (1992), that the materials you are required to use are culturally insensitive for your students; they give a distorted view, perhaps even a culturally oppressive view, of some societal groups.[8] Bigelow claims that the depiction of Christopher Columbus in children's literature is distorted and harmful. He notes:

> Children's biographies of Christopher Columbus function as primers on racism and imperialism. They teach youngsters to accept the right of white people to rule over people of color, of powerful nations to dominate weaker nations. And because the Columbus myth is so pervasive—Columbus's "discovery" is probably the *only* historical episode with which all my students at Jefferson High School are familiar—it is vital that educators analyze how this myth inhibits children from developing democratic, multicultural, and anti-racist attitudes. (p. 112)

When you, like Bigelow, discover materials that have the potential to develop distorted images of persons or societal/cultural groups, how can you transform these into culturally relevant instructional materials? One way to do this, according to Bigelow (1992), is to help students look critically and skeptically at certain accounts, "inviting children to become detectives, interrogating their biographies, novels, and textbooks for bias" (p. 119). This means helping your students understand that *discovering a country,* a phrase that suggests heroism and successful achievement from one perspective, may actually mean *invading other societies* from a different perspective. As a related example, *civilizing a nation* from one perspective may mean *genocide* from a different perspective.[9]

The value of using instructional materials that are culturally relevant to students is supported by a study conducted by Matthews and Smith (1994). Using instructional materials in science deemed relevant to Native Americans, Matthews and Smith reported that Native American elementary students who used these materials had more positive attitudes and higher levels of achievement than Native American students who used science education materials that were less sensitive to the cultural needs of these students. Related reports further suggest that using instructional materials and creating instructional environments that are sensitive to the cultural needs of students promote achievement and school success for some student groups.[10]

Because the textbook is central to many classrooms and because students use it most often for their main source of information at school, you should pay particular attention to its cultural relevance—that is, to how it reflects, if at all, the varied backgrounds, personal qualities, and perspectives of your students. To examine textbooks for cultural relevance, you first must address some larger questions about their widespread and essentially wholesale use. What is the essential purpose of textbooks? Should textbooks be the central clearinghouse for cultural literacy and therefore for giving all students the same information embedded within a single value system? That is, should textbooks relate a body of facts, lists, and concepts for students to master that make all students culturally literate in similar ways? Or should textbooks and other related materials "create the condition necessary for all [students] to participate in the creation and recreation of meaning and values" (Apple, 1993, p. 62)? Should textbooks help students question their taken-for-granted reality, to offer them alternative ways of thinking and believing?[11]

Addressing these two latter questions means rethinking traditional classroom instruction. In traditional instruction, you and your textbooks tend to prefigure meaning and selected values for students. To move away from this practice, you have to rethink classroom instruction in terms of a transformative, negotiated curriculum. Such a curriculum will include your voice, as well as those of your students, other educators, and textbook authors (and their publishers), who contribute equally to the construction of shared meaning in your classroom.[12] In such a curriculum, you and your students collectively create meaning as the voices and lives of students become part of your classroom curriculum.

We have suggested that the textbooks you use are tools. Consequently, we may have given you the impression that textbooks are lifeless until teachers and students act on them. The textbooks you use are not lifeless, however; they are alive with the values, beliefs, biases, and perspectives of authors and textbook publishers. Of importance here is the fact that of all the possible information that could be included in the textbook(s) you use, only a fraction of this information is actually included. This fraction has been carefully selected and crafted by persons who have values, beliefs, and biases that ultimately shape the content your students are expected to learn. To clarify this point, reconsider Bigelow's (1992) concern about how Christopher Columbus is depicted by biographers in children's books.

During the past two decades, textbook publishers have been increasingly sensitive to issues surrounding equitable representation of various social/cultural groups in textbooks.[13] In addition to their own corporate needs (profitability), publishers try to be responsive to many social groups—teachers, administrators, school board members, special interest groups, religious groups, to name just a few. In adjusting school textbooks to so many groups, textbook publishers often resist taking stands on issues that might involve controversy (e.g., to give the name *genocide,* when appropriate and needed, to actions that in school textbooks may otherwise be called *civilizing nations*).[14]

ACTIVITY 11.2   Examining Textbooks for Cultural Relevancy[15]

Locate several textbooks related to your classroom instruction. Use the textbooks to complete the analyses below. Because textbooks often are the central feature of classroom curricula, appraising them for cultural relevancy to students is of the utmost importance. Because of space limitations, we provide a rather simple set of analytical guidelines below. For a more comprehensive set of textbook analysis guidelines, see Grant and Sleeter (1989, pp. 104–109).

Topical Content Analysis

Pick several themes/topics that you have responsibility for teaching (e.g., Christopher Columbus/discovery, slave trade, contributions of scientists, language/arts, literature). The questions below can help you perform a content analysis on the theme or topic.

1. What content is included on the theme? How is the content depicted? Whose value system is represented in the content?
2. How is the presentation of a selected theme reflective of the students you teach?
3. Does the theme include a variety of perspectives? If not, how could you ensure that a variety of perspectives are taught with the theme or topic?
4. How does the depiction of the theme you explored help students connect with the content? How might the depiction alienate students from your lessons?
5. Using Bigelow's critique as a model, appraise the theme you explored. State whether you would teach the content as depicted, or whether you would change the content in some way to make it more culturally relevant.

Portrayal of Cultural Groups

One important feature of textbooks in a globalized society is that they depict various cultural groups in a positive and appropriate manner.[16] The rationale is that all cultural groups of students need to see their communities depicted in textbooks if they are to feel like they are part of the content. To determine this inclusion, you must look closely at how various persons are depicted in pictures, story problems, and anthologies. The following questions offered by Mary Atwater (1993, p. 34) can help you examine textbooks for appropriate portrayal of cultural groups.

Stereotyping

- Do Anglo American males hold the majority of the career-oriented positions? What are their careers?
- Are there differences between the roles that males of color fill and the roles that Anglo American males fill?
- Are there differences between the roles that females of color fill and the roles that Anglo American females fill?

Balance

- From whose perspective is the text written?
- Are predominantly Western terms used to describe other peoples and groups (e.g., *Indians* instead of *Native Americans, tribes* instead of *nations*)?
- Is the perspective slanted?
- Does the presentation provide the proper perspective on the contributions and struggles of underrepresented groups?

Unreality

- Does the text deal with controversial topics, such as discrimination and prejudice?
- Does it accurately reflect the real world?

Infusion

- Are the contributions of people of color treated as unique occurrences (highlighted in a box or chapter), or are they integrated into the main body of the text? When depicted as unique occurrences, contributions of social groups can further perpetuate stereotypes.

- Does the presentation of people of color remove their contributions from the mainstream of history, writing them off as an interesting diversion?

Cross-Discipline Analysis

Now move beyond the specific subject area you examined above in a selected textbook to yet another part of the school curriculum. That is, if you reviewed an English or history book, then select a science, math, or technology textbook. Review this new book by using the same criteria above. Compare and contrast this book with the one you analyzed above and with others in the school curriculum.

CHALLENGES FOR DEVELOPING A CULTURALLY RELEVANT CURRICULUM

When you begin making your classroom curriculum culturally relevant to your students, you likely will face many challenges. Below we briefly describe some of them. Keep in mind that the items are not formidable barriers, but rather are challenges to your beliefs, habits, and predispositions for making a curriculum that helps all of your students learn from and connect with your classroom and school curriculum.

Overcome the Primacy of Former Schooling Experiences

If you completed elementary, middle, and high schools that were predominantly monocultural learning environments with only few other representative social groups (e.g., mostly Hispanic; mostly Asian; mostly Black; mostly White), you might not even have thought about the need to transform your curriculum into one that is culturally relevant. This lack is because all of your years of schooling may have been uniform, with little if any attention given to shaping curriculum and instruction to the needs of a culturally diverse classroom. In this instance, your former teachers may have presented basic content in a straightforward manner, only rarely adding supplemental information other than what was required by the school district and what students were required to know for standardized examinations. If this applies to you, you may have to make extra effort to overcome the primacy of your monocultural schooling experiences when creating culturally relevant curricula. Knowing that your former schooling experiences may cause you to unknowingly teach in ways that you were taught as a student is important in overcoming any negative consequences of former schooling experiences.

Make the Content You Teach Culturally Relevant

Strategically applying cultural resources in your classroom curriculum is a strategy you should do regardless of whether you teach high school science, middle school reading, or elementary school mathematics.[17] This also holds true whether you teach in schools with predominantly one social group of students or many distinct social groups.

Some subjects, such as history and government, seem to lend themselves naturally to cultural relevancy. Yet, as the example of Christopher Columbus mentioned earlier suggests, even these areas can be problematic when helping students understand how subjects such as history are organized around values and beliefs of authors. Other subjects, such as science and mathematics, may appear more objective and factual. Consequently, these subjects may be perceived as being absolved from cultural relevancy. However, continual underrepresentation of some cultural groups in science and mathematics, both in school and later as careers, suggests that these areas are most in need of culturally relevant curriculum materials.[18] Making your classroom curriculum relevant to your students regardless of the content and grade level is supported by the work of Gay (1988), who notes:

> At its best, multicultural education permeates the entire school curricula, in that essential knowledge, skills, concepts, and ideas of the various subjects are taught through examples, illustrations, content, experiences, and perspectives selected from different ethnic and cultural group heritages. (p. 332)

Become a Proactive Curriculum Maker

Proactive teachers who make their classroom curriculum relevant to the needs of their students frequently create their own teaching materials. If these teachers do not create their own materials, then they greatly enrich their existing materials with information relevant to students' cultural lives so that these materials are more personally meaningful for the students they teach. This practice was demonstrated by all of the teachers we described in Chapter 7 and for effective teachers described elsewhere.[19]

We have taken the idea of being a curriculum maker from the work of Clandinin and Connelly (1992), who compare teachers who make their own classroom curriculum with those who implement and manage prescribed classroom curriculum. These latter teachers (implementers and managers) transmit information to students in a linear fashion, from teacher as content authority to student as unknowing learner. Teachers who see themselves as content authorities tend to put content first and the needs of students second.

To make classroom curriculum culturally sensitive, you must know where students are relative to what is being taught. You also must know how to bring students' voices into curricular decision making through the careful selection of instructional materials, activities, and information (Boomer et al., 1992). This tactic requires you to know your students, not just by name and by a few personality features, but by culture, family, and home. Joanie Phillips, whose teaching is described in Chapter 7, got to know her students by having them write about their home experiences and by actually visiting students' homes and families.

Create a Transformative Curriculum

An important feature of any curriculum that is truly culturally relevant is its transformative nature.[20] Banks (1993) notes that a transformative curriculum helps students "view concepts, issues, events, and themes from the perspectives of diverse ethnic and cultural groups" (p. 199). This kind of curriculum involves far more than focusing on heroes, holidays, and discrete cultural events, what Banks calls the "contributions approach," which perpetuates stereotypes of some social groups. And it involves more than merely adding content, concepts, themes, and perspectives to the curriculum without changing its structure, what Banks calls the "additive approach." In these two approaches, the basic structure of the curriculum remains the same; only cultural content is added. For example, you are probably familiar with the additive approach called Black history month, which usually means adding specific content about African Americans to an existing curriculum. In this manner, Black history becomes an anomalous part of the curriculum, as an afterthought, rather than an integral part that has been carefully and thoughtfully woven throughout an entire curriculum. Moreover, adding anomalous lessons to an existing curriculum without careful forethought and planning keeps the content of these lessons outside the regular curriculum; thus their perceived value is minimized.

Rather than append content to an existing curriculum, such as adding lessons on various aspects of African American cultures, a transformative curriculum changes the basic structure of the curriculum, including content and reading material. Content is presented throughout the school year so that students see it from multiple perspectives. As one example of a transformative curriculum, rather than teach literature representative of authors from primarily one or two countries, you might teach literature over time that is reflective of authors from many countries and many cultures.

Engage Students Culturally and Academically

When you make a transformative curriculum, you very likely will engage students more effectively in the content. Although you might not be able to connect every fact, sentence, story, or formula you teach with students' cultural backgrounds—nor should you be expected to—you nevertheless must remain mindful that the less often you do this connection, the more you risk alienating students from your lessons academically. Students alienated from your lessons most likely will not be motivated to learn, participate, or even pass the course.[21]

Perhaps even more important here is the idea that you may have every kind of culturally relevant material for your students, but if you don't use them effectively, the materials will be of no value. Ineffective use of such materials can even be counterproductive in the learning process; thus stereotypes and biases that students have toward other cultural groups are further ingrained. If culturally relevant curriculum materials are used effectively, however, they hold the potential of helping your students connect personally, culturally, and academically with the content you teach.[22] They also hold the potential for helping your students understand how any biases and stereotypes they may have for students from other cultural groups can influence their interactions with students from these groups.

Understand Equity and Excellence in Curriculum

Educators often become confused when they talk about the notions of equity and excellence in education. Some even hold the misconception that excellence, which is often translated into high achievement scores and higher academic standards, is compromised when issues of equity surface, that the curriculum has to be "watered down" for some student groups who aren't in the mainstream culture. Such students often are given derogatory labels, such as racial minority, inner-city youth, handicapped, learning disabled, economically disadvantaged, and language-minority students. Few teachers' misconceptions have had such widespread damaging consequences for learners as thinking the curriculum must be "watered down" for some students but not for others. Teachers who really think in this way usually expect less from their "disadvantaged" students.[23] These students are then viewed as having deficits to overcome, rather than strengths to build on. Many teachers who hold this deficit view tend to stereotype their students as low-level learners, thus lowering the expectations they have for some students.

To clarify the confusion over equity and excellence, we turn again to the work of Geneva Gay. Gay (1988) notes:

> Excellence finds expression in common standards and expectations of high achievement for all students, and equity translates into appropriate methodologies and materials according to specific group or individual characteristics. Excellence occurs when individual students achieve to the best of their ability, and equity is accomplished when each student is provided with learning opportunities that make high level achievement possible. (p. 328)

Gay further describes how both equity and excellence in classroom curriculum can be maintained for all students:

> Equity as comparability in curriculum means (1) the right of diverse learners to have learning opportunities and experiences that are as likely to succeed for them as those of middle-class Anglo students are, and (2) the selection and allocation of instructional resources, materials, and methodologies that are representative of a wide variety of different ethnic and cultural group experiences. (pp. 328–329)

Watering down a curriculum, according to Gay (1988), is clearly not the answer to meeting the needs of culturally diverse groups of students. One possible answer is believing that all students, regardless of their cultural backgrounds or the labels they are forced to wear, can reach high levels of excellence if they are provided with a curriculum that acknowledges in various ways their ethnic and cultural group experiences. When viewed in this way, as students are viewed at Brown Barge Middle School (see Chapter 6), academic excellence is contingent on knowing how to respond instructionally to issues of equity and how to establish a sociocultural learning environment that offers all students a chance to engage in meaningful social and academic experiences.[24] Academic excellence is therefore contingent on whether you know how to best communicate content to every one of your students, not on whether you know how to dilute your curriculum and lower expectations for learning.

Know the Limitations of Your Classroom Curriculum

The success or failure of students in school quite obviously depends on limitations that surround your classroom curriculum. These limitations are not only related to selection of content; they are much broader. They are related, for example, to how you structure learning activities, how you permit students in class to help each other with their expected learning, and how you respond to students' individual learning styles. These items above emphasize the necessity of knowing enough about your students (equity issues) to help each of them succeed in school (excellence issues). Erickson (1982) provides an example of how one dimension of a classroom curriculum—specifically, the social dynamics of the learning environment—increases the perplexity of solving a mathematics problem.

> If the subject matter task at hand (e.g., an addition problem being done in a classroom) requires carrying from the "ones" column across to the "tens" column, and the student is confused when at the point of carrying, if the social task environment prohibits asking another child for help (because that is defined as inappropriate in the social participation structure), the overall learning task at that point has become more complex. How is the child to get the needed information about an arithmetical operation in a socially appropriate way? This is an example of a sequentially arrived at point at which the learner gets "stuck" because of contradictory demands across the social and academic task dimensions. These sequential points of "stuckness" can become more salient for the learner than the overall task itself. (p. 172)

Another factor related directly to the limitations of your classroom curriculum is how you and your students socially construct the information to be learned. The nature of this information, including the kind of information and its level of difficulty, delimits their thinking and their understanding. Once again, consider Bigelow's critique of how Christopher Columbus is depicted in classroom learning materials. When students learn only the story of Columbus depicted by a single biographer without questioning the value-laden intention of that biographer, they learn only the perspectives associated with this view. Although every curriculum limits students' understanding in some way, such as the social portion of the curriculum described above by Erickson or the content portion of the curriculum described by Bigelow, your primary responsibility as a teacher is to move students from one level of understanding to another level. This movement loosens the limitations that inherently frame and likely constrain your curriculum.

Ground Your Classroom Curriculum in Psychology and Anthropology

As a teacher, you wear many hats. One hat is that of a psychologist. In fact, most teacher preparation programs require preservice teachers to complete a course in educational psychology. Teacher education has an obvious preoccupation with beginning teachers becoming pedagogical technicians who know how to apply psychological principles of learning in the classroom.

We admit the importance of your wearing the hat of a psychologist when you teach; we would be foolish to hold any other position. What we wish to suggest here, however, is that knowing about the psychology of learning without placing this psychology within a framework of anthropology is futile. Without being teacher as anthropologist while at the same time being teacher as psychologist, you run the risk of decontextualizing student learning. This decontextualizing leads you to have one size of instruction (based on your psychological assumptions for student learning) that promises to fit all sizes of students; in short, your classroom curriculum begins ringing with an assimilationist tone. With this tone, you run the risk of alienating students from the very content you intend for them to learn.

How can you become teacher as anthropologist, especially when few teacher preparation programs and few in-service workshops for experienced teachers offer any kind of instruction in the anthropology of learning? First, you must assume responsibility for learning about the social, political, and cultural dimensions of your students as these dimensions are embedded in the immediate learning environment and as they are acted out in the lived experience of daily classroom life.[25] Second, you must take time to learn about the home lives of your students, just as Joanie Phillips demonstrated in Chapter 7. Learning about home lives helps you communicate better with students on many levels, most especially on a cultural level. Finally, you must inform yourself about the cultural backgrounds of your students. You can do this by reading various resource books about the representative cultures of your students.

ACTIVITY 11.3   Addressing the Challenges for a Culturally Relevant Curriculum: Voices of Experienced Teachers

The challenges discussed above give you an idea of the important points you must consider when you move your classroom curriculum toward one that is culturally relevant. In Figure 11–1 are listed the challenges discussed above. For each challenge, we have developed a set of questions. You will most likely be able to add other questions to those we suggest. These questions can serve as a framework for interviewing experienced classroom teachers about challenges they face in making their curricula culturally relevant to students. The overall purpose of this interview is to help you understand how experienced teachers address these challenges in their own classrooms. A second purpose is to determine to what extent the teachers you interview have moved toward creating a culturally relevant curriculum.

The greatest insights will be gained from this activity when you interview two or more teachers. Select a teacher who teaches or has taught in culturally diverse settings where students from many different cultural groups are represented. Select another teacher who teaches or has taught in classrooms that are primarily homogeneous—that is, where students are mostly from one cultural group. You might have to go to different schools to locate these teachers.

The position we take in this book is that all teachers, regardless of school location (urban, suburban, rural) and level of student diversity (homogeneous, heterogeneous), must help students develop an informed, respectful, and tolerant view of cultural diversity in society. The value of interviewing teachers in different types of schools is to explore how teachers whose students have varied academic and cultural needs address the challenges we have posed.

After completing the interviews, determine how the teachers are meeting the challenges described in this chapter. What additional challenges did you discover for these teachers that are not discussed in this chapter?

---

1. Overcome the primacy of former schooling experiences.
   1a. What is the relationship between the classroom curricula you had as a precollege student and the class-room curricula you now use?
2. Make the content you teach culturally relevant.
   2a. Does the content you teach lend itself naturally to helping students learn about multiple perspectives of various social groups?
3. Become a proactive curriculum maker.
   3a. How much of your classroom curriculum do you actually create? How much of your classroom curriculum do you implement that is already prepared (e.g., textbook, commercially prepared handouts)?
4. Create a transformative curriculum.
   4a. Does your classroom curriculum give students an ongoing opportunity to understand how the content you teach is relevant to all cultural groups?
   4b. Do you think the nature of your classroom curriculum might alienate some students? Why or why not?
5. Engage students culturally and academically.
   5a. How does your classroom curriculum engage students both culturally and academically?
   5b. Does the academic portion of your classroom curriculum reflect the perspectives of diverse cultural groups in society?
6. Understand equity and excellence in curriculum.
   6a. How is equity part of your classroom curriculum?
   6b. What is the relationship between equity and excellence?
   6c. What strategies do you use to achieve equity and excellence simultaneously for all of your students?
7. Know the limitations of your classroom curriculum.
   7a. How does your classroom curriculum broaden students' perspectives about the content you teach?
   7b. How does your classroom curriculum limit students' perspectives about the content you teach?
8. Ground your classroom curriculum in psychology and anthropology.
   8a. What psychological assumptions, if any, do you hold for student learning?
   8b. What anthropological assumptions, if any, do you hold for student learning?

Figure 11–1   Challenges for developing a culturally relevant curriculum

TOWARD A CULTURALLY RELEVANT CURRICULUM

Now that you have considered the sociocultural dimensions of curriculum and have thought about some of the challenges you face in implementing a culturally relevant classroom curriculum, you should have a better idea of how such a curriculum applies to your classroom. The model in Figure 11–2, which incorporates much of what we have discussed throughout this chapter, is intended to help you think more extensively about creating a culturally relevant curriculum for your classroom. The model is not intended to be a stepwise, foolproof procedure for developing curriculum; rather, as a heuristic it is intended to help you consider some of the key factors that frame (and in some instances, constrain) the kind of classroom curriculum you want to create. As you actually create your classroom curriculum, this model can help you focus on factors that foster both equity and excellence for your students. A brief description of the model is shown in Figure 11–2. At the end of this chapter is a suggested research project in which you apply the model to actual classroom curriculum.

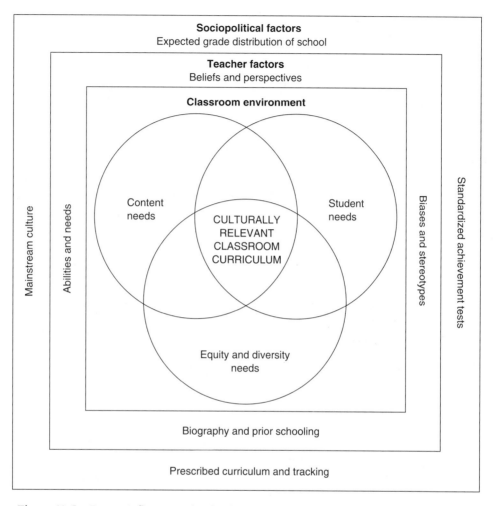

Figure 11–2 Factors influencing the development and implementation of a culturally relevant curriculum

At the beginning of this chapter, we implied that your classroom curriculum, particularly the information you teach, is framed by sociopolitical factors. Such factors that reportedly have an important influence on your curriculum include the values, norms, and social class of the prevailing (mainstream) culture, the curriculum prescribed by your school district (or state education agency), ability grouping, standardized achievement tests, and expected student outcomes of the school (see Figure 11–2). Many of these factors are powerful and unquestionably constrain how and what you teach.

Embedded within the sociopolitical factors is a second set of factors. These second factors, which we call *teacher factors,* set the tone for your classroom learning environment. Embedded within the political climate of the school, your personal qualities have a powerful influence on the kind of social and academic climate you establish for students. These factors include your autobiography, your teaching ability, and your personal needs that are met, if at all, by becoming a teacher. Other factors include biases or stereotypes you might have for students, your beliefs and perspectives about how students learn, and your level of content knowledge.

Your classroom learning environment, therefore, is framed by political factors and personal teacher factors. Although highly complex and exceedingly dynamic, these factors contribute to how you shape your classroom curriculum. These factors also determine how specific student needs are met in the actual classroom environment. In Figure 11-2 we identify three areas that each have special classroom needs: content needs, student needs, and equity and diversity needs. Notice that the relationships among these areas are dynamic. Consequently, as the nature of diversity changes from one student group to another, student needs change, equity issues change, and informational (content) needs change. The dynamics of these areas of need, as framed by sociocultural and teacher factors, suggest the kind of culturally relevant classroom curriculum you need to create and implement. Moreover, these areas of need give rise to pressing questions about planning and delivering your lessons. Below are questions for each area that help you consider more closely how to make your curriculum culturally relevant.

Content Needs

- Is the selected content relevant to students' family and cultural backgrounds?
- From which standpoint (e.g., value system, social group, prevailing culture) is the content being told?[26]
- Should other standpoints be introduced to students to provide them with alternative perspectives for understanding the content?
- In what way does the content enlighten students to help them better understand cultural pluralism?
- In what way does the content constrain student enlightenment, perhaps keeping them from understanding cultural pluralism?
- Which students, if any, might the content alienate?
- How will the content be presented to students so that the potential for alienation is minimized?
- If the content is not culturally sensitive, how can it be transformed into content that is culturally sensitive?

Student Needs

- What are the sociocultural features of students (e.g., culture, race, class, religion, gender, first language)? Which content might be best suited to these features?
- Are students put into groups based on ability levels (e.g., tracking)? If so, how does this grouping affect the social construction of your classroom curriculum?
- What are students' learning styles?
- What is the developmental readiness of students?
- What constitutes excellence in student learning?

Equity and Diversity Needs[27]

- In what way does the classroom curriculum affirm all students' cultural backgrounds?
- In what way does the classroom curriculum help students understand the value of cultural backgrounds other than their own?
- Is each student provided with learning opportunities that make high levels of achievement possible?
- How are learning opportunities differentiated, especially where the district prescribes classroom curricula, to reflect the characteristics of the students for whom they are intended?
- Does the classroom curriculum maintain high expectations for all students?
- Can cultural pluralism be promoted and still build a sense of cohesion with the classroom curriculum?

These questions, which focus specifically on creating a culturally relevant classroom curriculum, help you think more deeply about the nature of the lessons you develop for students. Signing a contract, however, in most school districts implies an agreement to teach the standard curriculum. Most teachers, especially beginning teachers, focus on trying to cover the required content and may not have the freedom, time, or collegial support to implement a curriculum that varies from the one prescribed by the district. Reviewing specific examples of how you can develop lessons that attend to the three kinds of needs above can be very helpful in making your classroom curriculum more sensitive to the backgrounds of your students. Suggestions for doing this can be found, for example, in the work of Grant and Sleeter (1989); Banks (1994); Bennett (1990); Reiss (1993); Nieto (1992); and others.

SUMMARY

Do not be disheartened if you are unable to immediately create a classroom curriculum that meets the diverse needs of your students. And do not be discouraged by the overpowering strength of political factors that constrain your desire to make your curriculum sensitive to the cultural needs of your students. Creating culturally relevant curriculum takes time, continual effort, patience, perseverance, and ongoing reflection about your teaching. The purpose of this chapter was not to provide you with a means to reduce time, effort, and reflection or to provide you with a stepwise algorithm for making a culturally relevant classroom curriculum. Our purpose was to heighten your awareness of factors that must be addressed when you create new curricula and transform existing curricula into those that are more culturally relevant.

Concomitant with understanding and developing a culturally relevant curriculum is being a multicultural person.[28] Being this kind of person means that you see classroom curricula from different perspectives and that you have some awareness of how students' ethnic perspectives (e.g., Asian, Hispanic, Latin, Black, Native American, White) cause them to respond to your classroom curriculum in unique ways.[29] This awareness is requisite to knowing how your classroom curriculum limits learning for some students and fosters learning for others.

At times you may feel alone in your effort to make a culturally relevant curriculum. In various ways, each teacher described in Chapter 7 felt alone in his or her efforts to create classroom curricula that were culturally sensitive. The teachers around you may be less sympathetic to the needs of diverse student populations. Thinking in new ways about classroom curriculum, in culturally sensitive ways, may require you to develop a personal agenda for how to do this. Certainly, it will require a personal transformation in your perspective about what students learn and how you help them learn it.[30] If enough teachers begin thinking about their classroom curricula in new ways, in transformative ways, then widespread curriculum transformation is inevitable. Implementing culturally relevant curriculum, then, begins with you.

RESEARCH TOPIC

Assessing Classroom Curriculum for Cultural Relevancy

Problem Posing

Throughout this chapter, you became familiar with factors that influence the cultural relevancy of your classroom curricula. We identified sociopolitical factors and teacher factors that frame the kind of curriculum you implement. And you considered specific challenges you face when creating and implementing a culturally relevant curriculum. After considering various dimensions of classroom curriculum, completing the activities in this chapter, and reviewing selected readings in the endnotes of this chapter, you should now realize how complex, how very political and cultural, is the curriculum you implement.

In this research project, you explore how the many factors described in this chapter influence curriculum in a selected school and classroom. On the basis of the model shown in Figure 11–2, we pose the following questions for this research: (a) How do sociopolitical factors and teacher factors influence a selected school and classroom learning environment? (b) What is the nature of a classroom curriculum in this environment? (c) What student needs, diversity needs, and content needs are met with the classroom curriculum you observe?

Exploration and Discovery

To answer the questions above, locate a school where you can gather various types of information. Also identify a classroom in this school, perhaps one of the classrooms you used to complete the activities earlier in this chapter. From this school and classroom, you explore (a) how sociopolitical factors of the school and classroom influence the classroom environment, (b) how teacher factors influence the classroom environment, (c) how student needs, equity and diversity needs, and content needs influence the classroom environment, and (d) how all of these factors shape the classroom curriculum. With this information, you then determine the degree to which the classroom curriculum is culturally relevant.

Sociopolitical Factors. To explore sociopolitical factors influencing the school and classroom environments, hold a conversation with one or more of these persons: a curriculum director for a district or school, an experienced teacher who has been teaching in the district for several years, an administrator. With the model in Figure 11–2 as a guide, explore what freedom the school district gives teachers to create their curricula. Find out how each of the following influences the school curriculum: prescribed curriculum of the district, academic tracking, and expected grade distribution that teachers are expected to meet. Ask about the value system of the predominant culture (mainstream culture) and how these values influence the school and classroom curricula.

Teacher Factors. After you have gathered information about sociopolitical factors, hold a conversation with a classroom teacher. If you talked with a selected teacher about sociopolitical factors, this same teacher can provide you with information here. Ask the teacher how each of these items influences her or his classroom curriculum: prior schooling of teacher, autobiographical experiences outside school, beliefs about learning, teaching abilities, personal needs of being a teacher, and any biases/stereotypes the teacher might be willing to acknowledge.

Classroom Environment. Ask the teacher to describe her or his classroom environment and classroom curriculum. Ask the teacher to describe which of the following factors have the greatest influence on the classroom curriculum: content to be taught, student needs, equity and diversity issues. Ask about the nature of the students: their cultural backgrounds, their social classes, and the languages they speak; explore what personal needs these students may have.

Review the tools (e.g., textbooks, instructional materials) the teacher uses throughout the year to teach content to students. Activity 11.2 can help you determine the cultural relevancy of these tools.

Culturally Relevant Classroom Curriculum. After you gather information on sociopolitical factors, teacher factors, and the classroom environment, think about how each of these influences the classroom curriculum. Observe the teacher's classroom instruction over a period of several weeks. Determine the nature of the classroom curriculum, including the social interactions that occur between students and teachers and between students and other students. Observe how the room is decorated and get a sense of the tone of the classroom. As you observe classroom instruction, watch for indicators that suggest cultural relevancy of the classroom curriculum. Determine how the classroom curriculum meets the needs of the students.

If you discover that the selected classroom curriculum you are observing is limited in its potential to be culturally relevant, you might also discover that other classes in the school or various extracurricular activities are designed to help students feel more connected with the school environment. Therefore, you should determine the degree to which the whole school curriculum meets the needs of the students. This is especially important if the school has students from many cultures.

Reflection and Modification

From your conversations about the sociopolitical climate of the school, from your observations of classroom teaching, and from your conversations with teachers (and/or other educators) about classroom curricula, did you discover that a culturally relevant curriculum is promoted at the school level and at the classroom level? What indicators suggest the school is or is not promoting such a curriculum? How much does the mainstream culture of the school predominate what is taught and how it is taught? Are multiple perspectives reflected in school and classroom practice? What specific evidence did you gather that suggests the school administration and the teacher you observed know about culturally relevant curricula? What changes might the school administration make to enhance cultural relevancy for students? What changes might the teacher make to enhance the cultural relevancy of the classroom curriculum?

During this research project, you presumably developed insights about culturally relevant classroom curricula. Record these insights below and describe how these insights will help you develop your classroom curriculum.

1. _____

2. _____

3. _____

4. _____

What modifications have you made in your beliefs about culturally relevant curricula during this research project? After considering various aspects of classroom curricula, are you prepared to make and implement one that is culturally relevant?

Description and Speculation

In this chapter, you began to explore the many dimensions of a culturally relevant curriculum. From what you learned in this chapter, what additional questions and research projects would further enrich your understanding of how to make and implement a culturally relevant curriculum? Write below several research projects and questions based on what you discovered from doing this research project.

1. _____

2. _____

3. _____

4. _____

NOTES

1. See Eisner's discussion of the null curriculum: Eisner, E. (1979). *The educational imagination*. New York: Macmillan. See also Peshkin, A. (1992). The relationship between culture and curriculum. In P. Jackson (Ed.), *Handbook of research on curriculum* (pp. 248–269). New York: Macmillan.

2. For discussions of constructivism, see Goodson, I. (1991). Studying curriculum: A social constructionist perspective. In I. Goodson & R. Walker (Eds.), *Biography, identity,*

and schooling: Episodes in educational research (pp. 168–181). New York: Falmer Press. See also Bruffee, K. (1986). Social construction, language, and the authority of knowledge: A bibliographical essay. *College English, 48*(8), 773–790; Gergen, K. (1985). The social constructionist movement in modern psychology. *American Psychologist, 40*(3), 266–275.

3. For a fuller discussion of classroom negotiations, see Boomer, G., Lester, N., Onore, C., & Cook, J. (1992). *Negotiating the curriculum: Educating for the 21st century.* Washington, DC: Falmer Press.

4. Erickson, F. (1982). Taught cognitive learning in its immediate environments: A neglected topic in the anthropology of education. *Anthropology and Education Quarterly, 13*(2), 149–180.

5. These questions were derived from Apple, M. (1983). *Official knowledge: Democratic education in a conservative age.* New York: Routledge, p. 41.

6. Garcia, J., Powell, R., & Sanchez, T. (1991). Multicultural texts as tools: Teachers as catalysts. *Ethnic Forum, 11*(1), 18–30.

7. Reading ethnographies of school classes and then discussing these ethnographies with peers can help you develop important insights into culturally relevant and irrelevant classroom curricula. In addition to the report by Erickson (1987), see reports by Au (1980); Contreras and Lee (1990); Fine (1991); Gibson (1988); Jordan (1985); Kleifgen (1988); Villegas (1988); Wilson (1991).

8. Swartz, E. (1992). Cultural diversity and the school curriculum: Content and practice. *Journal of Curriculum Theorizing, 9*(4), 73–88. See also Reiss, M. J. (1993). *Science education for a pluralist society.* Philadelphia: Open University Press.

9. For additional reports of how some curricula are culturally insensitive, see Watkins (1993) and Swartz (1992).

10. Au (1980); Dillon (1989); Erickson and Mohatt (1982); Jordan (1985); Noordhoff and Kleinfeld (1993).

11. Greene, M. (1983). Openings to possibility: The common world and the public school. In J. Frymier (Ed.), *Bad times, good times* (pp. 81–95). West Lafayette, IN: Kappa Delta Pi.

12. See discussions of transformative curriculum provided by Banks (1994) and Doll (1993).

13. See Garcia, J. (1993). The changing image of ethnic groups in textbooks. *Phi Delta Kappan, 75*(1), 29–35.

14. See Swartz (1992) for other examples.

15. To supplement this activity, we recommend reading the following items: Chapters 1 and 4 in Apple, M. (1988). *Teachers and texts: A political economy of class and gender relations in education.* New York: Routledge; Apple, M. (1992, October). The text and cultural politics. *Educational Researcher, 21*(7), 4–11; Bigelow, W. (1992). Once upon a genocide: Christopher Columbus in children's literature. *Language Arts, 69*(2), 112–120; Garcia, J. (1993). The changing image of ethnic groups in textbooks. *Phi Delta Kappan, 75*(1), 29–35; Gay, G. (1990). Achieving educational equality through curriculum desegregation. *Phi Delta Kappan, 72,* 56–62; Chapter 4 in Giroux, H. (1992). *Border crossings: Cultural workers and the politics of education.* New York: Routledge.

16. See Powell, R., & Garcia, J. (1985). The portrayal of minorities and women in selected elementary science series. *Journal of Research in Science Teaching, 22*(6), 519–533.

17. See Moll and Diaz (1987).

18. See Atwater (1993).

19. See Ladson-Billings (1990).

20. See Banks, 1993, p. 199. See also Suzuki, B. (1984). Curriculum transformation for multicultural education. *Education and Urban Society, 16*(3), 294–322.

21. Gay, G. (1990). Achieving educational equality through curriculum desegregation. *Phi Delta Kappan, 72,* 56–62.
22. See the study by Matthews and Smith (1994).
23. See Sonia Nieto's (1992) discussion of curriculum in *Affirming diversity: The sociopolitical context of multicultural education.* White Plains, NY: Longman, pp. 74–7.
24. See Wilson, P. (1991). Trauma of Sioux Indian high school students. *Anthropology and Education Quarterly, 22,* 367–383.
25. The notion of becoming teacher as anthropologist was derived from the work of Frederick Erickson. See Erickson, F. (1982). Taught cognitive learning in its immediate environments: A neglected topic in the anthropology of education. *Anthropology and Education Quarterly, 13*(2), 149–180, especially pages 173–174.
26. For a discussion of standpoint theory, see Harding, S. (1991). *Whose science? Whose knowledge? Thinking from women's lives.* Ithaca, NY: Cornell University Press.
27. See Gay (1988).
28. See Nieto (1992, p. 275).
29. See Hannan's (1982) discussion of a multicultural curriculum: Hannan, B. (1982) The multicultural school: Or schools in search of their culture. In G. Dow (Ed.), *Teacher learning* (pp. 79–110). Boston: Routledge & Kegan Paul.
30. Kincheloe, J. (1993). *Toward a critical politics of teacher thinking: Mapping the postmodern.* Westport, CT: Bergin & Garvey.

REFERENCES

Apple, M. (1993). *Official knowledge: Democratic education in a conservative age.* New York: Routledge.

Apple, M. (1988). *Teachers and texts: A political economy of class and gender relations in education.* New York: Routledge.

Apple, M. (1992, October). The text and cultural politics. *Educational Researcher, 21*(7) 4–11.

Atwater, M. (1993). Multicultural science education. *Science Teacher, 60*(3), 33–37.

Au, K. Hu-pei. (1980). Participation structures in a reading lesson with Hawaiian children: Analysis of a culturally appropriate instructional event. *Anthropology and Education Quarterly, 11*(2), 91–114.

Banks, J. (1993) Approaches to multicultural curriculum reform. In J. Banks & C. Banks (Eds.), *Multicultural education: Issues and perspectives* (2nd ed., pp. 195–214). Boston: Allyn & Bacon.

Banks, J. (1994). *An introduction to multicultural education.* New York: Longman.

Bennett, C. (1990). *Comprehensive multicultural education* (2nd ed.). Boston: Allyn & Bacon.

Bigelow, W. (1992). Once upon a genocide: Christopher Columbus in children's literature. *Language Arts, 69*(2), 112–120.

Boomer, G., Lester, N., Onore, C., & Cook, J. (1992). *Negotiating the curriculum: Educating for the 21st century.* Washington, DC: Falmer Press.

Bruffee, K. (1986). Social construction, language, and the authority of knowledge: A bibliographical essay. *College English, 48*(8), 773–790.

Clandinin, J., & Connelly, M. (1992). Teacher as curriculum maker. In P. Jackson (Ed.), *Handbook of research on curriculum* (pp. 363–401). New York: Macmillan.

Contreras, A., & Lee, O. (1990). Differential treatment of students by middle school science teachers: Unintended cultural bias. *Science Education, 74*(4), 433–444.

Dillon, D. (1989). Showing them that I want them to learn and that I care about who they are: A microethnography of the social organization of a secondary low-tract English-reading classroom. *American Educational Research Association, 26*(2), 227–259.

Doll, W. (1993). *A post-modern perspective on curriculum.* New York: Teachers College Press.

Eisner, E. (1979). *The educational imagination.* New York: Macmillan.

Erickson, F. (1982). Taught cognitive learning in its immediate environments: A neglected topic in the anthropology of education. *Anthropology and Education Quarterly, 13*(2), 149–180.

Erickson, F. (1987). Transformation and school success: The politics and culture of educational achievement. *Anthropology and Education Quarterly, 18,* 335–356.

Erickson, F., & Mohatt, G. (1982). Cultural organization of participation structures in two classrooms of Indian students. In G. Spindler (Ed.), *Doing the ethnography of schooling: Educational anthropology in action* (pp. 132–174). New York: Holt, Rinehart & Winston.

Fine, M. (1991). *Framing dropouts.* Albany: SUNY.

Garcia, J. (1993). The changing image of ethnic groups in textbooks. *Phi Delta Kappan, 75*(1), 29–35.

Garcia, J., Powell, R., & Sanchez, T. (1991). Multicultural texts as tools: Teachers as catalysts. *Ethnic Forum, 11*(1), 18–30.

Gay, G. (1988). Designing relevant curricula for diverse learners. *Education and Urban Society, 20*(4), 327–340.

Gay, G. (1990). Achieving educational equality through curriculum desegregation. *Phi Delta Kappan, 72,* 56–62.

Gergen, K. (1985). The social constructionist movement in modern psychology. *American Psychologist, 40*(3), 266–275.

Gibson, M. (1988). *Accommodation without assimilation: Sikh immigrants in an American high school.* Ithaca, NY: Cornell University Press.

Giroux, H. (1992). *Border crossings: Cultural workers and the politics of education.* New York: Routledge.

Goodson, I. (1991). Studying curriculum: A social constructionist perspective. In I. Goodson & R. Walker (Eds.), *Biography, identity, and schooling: Episodes in educational research* (pp. 168–181). New York: Falmer Press.

Grant, C. A., & Sleeter, C. E. (1989). *Turning on learning: Five approaches for multicultural teaching plans for race, class, gender, and disability.* New York: Merrill/Macmillan.

Greene, M. (1983). Openings to possibility: The common world and the public school. In J. Frymier (Ed.), *Bad times, good times* (pp. 81–95). West Lafayette, IN: Kappa Delta Pi.

Hannan, B. (1982). The multicultural school: Or schools in search of their culture. In G. Dow (Ed.), *Teacher learning* (pp. 79–110). Boston: Routledge & Kegan Paul.

Harding, S. (1991). *Whose science? Whose knowledge? Thinking from women's lives.* Ithaca, NY: Cornell University Press.

Jordan, C. (1985). Translating culture: From ethnographic information to educational program. *Anthropology and Education Quarterly, 16,* 105–123.

Kincheloe, J. (1993). *Toward a critical politics of teacher thinking: Mapping the postmodern.* Westport, CT: Bergin & Garvey.

Kleifgen, J-A. (1988). Learning from student teachers' cross-cultural communicative failures. *Anthropology and Education Quarterly, 19,* 218–234.

Ladson-Billings, G. (1990). Like lightning in a bottle: Attempting to capture the pedagogical excellence of successful teachers of Black students. *Qualitative Studies in Education, 3*(4), 335–344.

Matthews, C., & Smith, W. (1994). Native American related materials in elementary science instruction. *Journal of Research in Science Teaching, 32*(4), 363–380.

Moll, L., & Diaz, S. (1987). Change as the goal of educational research. *Anthropology and Education Quarterly, 18,* 300–311.

Neisser, U. (1976). *Cognition and reality.* New York: Freeman.

Nieto, S. (1992). *Affirming diversity: The sociopolitical context of multicultural education.* New York: Longman.

Noordhoff, K., & Kleinfeld, J. (1993). Preparing teachers for multicultural classrooms. *Teaching and Teacher Education, 9*(1), 27–39.

Peshkin, A. (1992). The relationship between culture and curriculum. In P. Jackson (Ed.), *Handbook of research on curriculum* (pp. 248–269). New York: Macmillan.

Powell, R., & Garcia, J. (1985). The portrayal of minorities and women in selected elementary science series. *Journal of Research in Science Teaching, 22*(6), 519–533.

Reiss, M. J. (1993). *Science education for a pluralist society.* Philadelphia: Open University Press.

Suzuki, B. (1984). Curriculum transformation for multicultural education. *Education and Urban Society, 16*(3), 294–322.

Swartz, E. (1992). Cultural diversity and the school curriculum: Content and practice. *Journal of Curriculum Theorizing, 9*(4), 73–88.

Villegas, A-M. (1988). School failure and cultural mismatch: Another view. *Urban Review, 20*(4), 253–265.

Watkins, W. (1993). Black curriculum orientations: A preliminary inquiry. *Harvard Educational Review, 63*(3), 321–338.

Wilson, P. (1991). Trauma of Sioux Indian high school students. *Anthropology and Education Quarterly, 22,* 367–383.

PART III

Reflecting on Field Experience

Chapter 12
Synthesizing Your Personal Practical Philosophy for Teaching
Diverse Learners

Chapter 12

Synthesizing Your Personal Practical Philosophy for Teaching Diverse Learners

Critical reflection is an ongoing responsibility of teaching and teacher development, not something to be dealt with safely and sporadically in occasional assignments on award-bearing courses.   (Hargreaves, 1994, p. 16)

There are beginnings. Some educators now realize that people cannot simply be viewed as representatives of groups or categories and, at the same time, as living beings with subjectivities and distinct vantage points.   (Greene, 1994, p. 2)

The profoundest of distances are never geographical.   (Fowles, 1965)

CRITICAL REFLECTIVE THINKING: GETTING IN TOUCH WITH YOUR PERSONAL PRACTICAL PHILOSOPHY FOR TEACHING DIVERSE LEARNERS

"Reflection—true reflection," writes Freire (1972, p. 41), "leads to action." What do you think about when you truly reflect on your teaching? And what educational action should you take after you engage in reflective thinking? One purpose for this kind of thinking is to help you understand the personal philosophy you have for teaching in schools. This philosophy frames your classroom learning environment, so getting in touch with it is an important step toward building a deeper understanding of your own teaching.

In this book, we equate Freire's notion of reflecting on practice and taking classroom action with the writings of contemporary writers in Canada and the United States—namely, Hargreaves (1994) and Greene (1994). Hargreaves's description of critical reflection above represents what you must do if you are to think reflectively: frequent, persistent, and wholehearted contemplation about your teaching. Critical reflection involves contemplating a teaching situation or event in ways you hadn't before. For example, if you think about the classroom interactions you have with your students or about the classroom interactions another teacher has with her or his students, you might discover yourself or your colleague responding more often in certain ways to students of one cultural group, such as Asian, than another group, such as Latino or White. Critical reflection about how one interacts with certain social groups involves more than only saying, "OK, I guess I do interact more often with Asians than Latinos." In contemplating your predisposition to interact more often, and perhaps more positively, with some students than others, you try to find out *how* you are doing this; perhaps more important, you search for *why* you are doing it.

When in the swift pace of the classroom you are at crucial moments of teaching concepts or ideas, you might not think about which students you most often interact with, although those students most likely are the ones who gain a better understanding of the concepts you are teaching. Your immediate concentration on academic, interpersonal, and instructional concerns at a particular moment in the lesson might not provide the opportunity you need to be reflective and interpretive. This uncertainty is why we believe reflective thinking is important.[1] Once you step from the busy pace of your classroom, you can begin thinking about why you might, for example, interact more often with some students than others. You may think more deeply about the nature of your interactions with students, and such thoughts can lead you to alternative classroom actions,[2] to new beginnings,[3] and to more academically and personally meaningful ways of interacting with all students.

Moreover, reflective thinking is not something you do only once or twice, perhaps because a university professor or school administrator asks you to think specifically about a particular classroom phenomenon. The reflective thinking we are talking about, called *critical reflection,* is a habit of mind and an attitude. It involves a willingness to challenge your own beliefs about teaching and those of your peers and colleagues. Dewey (1910/1991) described critical reflection as "active, persistent, and careful consideration of any belief or supposed form of knowledge in the light of the grounds that support it, and the further conclusions to which it tends" (p. 6). Although we realize that every person is not disposed to this kind of thinking, those who are will reconsider and possibly reconstruct their teaching on very personal levels.

Ongoing critical reflection on your classroom strategies and on your interactions with students helps you clarify your teaching beliefs and classroom actions, what Connelly and Clandinin (1988) call your *personal practical philosophy* for teaching.[4] One goal for this chapter is to help you clarify your personal practical philosophy for teaching diverse learners. To do this, we ask you to think about the new ideas and insights you gained earlier in this book. We especially encourage you to think about any insights you gained about the personal, cultural, academic, and social distances you might be keeping, though unintentionally, from some of your students and to consider why these distances might exist.

Although you likely have your own items to reflect on, we provide you with additional items below. Some of these items were part of earlier chapters. By refocusing on them in this closing chapter, new beginnings are very possible, beginnings that help you understand more clearly the predispositions your students have, what Greene (1994) calls *subjectivities and distinct vantage points,* for being successful in your classroom. Being aware of students' subjectivities and vantage points, which can be further viewed as students' personal ways of knowing and learning, helps you be more successful in communicating content to your students. Before turning to these items, consider the discussion of personal practical philosophy that follows.

YOUR PERSONAL PRACTICAL PHILOSOPHY FOR TEACHING DIVERSE LEARNERS

In the introduction to this book, we said that one of our foremost purposes was to help you become better acquainted with your own personal practical philosophy for teaching diverse learners. We also asked you to write about your philosophy; this was your initial philosophy. Return now to what you wrote about your initial philosophy and think about how your beliefs and perspectives changed, if at all, as you completed this book. In this chapter, you explore further your personal practical philosophy for teaching diverse learners and consider the many ways that your philosophy influences your classroom learning environment.

At one time or another, you have talked about your personal philosophies. You probably have said things like, "What he just said about teaching reflects my own philosophy," or, "I agree with the activities she uses in her classroom, so we must have the same philosophy for teaching." Using *philosophy* in this way is useful in helping you compare your views, actions, and beliefs about teaching with those expressed by other people. Now, we want you to move beyond this common use of *philosophy* and explore the idea of personal practical philosophy as described by Connelly and Clandinin (1986, 1988). Your personal practical philosophy for teaching, constructed over many years, influences your classroom learning environment in important ways, especially your predisposition to interact with students and to use alternative teaching strategies.

To understand the idea of personal practical philosophy, first think about the many activities you completed throughout this book. As you completed these activities in schools, classrooms, and communities, you explored how your personal beliefs about teaching influence your classroom interactions with diverse learners and constructed a personal knowledge of how diversity influences the whole school context. The personal knowledge you constructed about teaching, embedded in the school classroom context, has a prevailing practical dimension. Because you constructed this knowledge in ways that were meaningful to you, you personally own it, and now you have the moral responsibility that comes with this ownership.[5] Your personal knowledge base, socially constructed[6] from within the lived experience of school classes and coupled with your prior beliefs about teaching and your ability to transform these beliefs into practice, comprises your personal practical philosophy.

If someone asks you about your personal philosophy for teaching, you likely say something that reflects your deeper level beliefs. Connelly and Clandinin (1988) note, "Personal philosophy is what we respond with when someone asks us as teachers what we believe about children, about teaching and learning, or about curriculum. . . . [It is] our beliefs and values contextualized in our experience" (p. 70). Following this line of thinking, personal practical philosophy is clearly much more than a phrase. It reflects what you do in the classroom as a function of your personal history, your former teacher role models, and your current beliefs.[7] This personal history is why you must also consider your autobiographical experiences when you synthesize your personal practical philosophy for teaching diverse learners.

Personal practical philosophy is an important way to think about teaching diverse learners. This very philosophy, embedded within your beliefs and values for teaching, provides the framework for how and why you interact with specific students in a particular manner. Constructed from years of experiences in various educational, societal, and cultural settings, it also frames how you view yourself relative to a global society. What, then, is your personal practical philosophy for teaching diverse learners? The previous chapters of this book were intended to help you socially construct a personal knowledge base for answering this question. To answer the question, you must now think critically and reflectively about what you learned in these chapters.

THINKING REFLECTIVELY ON DIVERSITY IN SCHOOLS

As you completed the activities throughout this book, you participated in teacher research projects and you formulated questions about teaching diverse learners. To answer these questions, you gathered, explored, and interpreted selected information. This procedure helped you begin the process of reflective thinking.[8] The activities in this chapter help you extend and deepen this thinking.

ACTIVITY 12.1   Exploring the Theoretical Basis of Your Personal Philosophy

In this activity, you explore how your personal practical philosophy is shaped by five areas: teacher biography and related features, school environment, teaching, curriculum, and student learning. Working alone during this first step, think about each of these areas and record important thoughts and insights you make during this time. For example, as you reflect on school environment, examine your beliefs about the kind of school context that best serves the needs of diverse students. Now is a good time to revisit your earlier observations and the corresponding notes you recorded.

The second step is to share your thoughts and insights with peers and colleagues. Hearing others react to your thoughts and ideas and listening closely to yourself as you react to their thoughts helps you clarify and verbalize your beliefs that frame your personal philosophy.

Teacher Biography and Related Features

- *Your autobiography influences your classroom learning environment.* Consider how your prior experiences inside and outside school are transformed into your classroom strategies. Which of these experiences, whether positive or negative, shape your teaching self and your classroom learning environment?
- *Your autobiography might influence your predisposition to interact more positively with some students than others.* Consider positive and negative experiences you have had at various times of your life with cultural and ethnic groups (e.g., Black, Asian, Hispanic, Native American, White) other than your own. What is the extent of these experiences, and how might they influence your ability and willingness to work with all of your students?
- *You think about teaching.* The teaching profession gives you so much to think about: managing learning environments for optimal learning of all students, developing appropriate learning outcomes for learners, implementing culturally relevant curriculum effectively, assessing student learning—the list goes on. In what ways, if any, do you think reflectively and critically about teaching in contemporary schools, especially about your moral and ethical responsibility to help all children learn? Consider the nature of your thoughts about teaching. In what way does your thinking reflect the metaphor of teacher as authoritarian and technician? In what way does your thinking reflect the metaphor of teacher as reflective professional? Does your thinking ever take on a critical perspective, questioning some traditional teaching methods? Do you believe that critical reflective thinking and teaching are constructive? Why or why not? How often and in what ways do you think critically about aspects of schooling and teaching?
- *You develop your personal beliefs for teaching students throughout your whole life.* What are your personal beliefs for teaching all students? Where did you develop these beliefs? Why are your beliefs appropriate (or inappropriate) for your immediate teaching context? How do your beliefs compare with those expressed by peers?

School Environment

- *The political realities of teaching are deeply embedded within cultural contexts of local communities.* Consider how your teaching is influenced explicitly and implicitly by the communities where students live. What is your level of awareness of the cultural values and local politics of the school's community? Lacking an awareness may limit the kinds of classroom interactions you have with students that help them be successful learners.
- *Diversity in contemporary school classrooms has increased, even in remote rural schools.* Consider how society and all of its schools have become more global, incorporating the values, habits, languages, and customs of various cultures. What is your level of tolerance for the globalization of schools and your level of tolerance for teaching in these schools?

- *Schools within and between districts contain fiscal inequities.* Think about some of the fiscal inequities that might exist in your school district. Many teachers in less advantaged schools experience problems getting paper and simple supplies. These same teachers may not have enough books or equipment and may be cramped with large classes in small rooms. There may be no playground equipment, and all field trip buses may be assigned to the "other side of town." You might be working in a district where one school has managed to be "adopted" by a major business or corporation and thus has acquired thousands of dollars for computer technology, special programs, or other advantages, whereas another school in the same district, perhaps your own school, has had to ration chalk because of budget cuts. Blatant and subtle discrimination continues to be reflected in a lack of opportunity that will affect teacher, as well as student. Part of your personal philosophy must be an opinion on this inequity and a plan for addressing it in some way during your career.

Teaching

- *Learning to teach diverse learners is a complex, yet highly rewarding experience.* Consider the argument made by Gomez (1993) that no single activity, unique teacher education course, or real-life experience among other cultural groups is sufficient to adequately prepare you to teach diverse student populations. Many different experiences over time in various settings are needed with ongoing reflective thinking, while alone and while with peers, to make the kinds of beginnings mentioned by Greene (1994) at the opening of this chapter. What additional experiences might you need to better understand the learners in your school and classroom learning environments?

- *You might be distancing yourself culturally and academically from some students in your classroom.* Consider how and why you might interact with some students more often and more positively than other students. In this chapter, we call this *distancing yourself from students.* For example, you might unknowingly give less attention and less assistance to students who have limited-English-speaking skills. In doing this, you "distance" yourself from these students. You create a chasm between them and you and, consequently, a chasm between them and the content you teach. How and why might you be doing this?

- *You become a "cultural worker"[9] when you enter contemporary classrooms as a teacher.* Consider the metaphor of cultural worker for yourself as a teacher. What does this metaphor mean to you? To what extent does being a cultural worker influence how you help students learn important academic content? To broaden this metaphor, think of yourself as interacting with various cultures, not only those framed by race or ethnicity but also those based on, for example, lifestyles or religious beliefs. What is your level of readiness for working with various cultures?

- *Culturally sensitive teachers view themselves as facilitators of student learning.* Following the work of Giroux (1992), we use the metaphor teacher as cultural worker to describe the work you do in contemporary school classrooms. Two alternative metaphors representing different teaching strategies and different ways of interacting with students are (a) teacher as facilitator for learning and (b) teacher as conduit for transmitting information. The classroom interactions that result from both metaphorical views of teaching are useful, yet both have limitations. Which metaphor aligns more closely with your perspective of teaching? Why might one metaphor be more appropriate for your specific teaching situation than another?

- *Your academic and personal interactions with students have a moral purpose.* Many educators believe that teaching is a moral act. In what ways, if any, do you view teaching as being a moral act? What are the moral dimensions of teaching? How do you enact such dimensions in your own classroom?
- *As a teacher, you are faced with broad challenges, including technical, political, and emotional challenges.*[10] Consider the many challenges you have in your classroom, in addition to the challenge of teaching academic content effectively.[11] How aware are you of these challenges? How willing are you to deal with them on a daily basis?
- *Any biases and stereotypes you might have for cultural groups interfere with how you teach students from these groups.* Consider biases or stereotypes you might have for student groups. How might these stereotypes interfere with your ability to teach some students? How can you overcome your stereotypes?

Curriculum

- *Traditional, content-centered curriculum and instruction may be inappropriate for some students.* Consider the nature of instruction in which content is transmitted to students directly, most often in the form of teacher-directed activities (teacher as conduit). Why might this instruction be inappropriate for some of your students but appropriate for others?
- *Classroom curricula can distance students from classroom activities and from the content you are teaching.* Consider how some school curricula, either in product or process, can distance, or marginalize, some students from the content you teach. How can you change the curriculum so that you close any gaps that exist between students and your classroom curriculum?

Student Learning

- *Students' subjectivities and distinct vantage points influence how they interact with you and your classroom curriculum.* Consider the personal perspectives of your students and how these perspectives, framed by cultural values, give your students distinct vantage points for learning the content you teach.[12] How aware are you of these subjectivities and vantage points? How willing are you to alter your teaching strategies to better relate to students' subjectivities?
- *Teaching is context specific and thus is shaped by the local needs of students.* Consider how teaching in a remote rural community school that has mostly a culturally homogeneous student population would be different from teaching in an urban city school that has a heterogeneous student population. In what ways, if any, would you need to vary your teaching strategies and classroom curriculum for these two settings? In what ways would they be the same?

Thinking by yourself on the areas above and then discussing your thoughts with a colleague helps you think more deeply, certainly more theoretically, about the underlying beliefs that frame your personal practical philosophy for teaching diverse learners. This kind of thinking also helps you become aware of the historical and professional experiences from which you have constructed and continue to construct your personal practical philosophy. An important point to remember is that every teacher's personal practical philosophy allows for both strengths and weaknesses in classroom teaching. This allowance is why you must continuously think about—and whenever necessary, reconsider—the status of your ever-developing personal philosophy.

Although the processes of critical thinking and open discussion help you understand the teaching beliefs that underlie your personal practical philosophy, these processes reveal only part of the mental scaffolding that frames your personal philosophy. To more fully understand your philosophy, you must explore how your personal practical philosophy is enacted in actual classroom teaching. Connelly and Clandinin (1986) note that your personal practical philosophy is brought to life when your underlying beliefs, whether expressed or unexpressed, are transformed into classroom practice. How you transform your beliefs into practice, either consciously or unconsciously, in the face of political, administrative, and curricular constraints of your local school context is a crucial factor in determining the degree of alignment between your beliefs as expressed explicitly and your beliefs as enacted in real classroom life.

ACTIVITY 12.2   Exploring Your Personal Practical Philosophy in Action

An important point must be made here regarding personal practical philosophies. You do not construct these philosophies by yourself; you socially construct them. That is, you construct your personal practical philosophy for teaching through personal and professional interactions inside and outside school. Your personal philosophy is always embedded, therefore, in a specific social context, and your philosophy is given life by this context. To adequately explore your personal practical philosophy for teaching, you must examine your actions within the social context of school classrooms, as you actually teach students. Because your personal practical philosophy for teaching is socially constructed, you will need to mutually reconstruct your philosophy over time with another person, preferably a trusted colleague (e.g., experienced teacher, preservice teacher, researcher, supervisor).[13]

Ask a colleague to observe your classroom instruction over time. Because this observation should be done on several occasions, you might need to videotape yourself teaching in the classroom and then view the videotape with your colleague at a later time. You and your colleague should explore your classroom teaching together, as a collective effort. Explore with your colleague why you are doing certain activities and why you are interacting with students in a specific manner. Talk extensively about any beliefs you have that correspond with your classroom actions. Try to identify historical antecedents to your actions, such as former school experiences, university courses, personal experiences outside school, or perhaps the confluence of all of these things. As you and your colleague talk about your teaching and as you "jointly come to think about [your] work,"[14] describe your personal practical philosophy.

Compare your personal practical philosophy with any comments you recorded in Activity 12.1. Determine the correspondence between your theoretical ideas about teaching diverse learners (Activity 12.1) and your actual classroom practice (Activity 12.2). To what degree do your theoretical notions of teaching and your personal practical philosophy, as expressed in your classroom teaching, align? Does your personal practical philosophy for teaching, as you and your colleague have jointly constructed it and as it is transformed into classroom instruction, connect you with all of your students? How does your personal practical philosophy distance you from some students while bringing you closer to others?

SUMMARY

This chapter and those that preceded it have been an attempt to help you understand your beliefs, predispositions, personal theories, and personal philosophies for teaching in a pluralistic society. This book has also been an attempt to help you learn about distances: the cultural distances you might be keeping from some of your students, either through your personal interactions with them, your classroom curriculum, or your classroom learning environment.

Underlying this book is our conviction that you as a classroom teacher must make a sincere, passionate attempt to help every one of your students be successful in school. Although this is a complicated task even for the best of teachers, your attempt to do this will be more successful when you better understand personal factors (e.g., beliefs, values, classroom behaviors) that widen any existing gaps between you and your students.

Understanding cultural distances between you and your students, through self-searching critical reflection over many months, makes you continuously wonder about your teaching. Boomer (1992) explains the value of this kind of wondering:

> To know "what is going on," or even to wonder what might be going on, means having an all-encompassing fish-eye-lens taking in the backgrounds, capabilities and aspirations of the learners and their parents, knowing the structures, habits and values of the school, reading the wider politics of the system and society (particularly its economics), and understanding the ebb and flow of interactions and struggles in the arenas of gender, race, ethnicity and class. (p. 281)

Teachers who are deeply committed to their work continuously wonder about their classrooms. They think critically about their practice, always looking for ways to begin anew. They do this because they understand, as Boomer does above, that any distance between them and their students, regardless of the cause, interferes with learning.

Throughout this book, you should have come to realize that becoming a culturally sensitive teacher may require you to make a transition from one kind of thinking about teaching (e.g., traditional, authoritarian, content centered) to another kind (e.g., contemporary, negotiable, student centered). Do not think, however, that you must make this transition overnight or even in a few weeks. Moving from one kind of professional thinking to another can be threatening to your sense of security as a teacher and thus cause you to quickly retreat to what feels secure and what protects your self-confidence as a teacher. Making the transition to being a more culturally sensitive teacher should be approached carefully, thoughtfully, and with determination and wholeheartedness. About the idea of transition, Silko (1977) writes, "It is a matter of transition, you see: the changing, the becoming must be cared for closely"

(p. 130). As you move toward becoming more culturally sensitive in your curriculum and instruction, continuously reflect on your personal practical philosophy for teaching diverse students. This reflection will help you nurture and care for changes in your teaching practice without running back to ways of teaching that might be less effective for your students.

A final note needs to be mentioned about what you have learned from this book and from doing the activities and research projects we suggested about teaching culturally diverse students. In a profoundly rich book on Native American culture written by Storm (1994), Estcheemah, the teacher of Lightningbolt, says: "Discernment and decision shape what you have learned, not what you believe you have learned" (p. 372). What you have truly learned about teaching culturally diverse student populations in today's schools will be apparent in the daily decisions you make about engaging every one of your students as individual human beings, not as stereotypical members of cultural groups, in the learning process. A key feature in making these decisions is discernment, knowing what to do and say at the right classroom moment to engage all learners and knowing what not to do. This kind of knowing is constructed from real-life experiences, the kind of experiences we offered you in this book.

In theory-based academic courses on diversity and multiculturalism—those that are encapsulated in colleges and universities and those that rarely require you to study real school classrooms—you often come to believe that you have learned specific skills for interacting more proficiently as a teacher among diverse students. What you believe you have learned, however, will not always transfer to the reality of practice, given the political and contextual constraints in which you work. This book, with its numerous activities and classroom-based research projects, is an attempt to help you distinguish between what you have truly learned and what you think you have learned. What you have truly learned about yourself, about schools, and about teaching culturally diverse students will become apparent in the daily decisions you make to create a learning environment that engages all students in meaningful, productive, and relevant instruction.

NOTES

1. See Bullough (1989); Kincheloe (1993); and Zeichner (1982, 1987).
2. See Dewey (1910/1991).
3. See Greene (1994).
4. See also Connelly and Clandinin (1986).
5. See Richardson's (1994) discussion of conducting research on practice.
6. We do not mean to imply that "others" (e.g., university professor, classroom teacher, peer, administrator) played an insignificant role in the knowledge you gained, but rather that you were the proactive agent in acquiring this knowledge and that "others" took the role of facilitator.
7. See Powell (1994) and Knowles (1992).
8. See Kemmis and McTaggart (1988, p. 85).
9. See Giroux (1992).
10. See Hargreaves (1994).

11. See, for example, Powell, Zehm, and Kottler (1995).
12. The notion of students' distinct vantage points can be further explored in the work of Statzner (1994).
13. See the discussion of personal philosophy and narrative unity offered by Connelly and Clandinin (1986, pp. 6–7).
14. See Connelly and Clandinin (1986, p. 7).

REFERENCES

Boomer, G. (1992). Negotiating the curriculum reformulated. In G. Boomer, N. Lester, C. Onore, & J. Cook (Eds.), *Negotiating the curriculum: Educating for the 21st century* (pp. 276–289). Washington, DC: Falmer Press.

Bullough, R. V. (1989). Teacher education and teacher reflectivity. *Journal of Teacher Education, 40*(2), 15–21.

Connelly, F. M., & Clandinin, D. J. (1986). On narrative method, personal philosophy, and narrative unities in the story of teaching. *Journal of Research in Science Teaching, 23*(4), 293–310.

Connelly, F. M., & Clandinin, D. J. (1988). *Teachers as curriculum planners: Narratives of experience.* New York: Teachers College Press.

Dewey, J. (1991). *How we think.* Buffalo, NY: Prometheus Books. (Original work published 1910).

Fowles, J. (1965). *The magus.* Boston: Little, Brown.

Freire, P. (1972). *Pedagogy of the oppressed.* Auckland, NZ: Penguin Books.

Giroux, H. A. (1992). *Border crossings: Cultural workers and the politics of education.* New York: Routledge.

Gomez, M. L. (1993). Prospective teachers' perspectives on teaching diverse children: A review with implications for teacher education practice. *Journal of Negro Education, 62*(4), 459–472.

Greene, M. (1994, April). *Beginnings, identities, and possibilities: The uses of social imagination.* Paper presented at the Annual Meeting of the American Educational Research Association, New Orleans.

Hargreaves, A. (1994, April). *Development and desire: A postmodern perspective.* Paper presented at the Annual Meeting of the American Educational Research Association, New Orleans.

Kemmis, S., & McTaggart, R. (1988). *The action research planner* (3rd ed.). Victoria, Australia: Deakin University Press.

Kincheloe, J. L. (1993). *Toward a critical politics of teacher thinking: Mapping the postmodern.* Westport, CT: Bergin & Garvey.

Knowles, J. G. (1992). Models for understanding pre-service and beginning teachers' biographies: Illustrations from case studies. In I. F. Goodson (Ed.), *Studying teachers' lives.* New York: Teachers College Press.

Powell, R. R. (1994). From field science to classroom science: A case study of constrained emergence in a second-career science teacher. *Journal of Research in Science Teaching, 31*(3), 273–291.

Powell, R. R., Zehm, S., & Kottler, J. (1995). *Classrooms under the influence: Addicted parents, addicted students.* Thousand Oaks, CA: Corwin Press.

Richardson, V. (1994). Conducting research on practice. *Educational Researcher, 23*(5), 5–10.

Silko, L. M. (1977). *Ceremony.* New York: Penguin Books.

Statzner, E. L. (1994). And Marvin raised his hand: Practices that encourage children's classroom participation. *Anthropology and Education Quarterly, 25*(3), 285–297.

Storm, H. (1994). *Lightningbolt.* New York: Ballantine Books.

Zeichner, K. M. (1982). Reflective teaching and field-based experience in teacher education. *Interchange, 12*(4), 1–22.

Zeichner, K. M. (1987). Preparing reflective teachers: An overview of instructional strategies which have been employed in preservice teacher education. *International Journal of Educational Research, 11*(5), 565–575.

❈ Index